NSEQUENCES

SALLY HUBBARD HARRIS

(SALLY WILLIAMS)

Consequences

Memoir of a Dowser

Sally Hubbard Harris

(Sally Williams)

Brontovox Publications

www.brontovox.co.uk

Dedication

FOR
ALL DOWSERS
PAST, PRESENT AND FUTURE
AND
ANYONE ELSE
INTERESTED IN
THIS, THAT AND THE OTHER!

May the faith that gives us hope,
May the Love that shows the way,
May the Peace that cheers the Heart,
Be yours this day.

Table of Contents

1. Preface 6
2. Introduction 7
3. Geopathic Stress and Other unseen Energies 15
4. Shapes, Symbols and Signs or Checking Your Signals 35
5. Protection Symbols 44
6. Sparsholt Agricultural College, Winchester, 1992 47
7. College of Ripon and St. John, York, 1993 68
8. Royal Agricultural College, Cirencester, 1994 121
9. The Birth of the Sussex Dowsers 1995 140
10. Free Will 1995 143
11. Lincoln 1995 153
12. A May Adventure 162
13. Glasgow and Iona 1996 171
14. Hawkwood 1996 241
15. Cirencester Again – October 1997 271
16. Ascension Day '98 283
17. Ripon 1998 286
18. White Horses and Crop Circles 306
19. Kosmed 312
20. Ripon 2000 320
21. Jubilee 2003 336

22. Denman College..342

23. Postscript...344

24. The Stepping Stones..346

25. Index..349

1. Preface

Consequences is a tribute to the many wonderful people I met when a member of The British Society of Dowsers, many of whom are no longer on Planet Earth, also all the others who were stepping stones, and sadly again many are no longer on our beautiful Blue Planet.

The British Society of Dowsers was born in the year 1933 under the parentage of Colonel Bell, D.S.O., O.B.E., and I was born in the year 1933, through the union of my Mother, Ethel May Hubbard to my Father, Frederick Vivian Harris, M.C.. There are many Sally Williams on our Planet, and so, to save confusion, I'm using their surnames.

2. Introduction

> O, learn to read what silent love has writ
> O hear with eyes belongs to loves fine wit
> *Sonnet 23, Shakespeare*

> Knowledge is power, and is a mighty lever to
> stir the world. It may be acquired in various ways,
> but not without industry and perseverance.
> *Echoes, James Hoggarth*

> Knowledge wants toiling for, God means it so,
> He does not make the man with wisdom full;
> He places it within the reach of all,
> And the first step to get it is to try;
> *Echoes, James Hoggarth*

This is primarily a story book but includes a few tips on how to dowse for things which maybe harmful and discoveries I've made. The stories are of what happened to me after I became a dowser in 1986. In 1991 I joined the British Society of Dowsers (B.S.D.). I dowse with a Pendulum, something with a weight on the end, which could be a bunch of keys or a shopping bag or just my arm!

I think there is a beautiful description of this in Amos 7, v.7.

'This is what the Lord showed me: there was a man standing by a wall with a plumb-line in his hand. The Lord said to me,'What do you see Amos?' 'A plumb-line' I answered. and v. 17 goes on to state that the 'Your land shall be divided up with a measuring-line.'

Anyone who knows how to hang wallpaper will know what a plumb-line is, but if you don't, it is made with a piece of string with a weight on the end, that's a pendulum, then drawing a straight line on the wall. Now this bit of vital information came my way on 5 October 1991. At 8.35 am I was having a bath, pondering on the forthcoming week – I suddenly realised that if I was going to a service at Holy Trinity, Cuckfield, it had to be there and then. I hopped out the bath, flung on a very full red skirt, white blouse and white gloves – they were used for cleaning the silver but had just been washed.! Thus apparelled I'd hopped on my bicycle, pedalled furiously, skirt billowing out, the shadow reminded me of St. George going off to fight his dragon! Then low and behold when Valerie Hollingshurst read the lesson, that was IT. That service was the first the Revd. Nicholas Wetherall took in Holy Trinity but his title now is Revd. Canon Nicholas Wetherall, which he became in 2008.

The other bit of info which may help those who feel that dowsing maybe the work of the devil is the belief of the Catholic Church that if done for love in peoples homes, there is no harm in it.

On 26 March 1942 the Catholic Church stated that if a Christian wanted to do God's will and help himself and others by dowsing for water and examining homes, then this work was blessed by the Church. However the Church warned people not to use dowsing for evil or solely for gain, but only for works of love. (1)

The image people usually have, if they know what a dowser is, is of someone holding rods or a forked twig to find water, even if they don't know the name is dowsing or divining but people often think I'm saying I'm a DANCER but I'm not!

All Souls Day 1990, standing on a bend of Cuckfield High Street, I'd met an elderly man, Ernie Malins, who'd enquired how I was a-doing.

"I'm a dowser now" I'd replied, and his reply simply stunned me.

"Should think that befuddles you, you know old Colonel Bell who lived in the Vicarage, he was a great dowser!"

At that point a large articulated lorry roared round the bend. Had I heard correctly?

"What did you say?" I'd gasped. He'd repeated.

"Old Colonel Bell was a great dowser".

We were standing in line with the Vicarage, I'd nearly fainted, he'd held me up. I'd rushed home, looked in Dowsing by W.H. Trinder, (2) discovered Colonel A.H. Bell, D.S.O., O.B.E., had founded the British Society.

Now Colonel Bell wore a black Homburg (a soft felt hat with a little brim,) and Jane Crampton told me how some mischievous girls leant out the low windows of the Huguenot house, The Sanctuary in the High Street, now the home of Cuckfield's famous cookery writer, Katie Stewart, trying to pour water into it as he'd walked with brief case and brolly to catch the bus!

My Beginnings!

I found I could dowse in 1986. For 9 years I had gone to a Homoeopathic Consultant. When young I'd made the decision that if ever I could afford such a thing, I would go to one. One day at the M.Y. Club (Mothers & Young) in Haywards Heath, one of the members came in looking very well; she hadn't been for several months. I asked questions, learnt she had been ill and had gone to a Homoeopath. I asked who and where she lived, and thus Joan Rene came into my life. She lived at Highley Manor, Balcombe. She diagnosed using a Pendulum over a long tape divided with names of the various parts of the body and diseases. Whenever it came to the brain, it whizzed round and she'd turn and say:

"You have a good brain".

This always surprised me for I had been backward at school. With her Pendulum she could pick up Cancer when the size of a pin head and her treatment for that had been infusions of Sweet Violet leaves – Viola Odorata. Sweet violet leaves are one of the standard Herbal remedies for the background treatment of some Cancers, particularly of the lungs, throat and intestine (3)

In 1984, I had another bout of Cancer of the cervix. I'd refused a hysterectomy and tried alternative therapies. I went to the then

Complimentary Centre, Southampton and was treated by Dr. Julian Kenyon with Complex Homoeopathy.

I became a Vegan, following the recommendations of The Bristol Cancer Centre. The only thing I didn't do was drink carrot juice, which I'd tried when in Salisbury with Brenda Hawkins (Tills). I didn't like it, and now, I believe it is no longer recommended. The Bristol Cancer Centre has also changed it's name to The Penny Brohn Centre.

The diet had a brilliant effect upon my skin, the upper arms had those little pimples. For about three months I didn't like sleeping with myself, the smells emanating from me in the night were most unpleasant. My husband didn't have to breathe in that air. Due to his nightmares I'd already departed the matrimonial bed!

In 1986 I hadn't felt well again. I made an appointment with Miss Rene, I'd taken a basket crammed with the recommended foods for her to dowse. Several were not good for me, including soya milk.

This was the first time I had seen practical dowsing. Going to bed I'd wondered if I could do it, so I'd collected the foods. I'd found a Pendulum, in the form of a crucifix, held it over them; it whizzed round with the same result. I'd gone to bed euphoric, I could now look after myself! But don't use a crucifix in public. Marilynne Elliott warned me. I'd been spotted, twice, one thought I was in league with the devil and the other that I belonged to some alternative Christian sect and could I go and speak about it!

I then began to show my friends and they began dowsing but the only thing I **knew** then was holding a Pendulum over things which might be good or bad and seeing how it swung. Later I learnt more, but to save you having to wade through the stories I put it in here!

To determine how long the string or chain should be for dowsing, allow the Pendulum to slip through your finger and thumb until it swings happily, that will be the length it likes to work at. I like to have the chain over my forefinger but some people hold them just between the forefinger and thumb.

To learn one's signal one says "Show Me Yes" and whatever way a Pendulum swings that is your particular 'Yes' signal'. Then repeat saying 'Show Me No' and again whatever that signal is, that's your 'No'. I then ask: Do I have enough knowledge?

There are many ways of achieving this, maybe holding a Pendulum over something you know would be good for you and vice versa, or over each knee. Practice is the answer; when you know it, check, because in a different place there may be an energy which will switch it. T.C. Lethbridge wrote about this. (4)

In 1987, my friend Elaine, who'd become a dowser after I'd discovered my gift in 1986, was reading 'Here's Health Magazine'. She spotted an advertisement for an Advanced Dowsers Day Course with the late Jack Temple. She'd dowsed I should go, I did. I was so impressed I'd returned for the Beginners Course. One thing he later discovered was that if you lacked Aluminium it was a sign of Cancer.

This came about because I had dowsed the nutrients listed in the Bristol Diet Book (5) and Aluminium had come up as lacking. I'd said this on the first course, I'd repeated it on the second, and Jack had announced:

"Nobody should be lacking it, it's in tea and you've just had some!" Jack later learnt better!

Also in 1986 I'd wondered if there was some other reason why my problem kept returning, if there was an underlying cause. I'd mentioned this to Miss Rene. She suggested I had the house dowsed and so in due course I did.

Elaine was present when Mike Shaw and Eric Humeston came and dowsed the house for Geopathic Stress. They discovered two harmful Ley Lines. Watching how they were corrected, I'd known I could do the same thing. For several years I'd then carried in the boot of my car 18" lengths of angle Iron and my husband's heavy hammer, with the injunction not to lose it, alongside delicate wedding cakes. I'd wondered what the Police would say if they ever stopped me!

In due course the B.S.D. set up a Register of Dowsers working in this field. I was duly Registered, met some very interesting people and through dowsing discovered and resolved their problems.

Before Mike and Eric left, Mike said I should become a Healer. My rejoinder had been that I couldn't; I had two sons who were doctors! Well in spite of that, God saw that I did!

Tekels Park

In 1991 the B.S.D. held a course with Jack Temple at Tekels Park, Camberley. Friday evening I'd found myself sitting next to the then Assistant Secretary of the B.S.D. , Deirdre Rust. She had never known why the B.S.D. Journal was printed by Charles Clarke in Haywards Heath. I'd informed:

"Because Colonel Bell, who lived in the area, decided the Journal should be printed there, I imagine, in spite of being chairman of Bells Publishing!"

Saturday morning coffee break, I'd met the late Joy Austen, who'd requested I healed her dog! I was so surprised I didn't. think to ask what sort. It was an Alsatian! I was so shocked when faced with it, I couldn't think what to do, so just put my hands out, which apparently did the trick.

I'd found the Course so enjoyable I decided I owed it to Colonel Bell to join the B.S.D. The Council accepted me as a member in November 1991 under the name of Mrs. S. Williams. I resigned in 2005. At present I am a member of The Sussex Dowsers.

If I had a slogan, it would be:-

LONG LIVE DOWSING or DIVINING

Dowsing draws together, people from all sections of life, whose combined knowledge is of immense value to this troubled world. It is time it was appreciated and not derided or lampooned, but if this is not to happen dowsers must be vigilant and not allow themselves to be drawn into the hands of manipulators.

Dowsing led me to Spirituality, to dowse for Geopathic Stress and Harmful Energies, and Healing the Body through the early methods of Jack Temple. Jack was often derided but in 1989 he'd found the underlying cause of my then Pre-Cancer of the cervix, which was accepted by my Specialist, but this book is not about how I combated Cancer.

I hope you enjoy these adventure of mine but if some are not to your taste, or some bits, just skip and skip to another! The next is about Geopathic Stress, for I thought it would be a good to get it out of the way!

1. Are You Sleeping in a Safe Place? Dulwich Health Society, 5th Edition, 130 Gipsy Hill, London SE19 1PL

2. Dowsing, W. H. Trinder

3. Materia Medica, 1 year course, School of Herbal Medicine.

4. E.S.P. Time and Distance, T.C. Lethbridge

5. The Bristol Diet Dr. Alec Forbes, Century, ISBN 0 7126 0326 3

THE BRITISH SOCIETY OF DOWSERS

Registered Charity No. 295911
A Company Limited by Guarantee Reg. No. 2154580

Sycamore Barn, Hastingleigh,
Ashford, Kent TN25 5HW.

Telephone No: 0233 750253

THIS IS TO CERTIFY THAT

Mrs Sally V Williams

has been entered on the Society's Register of Practising Dowsers in the Section(s) given below for the period ending 30th June 1995, having paid the fee due and fulfilled all the conditions for entry on such Register.

Section 1: Site   Section 2: Healing

Signed *Michael Rust* (Secretary)

Date 1st June 1994

3. Geopathic Stress and Other unseen Energies

So what is Geopathic Stress? It is an umbrella term to cover all the so far known forms of adverse radiation emanating from above, around and below our planet and can be the underlying cause of much illness The energies in themselves may be good but when they come into conjunction with something else or be disrupted, they may become harmful. It is harmful because western man has been foolish and not learnt to live in harmony with Nature. Subterranean streams were there before we built our houses over them, but in the East man takes note of such things.

If you have ants entering your house and I hope not your pants, it maybe due to a black or negative Ley Line. Not everything dislikes adverse energies, cats, ants, some people thrive on them, others do not and you may have noticed ants left to their own devices often travel in straight lines. I certainly had ants entering my kitchen where the Ley Lines entered! Well that is what a Ley Line is, a straight line.

I had a young woman come to see me from many miles away. After she'd left I'd dowsed her bedroom, discovered the problem and healed it. Next day her mother phoned to say after she'd gone to work the CAT did not try to get into her room, she had always made a beeline before. I didn't even know they had a cat! This is an example how a dowser doesn't have to be on site to dowse.

Where there are positive radiations they may be used in healing. Ancient man certainly knew how to make the most of these energies, for good or bad and so I have heard did the Nazis.

I often meet people who do not want to believe in such things and think they must be a figment of a dowser's imagination! However, a special type of blood analysis was developed in Germany which I think proves the opposite.

A small amount of blood is put through a special process which includes distillation, separation and heating, to a high temperature, before being recombined. From the resulting clear liquid comes both analysis and medication. Drops on a glass slide form a crystalline pattern which can be 'read' by specially trained evaluators. When a person is under the influence of Geopathic Stress this shows straight lines. I found this very interesting as the energies are often found running thus!

The radiations go under a variety of names, sounding a bit like a can of Heinz 57 varieties. Ley Lines, Adverse Earth Radiations, Subterranean Streams, Hartman, Curry and Schumann Grids. No doubt as man progresses, more discoveries will be found to join this merry band.

Now what can be done if by some unfortunate quirk of fate one finds oneself living with one or more of this jolly lot. There are many ways as I discovered and it is up to each of us to decide how we want to tackle the problem.

As the years passed I learnt about using metal in the form of angle Iron and Copper banged into the ground, buying a gadget known as a RadiTech or Radi Corder, the use of Symbols, the Mind, Thought, Crystals and Stones.

I have seen these set in spherical resin in a combination tuned to help a particular person. I was told they could be very helpful but then I heard from another dowser they could have the reverse effect.

I do know that one needs to be careful when using any of these things because if someone is suffering from Heart trouble, to suddenly alter the energy can be detrimental. This maybe the reason why quite often people suffer a Heart attack whilst on holiday. They are sleeping in a different area. It is for reasons like this, that if everyone knew about the unseen hazards, they might be able to counteract them before they caused the onset of physical illness, including mental and emotional problems.

Now why are these radiations harmful to some and not to others? Why do some plants and animals like them and others not? Well they are energy and so is everything else. Some things need one type and others another. Our own body chemistry will determine what we require. Depending on our life style, what we eat, what we drink, where we have been, what vaccinations and illness's we have suffered, even what we have inherited, will all play a part on how we receive and utilise these energies. They have an affect upon how our bodies absorb nutrients. In some cases they stop it and in others leach it.

For years I took Vitamin E and when I tried to give it up I felt desperately tired for a few days. My young sons at the time thought it very funny when I said I thought I was suffering from withdrawal symptoms and then I wondered if there was a connection between Black Ley Lines and Vitamin E. I was certainly sleeping over them.

Ley Lines

It was in 1921 that Alfred Watkins had a flash of insight as to how these were formed. He worked out that Neolithic man made his first tracks by marking sighting points using staves from one hill to another, just as the Dodman is depicted on the Sussex Downs.

Watkins then looked at names on maps; he came up with 'Ley', the Saxon word for a straight line. It is actually quite easy to tell without being dowser where these tracks went, there is usually a V on the landscape, a dip in the hill line.

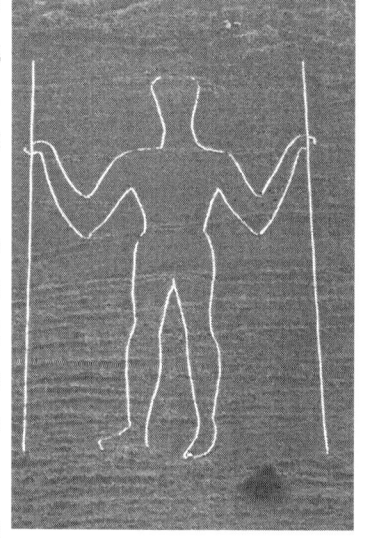

Prehistoric megalithic monuments like Stonehenge were built at the meeting points and subsequently Cathedrals and Churches upon the older places of ritual. Watkins thought it was the continual use of these paths which energised them but some people believe that ancient man was simply tapping into existing lines of energy. However by walking upon those lines he would have added his own energy, for everything leaves an energy imprint upon what it has touched

How did I know about them? I think I heard with half an ear, a radio programme. When I was ill in 1984, Miss Rene had also become very ill, partly due to a great deal of earth being removed from near her home; her neighbour was building an atomic bomb shelter! This upset the good Ley Lines, for if disturbed they become known as black, bad, inhospitable, negative or maybe any other word!

She knew there were Ley Lines because people would come dowsing for them. She lived on high ground, the place name: Highley!

In 1986 after I had worked really hard to get rid of my Cancer, I'd realised I wasn't well again and thought maybe there were other causes beside stress. If I had gone to the Bristol Cancer Centre I might have cottoned on a lot quicker about finding harmony in life, but Bristol cost money and I didn't feel I needed to spend all that on my health! Due to this aspect of myself, over the years I have discovered things by my own experience!

So what did my thoughts turn to. It was the previous inhabitants of our house and our neighbours!

Soon after we arrived my husband suffered traumatic nightmares and then depression. A previous owner had a baby born tragically with Leukaemia, another, according to local gossip, was an alcoholic. A neighbour's husband had died from Cancer and her father suddenly after sweeping the drive of snow.

I reported this to Miss Rene and she said I must get the house tested, and as you know, that is how Eric Humeston and Mike Shaw came into my life.

Then at a Cancer Contact Fund raising Coffee Morning, I met the late Marion Brown, told her I could now dowse with a Pendulum, and the possibility of Ley Lines. She said if I could do that, I could find out for myself! Well I was very busy at the time and didn't know what to do!

One Saturday morning, some months later, inspiration came. I dashed into my husband's empty bedroom, walking backwards across the room with my pendulum taking it from one side to the other and to my amazement found it went anti clockwise as it passed the bed, which was my signal for NO or BAD. I then tested the rooms on either side and found the same 5' band running through them. Either side of this band the Pendulum swung clockwise, my signal for Yes or Good. I then knew for certain something WAS wrong!

When husband was well out the way, into the garden shed I went, found two pieces of old Iron pipe, took them upstairs and hid them in a straight line under the bed. The Pendulum swung YES.

Next morning I ventured in to see his Lordship, enquired how he was, and to my astonishment he said in a very little voice:

"I'm alright!"

That was very different to my usual greeting!

"My God" I thought, "the Iron has worked". That was when I resolved to contact Eric again but I did nothing for a fortnight, kept putting it off! Then I got the urge!

Anthea Arnold had held a Colour Coding Party and I'd worn an emerald green velvet trouser suit. It had been a really interesting day but cycling home through Haywards Heath, I'd thought:

"I don't want to spend £30.00 on that, I know what colours I like to wear, I shall use that money to fund a fund raising party for the Royal Commonwealth Society for the Blind." Their headquarters are in Haywards Heath.

Back home, guilt set it, my poor house was neglected; I set about cleaning the outside dining-room windows and when some were looking better and I was also feeling better, bang on 5 pm. I had the urge to phone Eric. The other windows would just have to wait. I rang, he apologized for not having done anything before but then said:

"Hold on".

I did, and did, I could hear talking, presumed it was a customer but after a while he returned and said someone had just entered the shop who could help me.

That someone was Group Captain Mike Shaw, who amongst other things, used a Pendulum for healing purposes and corrected Ley Lines and Adverse Earth Radiation. He promptly dowsed, said I was quite correct but that my husband's bed was not entirely covered by the Iron pipes.

T.C. Lethbridge worked out with the aid of a long Pendulum that everything sends out its own ray for a specific distance. The rays of the Iron pipes did not reach one side, I hadn't centred them. I checked; he was correct. Mike was taught his dowsing skills by Bruce MacManaway, the father of Patrick, whom I later met!

Then I had the Fund Raising Lunch, raised over a couple of hundred quid, then I went with the money in a jam jar to their headquarters. As it was being counted, I'd wearily said:

"Do you ever sponsor medical students for their Electives?" The answer was:

"Yes".

So that's how one son, quite desperate as to where he was going, went on an Elective to India, leaving all his dirty washing behind. I'd been told some of his accommodation might not be up to standard. Next thing I heard on a postcard was that he was awaiting for his tea to be served in the garden, I seem to remember on a Silver salver!

So the Dowsers came, I saw what they did, as you have already read, told me I should become a Healer but they also told us about Gustav Freiherr von Pohl, a German scientist and dowser. What they said was quite frightening and when I tell people this I feel the need to put protection around us, so stop at this point reading, and do it for yourself if you feel the need. I use the thought of the protective Yellow Light.

An Underlying Cause of Cancer

In 1929 von Pohl dowsed the village of Vilsbiburg with a population of 3,300. He didn't go on site, he dowsed a map in his own home many miles away. He found 54 houses which had adverse radiations. Unbeknown to him, the local council did some research, researching where everyone who had died of Cancer had lived. The answer was in those 54 houses!

That sent a shiver down my legs when I heard that. Von Pohl published a book in 1932 detailing what he had found but his views were not acceptable in the Germany which was then emerging. Mike Shaw had also discovered the same thing as he'd dowsed peoples homes.

Valerie Lee lived in Crawley, had Cancer and was a member of Cancer Contact, founded by Kit Mouat, a Tribune Poet, who wrote about her in:

'Fighting for Our Lives' subtitled:' An Introduction to Living with Cancer. with a preface by Sheila Hancock'.(1)

'This is a fascinating book written by a Cancer patient who is one of the founder members of a self-help group for Cancer patients....I learnt a lot...I encourage you all to read it.' *NURSING TIMES.*

Valerie had been very sceptical about dowsing, then at the hairdressers she'd read about 'Are You Sleeping in a Safe Place' (2) which she promptly ordered then, discovered it was about dowsing and finding good and bad places to sit and sleep.

She made herself a Pendulum and got 'hooked'. Her Pendulum gave a NO swing in certain rooms. At the next meeting she spoke to the late May Cottington and Janet Willis. They told her what I had done for them, so she'd phoned. I said I would be able to tell her from my own home if there were lines and where they flowed. I don't think she believed me!

I agreed to survey her house but before going I wrote down where I thought the lines were, crossing in her sitting room and one going through her bedroom. I had never been to her house. She was amazed when I showed her the note, because that was where she had found them. A dowser plugs into the electro magnetic rays. When I asked about someone's house, stating the name and address, I got a tingling feeling in my hands. I felt 'plugged in'

Valerie lent me the book and the book was the reason Valerie came into my life. In due course I visited the Dulwich Health Society which turned out to be an electrical firm that turned its hand to make a gadget to deal with harmful earth radiations. The RadiTech.

I then wrote about Ley Lines and in June 1987 I wrote to Mike Shaw asking for verification. He filled me in briefly about Adverse Earth Radiations and not only von Pohl but the Austrian, Kathe Bachler.

Kathe had researched vast numbers of children and found that their problems could all be traced to Geopathic Stress. Due to this, the Austrian Government then made sure that children no longer sat in the same place for a whole school year, so there is something to be said for our large comprehensives, with pupils moving from classroom to classroom, not waiting for the teacher to come to them, as happened in my day

'Are You Sleeping in a Safe Place' (2) sited all the research done on the Continent proving that where you sleep or sit, does have a very important affect. Not only Cancer but so many of the other illnesses which mankind seems to suffer.

The day before visiting Valerie I'd dowsed where I had lived in my childhood. My Pendulum indicated there were two black Ley Lines intersecting just outside my bedroom and my mother's bedroom. My Father died of T.B in that bedroom and my Mother succumbed to breast Cancer. I was also very spiteful to my best friend and was backward.

My Mother's next home was a flat, a subterranean stream and Curry line ran through her bathroom and kitchen, she was reasonably well there, so they didn't upset her. Her last home in the centre of Chichester in a beautiful Queen Anne house had a very powerful line going straight under her bed towards the Cathedral and then she came here!

It was amazing that she kept going for 25 years and not surprising that the Cancer kept returning. The lady in the flat above my mother had psychiatric problems and regularly at midnight would make banging noises. Mum thought she was moving her furniture.

G.P.S. maybe the underlying cause of so much illness but I cannot stress how important the MIND and PRAYER is as a counteracting force. When she was undergoing treatment at the Middlesex Hospital in the 1960's, a doctor read all her 1948 notes, and commented that she should not have survived her initial treatment of Radium She had been a guinea pig at St. Bartholomew's Hospital. Her Consultant, Mr. John Beattie, thought he'd killed her! Just before the end of her life, I'd asked her why she hadn't died, she'd replied:

"I would not leave you an orphan"!

This Doctor felt that her life was not due only to the skill of the medical profession but her will power and faith.

Rolf Gordon wrote "Are you Sleeping in a Safe Place" (2) because his own son died of Cancer at 25. He was making good progress until he moved into a cottage and his bed was over a subterranean stream. Mr. Gordon felt that everyone ought to be made aware of what may be coming up at them and thus 'Are You Sleeping in a Safe Place' (2) was born and he invented the RadiTech.

What to do about it? Some dowsers say move house! That's drastic! Next advice, move the bed or seating to a safe area but this is not always possible, as in my house. What I believe needs to be done is for Mother Earth to be healed.

I did this through prayer, standing in the Kitchen with a sketch map of the place in question, oriented North and shut my Chakras down to an appropriate level. These are entrances of energy linked to the Endocrine Glands. I then said an appropriate prayer, invoking whoever came to mind. When an electrical problem was a fault, I found the Buddha was invoked. I would then ask questions as to what sort of problem and these are mentioned later in this chapter.

After Mike and Eric had banged in the angle Iron, a couple of months later I thought it might be a good idea to check my bedroom again. I did and to my horror the Pendulum swung NO. I didn't know what it could be.

I phoned Mike for help and enticed with the thought of a good lunch he returned and dowsed, which resulted in the knowledge there were Subterranean Streams crossed with Curry Lines sapping my bodies energy flow and nutrients!

Pendulum in hand Mike discovered the crossing points, which we marked by placing pieces of old Copper pipe on the carpet! One, under the large double bed, the other near my bed.

Two days later I'd breakfasted in bed, I'd felt like a bit of coddling, I'd been very busy making cakes, this was a free day. Then I'd pondered on how to spend it. I decided upon lunch with Rosemary Baxter. Rosemary and I have been friends for over 42 years, she moved to Cuckfield three weeks after we had, and lived further down the road. Another amazing woman who has done much in her life to help others and moved home several times whilst we stayed put.

That sorted, I'd then thought about the Copper pipes. I could not live with two pieces of pipe lying on the carpet, they'd get moved when cleaning!

I jumped up, rolled the heavy carpets back, found a convenient trap cut in one board but nothing under the large bed.

It was a case of taking to a saw, remembering to cut the floor board over a joist, which made it very difficult. My husband had been a real expert at this and I just wished I'd watched him. It was very hard work, a very hot day and I was reduced to bra and pants!

Half way through I went off to lunch, returning with a rather blunt little saw and eventually prized a section free. I then wiggled the Copper pipe under the felt insulation, and checked with my Pendulum it was at the correct angle.

I then wrote on the underside of the floorboard what I had done, why, and the date. I replaced the boards, countersinking the screws and got the room straight just before my husband returned. I knew only too well what he would say about my actions!

On reflection I realised it would be possible to alter these radiations by either going under a house or up into the loft which I did for some friends. Though I disliked heights and ladders I felt this was the only way to do it! However I have never been in our loft for there is no fixed ladder, so it did not occur to me to get up there.

Radiations rise and according to my Pendulum it appears that at whatever level a piece of angle Iron or Copper pipe is placed, it corrects the radiations upwards and downwards for about 15'. So that was how that problem was dealt with but in the fullness of time I learnt to do such work in another way, through prayer which cannot, hopefully, get moved!

I learn from doing things my way, in this case it was not quite blood, sweat and tears, but certainly a lot of sweat!

So how to do this for yourself. You could make a pair of dowsing rods from a pair of wire coat-hangers which people laugh at but are very effective but Mike taught me Teleradethsia which is talking to a Pendulum and asking questions and just to remind you, I've included them here again! Sadly Mike is no longer on Planet Earth.

Teleradethsia

These are them!

May I ?, Can I?, Should I?.

I also add:

Do I have enough knowledge?

I don't think there is any point in dowsing if you don't know what you are hoping to find out!

If having checked all signals, and getting a **YES** to all of them, then ask the first question and having asked it make your mind go **blank**. Julian Kenyon said this was difficult for someone who had knowledge on the subject, but for me with no scientific knowledge there would be no problem!

"Does this house suffer from Geopathic Stress?" If yes,

"Is it Ley Lines?" If yes,

"Is it one, is it two, are they black."

Then enquire where they are, asking in turn about each room.

If the answer to Ley Lines is NO, then enquire about Adverse Earth Radiations or Subterranean Streams. If yes, ask similar questions to the Ley Lines and find out which way they flow.

If the answer is 'No', ask if it is a Curry Line or some other. Don't forget, if you did discover black Ley Lines you also need to ask if there are any other Adverse Radiations, which Mike and Eric omitted to do on that first visit.

Having discovered there is a problem, then go to the rooms in question and walk backwards down the length and breadth, having first told the Pendulum to indicate where the harmful Ley Lines or sub streams etc. are, otherwise you may pick up things like Quartz clocks, which Valerie discovered. Not all affect a Pendulum, it depends on how the battery is fitted.

Well that's what you do if you are dowsing in situ, and having found the problem lines, you can ask if there are any other things in that room which are also harmful, if yes, then ask what!

Having found the line, one then has to discover which way the energy is flowing. Do this by sticking out you other arm and slowly turning or simply saying,:

"Are you flowing North – South, East – West etc. or just point at something.

Then if it is Ley Lines or crossing sub streams I go outside and trace the line. You need to be on the side of the house where the energy is entering. Then check the width of the line, then ask the Pendulum to show where the angle Iron should be placed. Retrace the line, the Pendulum should be swinging 'No'. When it gets to the centre of the energy flow it will change to 'Yes'. I then pick up the Iron, place it over the spot indicated, rotate it with one hand, until when in the correct position the Pendulum will forcibly swing backwards and forwards on the line of the energy. It will also do this inside the house. If there is no suitable place in the garden you may have to go to the next house, I have been as far as four houses away.

Parallel streams are a different kettle of fish. First Aid is to place angle Iron along the line of the streams, under a bed, in a loft but then I discovered that by drawing a line and putting a circle through it would do the trick, do this over whichever stream is higher.

Now to the Curry Lines named after Dr. Manfred Curry, a Medical Doctor and Biochemist. During the course of his research he discovered that just under the earth's surface there is an electromagnetic-magnetic grid running N.E. – S.W. and N.W. – S.E. Where these lines intersect the radiations are particularly strong. Get these on top of a sub. stream and there is real trouble.

Now I come to the last of the lines which I have read about, Hartmann, a grid found by Dr. Ernst Hartmann and the lines run N. - S. and E. - W.

Schumann waves were identified by Professor W.O Schumann and play an important part in health. Steel and concrete buildings, aeroplanes, all act as insulators from these resonances. Jet lag and a feeling of tiredness can be the result.

If map dowsing, then one asks the same questions, discover what and where, and draw in the appropriate lines, with arrows pointing in the direction in which the energy is flowing and having said the appropriate prayer, the problem is healed. **Voilà**.

Selenium

According to my Pendulum, Selenium is affected by sub. streams. I was tested for deficiencies by Julian Kenyon and he did not suggest I should take it. Strange for Selenium is considered very important for anyone with Cancer, as it combines with Vitamin E to stop damage occurring in the cells. Valerie Lee had read that Selenium should be taken before breakfast, and my Pendulum corroborated the fact. Then some months later I decided to check whether it still wasn't required and if not, WHY?

I held a little conference with my Pendulum:

"Is it all the healing I have done to my body? (I had been using the early methods of Jack Temple.) Answer:

"NO".

"Is it to do with the Ley Lines?"

No.

Is it to do with this bedroom?"

Yes.

"Is it to do with subterranean streams?"

Yes!

"Do I need selenium now?"

Yes.

When I was tested I wasn't sleeping in that bedroom!

If there is a connection between Geopathic Stress and absorption of nutrients, when you consider that an underlying cause of illness may be harmful radiations of one sort or another, no wonder it has been found that Cancer sufferers are low in particular nutrients.

David Holmes of the then Wessex Cancer Centre, (W.C.C) told me that the first thing the W.C.C. did was to give these nutrients to their patients to build up their blood levels and he had seen dramatic improvements. Even after the crossed sub. streams had been corrected, it took three months for my body to have enough Selenium. Radiation such as from a Laser has also an effect upon the absorption of Selenium.

I believe the energy lines Mike and Eric found in my house, two 'Black Crossing Ley Lines ' were in fact emitting a low electrical force, ELF or YIN which when the angle Iron was banged in altered to Yang or a higher electrical frequency, which is actually beneficial.

If underground cables meet an earth energy line, it is not the current, Electricity, but the metal of which they are comprised, Copper, which changes to a low frequency ELF and the element, which was Vanadium when the energy was Yang, now becomes one of five. I discovered this information between 5 pm and 5.15 on Thursday, 20th October, 1994.

1 = Hafnium No. 72 .... affects Sodium

2 = Mendelevium, No.101 ...... affects Magnesium

3 = Osmium, No76 .... affects Chromium

4 = Samarian, No.62 .... affects Selenium

5 = Xenon, No54 .... affects Calcium

Having discovered the above I felt I should check it out with a physicist Michael Watson whom I'd met in 1992 at my first Congress. He confirmed that the Copper wires could do this.

Subterranean streams may affect the availability of Nitrogen, Boron, Silica, Iron, Copper.

I got hooked on the Periodic Table years ago, once discovering when the energies flow through to us and the last one, which took a couple of days to achieve was Zirconium, No40, and it set my new electronic typewriter - which was switched on - moving. I was petrified!

1. Fighting for Our Lives, Kit Mouat, Heretic Books, PO Box 247 London N15 6RW. ISBN 0-946097-14-3

2. Are You Sleeping in a Safe Place? Dulwich Health Society, 130 Gipsy Hill, London, SE19 1PL ISBN 0 951 4017 0X

    Tel: 020 8670 5883 www.dulwichhealth.co.uk

Periodic Table This was dowsed during the week 14 March 1990 culminating with Zirconium at 2.30A.M. Friday 23 March.

<u>Violet - Crown Chakra</u>

Actinium	=	6 P.M. Midnight
Bismuth	=	" "
Bromine	=	" "
Cobalt	=	" "
Europium	=	6 A.M. - Mid-day
Gadolinium	=	Mid-day - 6 P.M.
Gallium	=	Mid-night - 6 A.M.
Lead	=	Mid-day - 6 P.M.
Lithium	=	6 A.M. - Mid-day
Radon	=	Midnight - 6 A.M.
Terbium	=	6 A.M. - Mid-day

Indigo - Brow Chakra

Polonium	=	Midnight – 6 A.M.
Potassium	=	Midday – 6 P.M.
Rubidium	=	6 A.M. – Midday
Strontium	=	" "

Blue - Throat Chakra

Caesium	=	Midnight – 6 A.M.
Indium	=	Midday – 6 P.M.
Oxygen	=	6 A.M. – Midday

Green - Heart Chakra

Barium	=	Midnight – 6 A.M.
Chlorine	=	Midday – 6 P.M.
Chromium	=	" "
Fluorine	=	6 P.M. – Midnight
Mercury	=	6 A.M. – Midday
Nickel	=	Midnight – 6 A.M.
Nitrogen	=	6 A.M. – Midday
Radium	=	" "
Tellurium	=	Midnight – 6 A.M.
Thallium	=	6 A.M. – Midday
Zinc	=	Midday – 6 P.M.

Yellow - Solar Plexus Chakra

Cerium	=	Midday – 6 P.M.
Gold	=	" "
Iodine	=	" "
Iron	=	6 A.M. – Midday
Lanthanum	=	" "
Magnesium	=	" "

Molybdenum	=	" "
Palladium	=	" "
Phosphorus	=	Midnight - 6 A.M.
Platinum	=	Midday - 6 P.M.
Rhodium	=	" "
Ruthenium	=	Midnight - 6 A.M.
Silver	=	" "
Sodium	=	" "
Sulphur	=	" "
Tin	=	" "
Titanium	=	Midday - 6 P.M.
Tungsten	=	6 P.M. - Midnight
Uranium	=	6 A.M. - Midday
Vanadium	=	" "

Orange - Sacral Chakra

Helium	=	6 P.M. - Midnight
Hydrogen	=	" "
Krypton	=	" "
Neon	=	Midday - 6 P.M.
Selenium	=	Midnight - 6 A.M.
Silicon	=	Midday - 6 P.M.
Xenon	=	6 A.M. - Midday

Red - Base Chakra

Aluminium	=	Midday - 6 P.M.
Antimony	=	" "
Arsenic	=	Midnight - 6 A.M.
Boron	=	" "
Cadmium	=	6 A.M. - Midday
Calcium	=	" "
Copper	=	" "

The remaining Elements in 1990 ****** Minor Chakras ****Time G.M.T

Left Foot - Dark Grey

Americium	=	6 P.M. - Midnight
Astatine	=	Midnight - 6 A.M.
Lutetium	=	" "
Manganese	=	6 A.M. - Midday
Promethium	=	6 P.M. - Midnight
Yttrium	=	Midnight - 6 A.M.

Left Thigh - Scarlet

| Thorium | = | 6 A.M. - Midday |

Left Hip - Apricot

| Beryllium | = | 6 A.M. - Midday |
| Thulium | = | Midday - 6 P.M. |

Left Shoulder - Dark Brown

| Argon | = | Midday - 6 P.M. |
| Rhenium | = | "   " |

Left Elbow - Beige

Berkelium	=	6 P.M. - Midnight
Hafnium	=	Midday - 6 P.M.
Mendelevium	=	Midnight - 6 A.M.

Junction Transverse Colon / Descending Colon – Cambridge Blue

Carbon	=	6 A.M. – Midday
Lawrencium	=	6 P.M. – Midnight
Niobium	=	Midnight – 6 A.M.

Spleen – Pink – Below Tummy Button

Dysprosium	=	6 P.M. – Midnight
Erbium	=	Midday – 6 P.M.

Above Left Brest – Leaf Green

Curium	=	Midday – 6 P.M.
Francium	=	6 P.M. – Midnight

Left side Throat – Turquoise

Einsteinium	=	6 A.M. – Midday
Fermium	=	Midnight – 6 A.M.
Plutonium	=	6 A.M. – Midday

Right Foot – Light Grey

Hahnium	=	Midday – 6 P.M.
Iridium	=	6 A.M. – Midday
Neodymium	=	" "
Nobelium	=	6 P.M. – Midnight

Right Knee – Gold

Osmium	=	6 P.M. – Midnight
Samarium	=	Midday – 6 P.M.

Right Hip – Copper

Rutherfordium   =   6 A.M. – Midday

Right Shoulder – Light Brown

Technetium   =   Midday – 6 P.M.
Ytterbium   =   "   "

Right Elbow – Wine

Californium   =   6 A.M. – Midday
Germanium   =   Midnight – 6 A.M.
Protactinium   =   "   "
Zirconium   =   "   "

Above Right Breast – Dark Green

Neptunium   =   Midday – 6 P.M.
Tantalum   =   Midnight – 6 A.M.

Right side Throat – Aquamarine

Holmium   =   6 A.M. – Midday
Praseodymium   =   Midnight – 6 A.M.
Scandium   =   Midday – 6 P.M.

4. Shapes, Symbols and Signs or Checking Your Signals

Well have you decided to become a Dowser? If you have and you turn out to be like me (I hope you are not saying "God Forbid") you might encounter some HAZARDS along the way. Things which can switch your signals and this is why it is so important to check whenever dowsing. Even if you don't want to be a Dowser you might just find the following of interest.

Furniture:

This is another problem. I had been invited to a lunch and afterwards dowse their home, and all the other guests bar me, played Bridge. I felt rather out of the conversation. Lunch over, my work began. There was a lot of antique furniture and over one piece I got a 'No' swing.

I dowsed how long it had been like that, it was sometime in the 19c. I asked the owners if it could be that age, and they said Yes. There were other pieces which I got a 'No' to, including a side table where we had sat at lunch. Another of the guests had felt she couldn't walk past it when she required a pee!

What to do about it. At the time I was recommending the RadiTech, but the owners didn't wish to have one.

As I came home I thought about the problem and eventually this lead me to finding symbols of protection.

Long Pendulums

I'd borrowed from the Library a book by T.C. Lethbridge and learnt one could use a long Pendulum to discover all sorts of things, depending on the measurement, including the sex of unborn babies!

I made one, over 40" long with a good weight on the end. Our first grandchild was on the way. The parents came to stay and my daughter-in-law was only too happy to be dowsed. I sat her down in the sitting-room by the door. The result was I thought we were going to have a little grandson and proudly told my son.

Having done this, I got an awful ribbing from my family.

"Only 50/50 chance of getting it wrong"

"What will you think of your Pendulum if you do get it wrong?"

This from youngest son who felt I was putting far too much trust in it

In the event we had a beautiful little granddaughter! On my return from helping the new Mum, I found my usual Pendulum placed on the kitchen waste-bin but at least it hadn't been thrown in!

Why did I make this mistake? I did not know then about asking questions, such as the VITAL one, **Show me Yes**. This is why I think it so IMPORTANT that people KNOW what they are doing when they hold a Pendulum. I eventually discovered it was the Black Ley Line that caused my downfall, which daughter-in-law was sitting over! However Dowsers know they learn from their mistakes.

It was because of this mistake that I was motivated into reading more. I wanted to KNOW why I had got it wrong.

The next book, 'E.S.P. Time and Distance' also by T.C. Lethbridge, (1) put me on the right track. I learnt that there were things which could alter the swing of the Pendulum. He had come across many, one of which was salt.

I found it lethal to dowse anywhere near this unless I was dowsing over my chopping board. Eventually I discovered that if I drew six pointed stars all around the salt container, this would stop the interference.

But why? I think it is something to do with energy, Magnetism, and shape but I do not have the necessary knowledge to be able to explain the phenomenon. However some months later Elaine and I discovered what appeared to be a reason for symbolism. It was a method of protecting the entrances of energy in the unseen, esoteric, body which I had just learnt about.

This body is known as the Aura and the energy enters through Chakras, The Base, Sacral, Solar Plexus, Heart, Throat, and Third Eye are all linked to Endocrine Glands.

The symbols stop adverse energies entering. They are like having a security pass to enter a place of high security. Others have made similar discoveries which Elaine and I had not come across

I first became aware that symbols can play an important part in some peoples lives when I iced a very unusual wedding cake. I had to put upside-down triangles all around the top tier. Instead of flowers there was a strange symbol atopping the edifice.

I mentioned this when John and Hazel Burgess were visiting from Australia. John stems from Sussex and Surrey, and he said:

"Oh that's to do with the Old Religion. There's a lot of it about in Sussex". I didn't know there was one! Many of my friends became quite worried about me decorating that cake. One afternoon a thunderstorm raged and I really became very frightened.

A strange thing occurred on the night of collection. I had gone to an evening party at Cuckfield Park and whilst there joined the Cuckfield Society as a Life Long Member for the princely sum of £5.00, quite the best investment I've ever made!

On my return I discovered a calamity had occurred. My husband had carried the top tier of the cake down the drive, there was a small pothole, his ankle went over and the **piece de résistance** fell off! Now he had never carried a cake down the drive! I came home to discover the bridal party sitting round the kitchen table trying to put it all together again.

I suggested flowers might be nice instead, but no, so at Midnight I made another topknot with different icing!

So what was atop this cake? The round sun, a crescent moon and a snake or perhaps I should call it a serpent!

The next bit of information came from Mike Shaw. I had been mucking around with lead on the T.V. I'd used the Mager Rosette to discover the colours emanating and the description of that little disk is in Chapter 16, Ripon 1998. The lead reversed the energies, which made it safe to sit in front of the box .

Now why was I concerned about sitting in front of the Box. Evelyn Ward had alerted me in 1985 about the dangers of this modern invention. She said that the German-born US physician Max Gerson maintained that if one had Cancer, then sitting in front of the magic box would result in death, but I had instinctively sat at the side of the box. On dowsing with the Mager disc I discovered the rays at the side were not harmful.

Mike said Bruce MacManaway could do it with a drawing. I didn't know if he had used a lead pencil for graphite can alter the swing, or whether it was a shape, whether the drawing was bending, absorbing or earthing the rays. If you read on, you will discover what the drawing was and what it did but it was several months before inspiration and enlightenment was to be mine.

Some months after the adverse radiations from the Ley Lines and Subterranean Streams were neutralised, I entered the dining room holding my Pendulum, it was an evening when I felt in need of a little drink! As I entered the Pendulum started swinging 'NO'! I wondered why for it wasn't because of the drink! I decided it was probably due to the upright piano. I got the drink!

It was weeks later when I decided to see what was the cause. It wasn't said piano, or any of the bits adorning the top, it was the reading lamp, circa 1940's, the sort with a half moon shade and arm which bends, 'growing' from a shaped base, something akin to a Heart. The bit the Pendulum didn't like was the base. I wondered why. I thought if I put a round object underneath the lamp, in some way this might complete the half moon of the shade. There was a hollow underneath the base and I placed a penny there. The swing altered.

I was so excited I phoned Elaine with the 'hot' news and we wondered what it was all about but then I decided I didn't want to know!

Then I discovered the kettle was also doing the same thing to the Pendulum but it wasn't the actual kettle, that I'd checked some months before, but it's lid. Again there was the same shape, one where the knob was fixed to lift the lid and the other the hole for the steam. I didn't do anything about this until some time later.

Elaine and I were dowsing. I reminded her about the effect the kettle was having on her dowsing. She made remarks to the effect of my "ruddy" kettle and my nerve to grumble about her house!

When she left I decided that something should be done. I thought of sticking a coin on the bottom but didn't feel that would be right. Then I had an idea, I would draw a circle. The kettle stood on a mat and that was where I drew it using a Biro. It did the trick! I duly informed Elaine that in future she could dowse in safety in my kitchen.

LAMP

KETTLE

LID

Then came a Friday. I felt it was my duty to remove some dust and dirt from the family home. Out came the Electrolux. By the time I got to the bedrooms my mind was on to wondering what Bruce MacManaway placed on a T.V. I decided to seek help from the Pendulum.

Was it a circle? No.

Was it a cross? No.

Was it a triangle? No.

Was it a star? Yes. What sort? Six pointed, the Star of David.

I drew one and took it downstairs, I didn't even cut it out. I removed the lead from the T.V. and the room. I held the Pendulum all round the set, it swung Yes.

I placed the drawing upon the set, still Yes all the way round. I switched on which resulted in a 'Yes' swing in front but a 'No' behind. When there was no drawing and no lead weight, the signals were reversed. I also got 'No signals from the hall and kitchen, so not good for anyone there!

So that's how that's done, I thought and returned to the Electrolux. In my travels to try and make sense of all this I eventually met the man who had told Bruce MacManaway, at which point I felt I had come full circle.

FLINT

I have had my allotment since 1967. In 1987 I dug up a piece of Flint. I looked at it in amazement, I felt it had been sent to me for a special reason. I looked at it very carefully. It was smooth on one side but with ridges on the other which had been cut. I thought it might have been a partially formed arrow head. It had certainly been abandoned. The first time I dowsed this stone it made me feel very woozy. Pat Pope dowsed it and she decided it was going to be a tool. My Pendulum agreed and indicated a man had been working on it.

The reason I wrote about it was because:

a. I found it overrode salt

b. It is an example of how you can discover things by asking questions.

I kept it on top of the fridge/freezer where there were a couple of salt cellars.

Why does it do this? The working of the Flint with I presume another piece, for Flint was the only tool of the day, energised it and the power of that energy was greater than anything else around.

It was the same with my chopping board but in that case it was the action of the knives energising it and I found that was the safest place to dowse but not if a knife was upon it.

I decided my Flint must have been a reject but never mind, I would always treasure it but treasure or not, I can't find it this morning! I did check another, ordinary piece, to see if it had the same effect, it didn't.

Then Cyril Pike (Vice-Chairman of Cuckfield Parish Council) came to help me with a problem on my allotment, and I learnt that the Cuckfield area had once been a Flint factory. He had studied the subject and had a collection of tiny flints, and one day the pair of us were to be seen in the High Street huddled together as I viewed them.

This is just one of the many instances which have happened since I became a Dowser. Information just comes without any searching from me!

Switchers!

I next discovered that my signals changed when dowsing near my old Olivetti typewriter, but if I crossed my feet, left over right, this didn't happen. It isn't any good doing the opposite unless you are left handed and holding the Pendulum in that hand. What happens when I do this I do not know but I feel there is a scientific explanation maybe to do with electromagnetism. Miss Rene always made sure her patients were sitting with nothing crossed.

When I stumbled upon this it got me thinking about how we cross our fingers. When children we would cross them if we told a fib. If asked if we were telling the truth we would say we hadn't got anything crossed! We cross our fingers or legs for luck. So maybe after all we haven't lost touch completely with what our ancestors knew; oh what a relief! Is there hope for us after all?

Some other switchers are Gold, Brass, depending on the shape, and objects which have absorbed radiation due to being in an area of harmful radiation or the very substance from which they were made came from such a place. Oaks like a Ley Line! Therefore furniture made from it might be harmful.

Now don't get paranoid, for you've lived with it, go on living with it, but you could try altering especially if you feel it might be harming someone or something!

How you do this will be up to you but there are many ways to overcome this, the greatest and cheapest being THOUGHT!

There is one hazard to dowsing, which I know of, and that could be YOU! For some reason - I rather think it is to do with the phases of the moon - a Pendulum may suddenly tell you a load of nonsense! It could suddenly say 'Yes' to a mixture of food which you know well isn't correct for you.

When this happens I hold the Pendulum about 6" in front of my chest or in front of my feet. If it makes no movement I know I have lost the power to dowse. I've been switched off. The first time this happened Jack Temple alerted me.

We were on the phone and he was checking levels of nutrients and he couldn't get a reading. This is an example of long distance dowsing. I had to use my hand and span from one part of my body which still had 'current' and then dowse what pills had to go on to get the energy flowing again. Well that method was only applicable when using Jack's methods of healing but there is another way.

I went to see Ann Higgins, a healer in Worthing, to have my Chakras balanced and she told me a very simple method. I had to say a few words which worked but I wasn't too happy just doing that, so I turned them into a prayer of supplication, and made the sign of the cross on completion, which for me, felt right.

Prayer: Dear Lord, if it by Thy Will, please let there be Harmony and Balance between my Head and Base Chakras, Harmony and Balance between my Throat and Sacral Chakras, and Harmony, Love and Balance between my Heart and Solar Plexus Chakras. Amen.

Request: There is Harmony and Balance in my Base Centre and all levels of my Being, there is Harmony and Balance in my Sacral Centre and all levels of my Being, there is Harmony and Balance in my Solar Plexus Centre and all levels of my Being, there is Harmony and Balance in my Heart Centre and all levels of my Being, there is Harmony and Balance in my Throat Centre and all levels of my Being, there is Harmony and Balance in my Anjna Centre and all levels of my Being, there is Harmony and Balance in my Crown Centre and all levels of my Being.

Why this should happen I do not know and I asked Edmund Harold, a Crystal healer, and he said it happened all the time to clairvoyants and such like and Jack had his views. Elaine was with me when I saw Ann and as she worked Elaine felt a cool current of air cross the room!

I then discovered if I was dowsing someone and they lost their 'current', if I placed my finger on them, they were switched on again, my energy re-energized them, rather like placing a jump lead between two cars to get the battery working again.

1. E.S.P. Time and Distance, T.C. Lethbridge.

5. Protection Symbols

One afternoon Elaine was sitting in my kitchen whilst I was decorating yet another wedding cake; we started thinking about symbols! The resulting table is what we came up with which solved the problem posed when those people did not want to buy a RadiTech.

I was so astonished from our experiments that yet once again I had to flee to my allotment to ground myself, for for me there is nothing like a bit of gardening or ironing, or cleaning, to do it!

Chakra	Colour	Gland	Symbol	Place to put it
Crown	Violet	Pineal	⊕ (sun-edged)	Walls, Pylons
Brow	Indigo	Pituitary	⊗ (sun-edged)	Furniture
Throat	Blue	Thyroid	⊙ octagon (sun-edged)	Vehicles
Heart	Green	Thymus	✚ (sun-edged)	Hoffman and Curry lines, TV, VDU, Microwave

Solar Plexus	Yellow	Pancreas	✡	TV, VDU, Microwave
Sacral	Orange	Gonads	△	Ley Lines, Radar
Base	Red	Adrenals	†	Subterranean Streams, Nuclear Industry, Radon Gas

The above were discovered in March 1990. Four more came from a friend in Holland.

Electricity

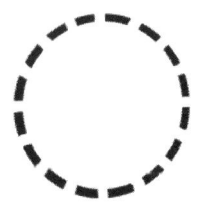

Cosmic man, Just above Heart Chakra to protect Core Star.

Five pointed star – Schumann Waves – Use when flying.

Tail Bone – Electricity in the body and Pituitary.

Television Aerials

On highest aerial place the symbol of a Golden Cock as seen on top of Churches. This cuts down the Magnetism coming from the set – try first measuring the extent to which it extends in the room. A Spider plant also helps.

Cocks: In Christianity Cocks greet the dawn of the sun of Christ in the East, Christ putting to flight the powers of evil and darkness; vigilance, hence used as a weather vane turning in all directions to watch for powers of evil; the gilded, solar cock guards the steeple through the hours of darkness when the bells are silent. (1)

Arrows:

It symbolises amongst other things lightning,(1) the last place you want it is on top of a spire, a steeple, it's usually the tallest thing in the area. Pointed pieces of metal attract harmful radiations. When swinging, an arrow may on top of a Church, cause the energies flowing through the cardinal points to go amok.

1. An Illustrated Encyclopaedia of Traditional Symbols, J. C. Cooper, Thames and Hudson, ISBN 0-500-27125-9

6. Sparsholt Agricultural College, Winchester, 1992

B.S.D. Congress and the Pillars of Light

So I'd joined the B.S.D. When notification arrived regarding the fifty ninth annual Congress, I'd dowsed whether I should go. I kept getting 'No', so did Elaine.

Here I would like to point out one point, one should always take the first signal/answer and not repeat the question! This I learnt at a London meeting from a lovely man, Bob Sephton.

Cheque written – decision time! I mentally thought:

"If I am meant to go, cheque will be posted".

I say this because I could see after the event, that maybe there were other powers interfering with our dowsing. When that occurs one has to rely on oneself.

So there I was on Friday 11th September 1992, stuck in an almighty traffic jam in Winchester, heading for Sparsholt Agricultural College. I was late, tired, worn out, I'd had a long day. I'd lunched with friends, Elizabeth and John Pilkington in Havant, then medical tests at the Complimentary Centre, Southampton. All had gone smoothly until entering Winchester, where pilgrims once gathered for their walk to Canterbury which I didn't realise till Monday.

Drawing near Sparsholt I'd suddenly hoped Joy might be there, I badly required a hug. I stopped near reception, there she was walking towards me, we were both in red! Then she took charge, I was billeted in her block – Brock!

Hauling my baggage from the boot, she then thought a key might be a good idea, so returned to Reception – me following like a little lamb. There was Deirdre Rust and soon her consort, Michael, the Secretary, appeared Part of me realised the key was taking a long time to materialise. Deirdre had been diverted but then she'd announced:

"I'm sure this lady will not mind being put in an en suite, but you're not to charge her!"

I had a little chuckle. I'd known all along I'd have one. I'd even wanted to book a room with bunk beds, but my husband had said:

"You can afford an extra fiver".

I'd booked to share!

We found my residence, Rose One, Rose my grandma's name. The room was not 'Rose' like; painted breeze block, cell like, due to en suite. Door furniture – red. We were in harmony.

Thus I arrived at my first Congress. I quickly made myself presentable and dashed to the President's Reception. As I was introduced to Sir Charles Jessel, I said I came from the same village as Colonel Bell. Then to my astonishment I was told that Colonel Bell couldn't dowse!

Next came dinner – a very glorified name for the repast we received, at a very inflated price! Not very good fish and chips. I just hoped the profit would go to some good cause at the College and its students.

The President's Opening Address, was followed by 'Ecology with Dowsing' by Bob Harris. A wide ranging talk on harmful earth energies. Atlantis cropped up, he'd dowsed and believed it might be in the area of Faro in Portugal, adding that one day he thought Atlantis would rise again. I wondered how. Little did I know that in 2009, I would be sent on a mission to Antarctica to do that on the etheric level, but that is not part of this story.

The Ankh

The ancient Egyptians popped up and their Ankh, crux ansata, the cross with a circle on top. They'd dowsed with it and it had led them astray! Some years before I'd seen one on television; I hadn't liked it. Was that the answer to my antipathy? Elaine wondered whether it had once led me astray! Lecture completed, up shot my hand.

I said I used symbols for harmful energies and what I felt about the Ankh and added in Oberammergau in 1990, after seeing the Passion Play, I'd had a double cross made, the cross of archbishops and patriarchs (2) which is slightly different from the cross of Lorraine, of the Free French. I'd been on a pilgrimage in Austria. Whilst looking at a painting of some cleric sporting one, I *knew* I required to one!

Meeting concluded, people rushed up, I'd been astonished. One said she was working on similar lines. I caught up with her at the last session and taken her to the station. An elderly gentleman, Will Hazell, a regular contributor to the Journal, plopped down beside me, wanting to know why I didn't love his beloved Ankh. The President himself joined in, informing Will that only the Pope had a cross with three bars!

Will then asked:

"Are you a 'drinking woman?"

"YES" I'd firmly replied.

He led me to a dark gloomy bar; I'd perched on a stool. He couldn't get over the fact I knew friends of his in Cuckfield. Then Major General Bill Cooper had walked past and Will had called to him:

"Major General, this is Mrs. Sally Williams, she comes from Cuckfield".

I jumped off my stool, I'd felt myself standing to attention, I'd really wanted to salute, but somehow managed to restrain my right arm. When home again I'd made the connection; it was the reaction of Colonel Bell to a brother officer!

I was often late for a seminar, not, I hasten to add, through my own fault . People with split second timing, just kept popping up in unexpected places, every one for a purpose. Sunday morning I completely missed Dr. Julian Kenyon, speaking on Scalar Fields – A Scientific Basis for Subtle Energies.

Already late, I'd spotted Deirdre Rust. We had unfinished business for I'd offered to make for the 1993 Congress a Diamond Anniversary cake. The size still had to be determined. and we determined on a small diamond, with a spare square. Michael would design the art work. That was a relief. I just had to make enough cake for three hundred!

For many years I'd made and decorated cakes and taught at Earnley Concourse, near Chichester. I'd just made enough cake to feed three hundred and Diane Stenning had helped me transform this into Holy Trinity, Cuckfield. We'd even put on our famous grave digger, Gordon Stewart, who is in the Guinness Book of Records. So I had a bit of experience under my belt!

Diane and Joyce King founded the Holy Trinity Young Mothers in 1966. We moved here from Beaconsfield in 1967 and I took my little boys to Holy Trinity. Joyce had given us a lovely welcome and invited me to join the club and then within a month, much to my surprise, I'd been invited to join the committee. I did, it changed my life, for at that first meeting Heather Stringer, who'd lived in

Barrowfield, had said:

"I would like to know how to ice a Christmas Cake!"

Without hesitation I'd piped up:

"I think I can show you that!"

and as its said, "the rest is history".

In 1968 Diane had the inspiration to start a pre school playgroup, which is where Marilynne Elliott and I met. Daphne Stewart, Gordon's wife, was Treasurer and so the Cuckfield Playgroup was the second in the area, the first being The Albemarle in Haywards Heath.

But and it is a big but, when I'd first met Diane, I'd managed to put my foot right into it. I'd knocked on her cottage door and enquired if I could speak to her FATHER!

"Do you mean my HUSBAND?"

"Well it's about the allotment, I gather Mr. Stenning no longer requires it." I'd thought Mr. Stenning was an old man and he couldn't manage it any longer! I was then enlightened.

"We have two, we only require one" and that is how I got my allotment. I have to admit we made a lot of decisions regarding the playgroup whilst doing our weeding, which the committee then usually agreed to!

Pendulum

Can you imagine anyone setting off to a Congress of Dowsers without a Pendulum? I did. I couldn't find the one I wanted, so decided a new one was required. Saturday morning I'd homed into a rock Crystal stocked by the B.S.D. for under £7. I showed it to Joy. She'd said:

"Better clean it before you use it".

I mentally cleansed, probably using the thought of Crystal water or salt water but it wasn't enough, so passing it to her she mentally popped it into her spring water; what else she did I do not know, but it was happy after that!

In the coffee break, we'd muscle tested various organs. My Gall Bladder was very weak (3) Coffee over, whilst listening to the next speaker, I'd held the Pendulum against it with a lapis lazuli and carnelian Crystal secreted in my pocket. Together they performed their magic; great warmth emanated. Rock Crystal, (4) can increase the healing powers of other minerals. Session over, she re-tested the muscle; it was much stronger.

Ileocaecal Valve

Saturday evening, I was just getting ready for dinner. There was a knock on the door and Tom Butler appeared. I'd talked to him earlier about my digestive health. He set about me! He'd dowsed that my Ileocaecal valve was in spasm, open. This accounted for the fact that my faeces were very, very loose, had been for a year or so. He pressed hard in that region and it popped closed. He promptly departed and so did the runny faeces!

HEALING THE CITY OF BATH

After dinner Bob Harris gave an unplanned workshop; 'Geomancy, the Art of Harmony of Building with Nature'. Around forty-five dowsers were present and we'd naturally formed groups. We were given a site plan of a particular area in a beautiful city. Great discord was reigning, shops wouldn't let, everything was wrong. A fire, ten years before, had resulted in new buildings being totally out of keeping with their surroundings, but we didn't learn this until afterwards.

We were set the task of finding what was wrong and how to correct it. I was with Joy and an elderly lady. Joy wielded a Pendulum, me a Biro which acted as a pointer and marker. My left hand got hot and I told Joy to get to the bottom of it. She did. Three thousand, four hundred years before Christ!

In one area we found a slab of stone. She knew what it was and we got it's measurements. I knew it required healing. I took the hands of the elderly lady, who'd taken no obvious part in our findings, and Joy's, and placed them between mine. I felt pain in my right toe, the Gall Bladder point..

"It's healing it," said Joy.

Then I saw white robed people around the stone and a human sacrifice, a child. I said it wasn't nice. I was totally shaken by the experience.

We were the last to say what we had found, what we had done – I'd sung very quietly, for my voice is a channel of healing. I was spokesperson. Nobody said anything, nobody came near us for the rest of the evening, even when we were in the bar.

It was an amazing experience and all the groups had homed or dowsed the area where the trouble emanated, exactly where we had our altar, on the exact line. They'd dowsed all the different things, some back to Roman times, some to the present and what was now required – broad flat leaved plants!

INTERRUPTION!

I was retyping this story on the Feast of St. John the Baptist, 24 June 2005. Suddenly as I typed, something said ' take care' so I put yellow light around myself. (It's a protective colour.) I'd wanted to stop typing and deliver the Church Magazines, but no, I had to continue. At the description of that plant, my huge Anthurium Scherzerianus, given on Mothering Sunday April 2nd 2000, toppled over, landed on the floor. Spooky!

It was thundering, the heatwave about to break. Shocked, I mopped up the desk, picked up the plant, put plant in its double pot into another one, stuck it in the dining room! I'd been wondering what to do with it whilst a guest was in that room; it had decided for itself!

THE HERMIT

Back to Saturday evening. After my presentation Joy and I should have stopped dowsing, we didn't, and we didn't ask permission. We hadn't obeyed that rule of dowsing!

May I, Can I, Should I.

Suddenly my legs began shaking, then the whole of me was!

"You're a hermit" Joy stated.

I beseeched a Scot, Doctor Flint for help. He just happened to be in front of us and I thanked God I'd met him earlier. He did, but didn't say anything but subsequently said his contribution had not been orthodox! He'd channelled energy to my Solar Plexus Chakra!

I beseeched the hermit for a remedy. He suggested, 'Pigs Wee'! I mentally swilled it and then thankfully recovered. We'd then taken Joy's dog for a walk. She then dowsed what I could drink, Grapefruit juice, diluted with her spring water. So much for the stiff Brandy I felt I deserved. Was grapefruit juice the choice, due to its colour or it's cleansing capacities?

I asked the hermit his name. Rhododendron. Well that's got broad flat leaves, just as my plant which toppled over! Joy said that would fit with what Britain was like then. It also gave me the clue for medication made by David Beale.

'Made for those with nervous problems. 'Going the wrong way'.

That applied to me and my nocturnal burps. At the time I'd thought 'many Welsh names start with Rh', that was a comfort.

Are you aghast at the thought of pig's wee. Well that little pig went wee, wee, all the way home, did he have a weak bladder or was he squealing! In 2005 reading 'Katherine' by Anya Seton, p.78 (5) I'd learnt the boy, when very ill, had been washed in Pigs Urine.

Urine is said to be a great healer, in fact I'd drunk my own earlier in the year; rather oily! Once over my initial distaste it was quite enjoyable! Joy also knew a doctor who believed in drinking his urine!

Some people believe we are all part of one another, we contain threads. Thus at times we home into something or somebody, and healing may be achieved.

I have told this tale as a warning. I was frightened by the experience. I hadn't sought it, it happened, and it happened through dowsing, which can make the unseen, seen. Luckily I was with people who knew what to do.

Michael Bentine wrote in 'Doors of the Mind', (6) one should only delve into the past in the company of others, to act as a safeguard, bringing you back to the present time if needed.

In 1990 I did a couple of courses in Heathfield with a very well known healer, Ruby Tonks. I had to persuade her that I really needed to come, for I'd missed the 'Beginners' course in the Autumn. One course was devoted to 'Far Memory', taking people back to previous lives and it was amazing how they related to their present lives.

SUNDAY MORNING

Still in bed I thought about that child sacrifice and wondered whether I had been that child. I wasn't but I did an involuntary gasp, something departed. A well read friend said child sacrifice was quite the norm, the first born, which gave mothers great trauma.

Then many things happened, very fast. I met Michael Watson, me in dressing-gown, he with attaché case! A physicist, who'd spoken on Saturday afternoon on J.C. Mabey and L.G.V. Rota. He'd slept the night in the room next door. We filled each other in with the relevant details about Colonel Bell and J. C. Mabey, a scientist, who Bell had fallen out with!

Late for breakfast, Joy felt I required Homoeopathic pills and we used Jack's method, placing them on the skin. Dowsers are amazing people and in group situations often try to help each other. This was a result of another kind dowser, who'd discovered something the night before but what, I haven't a clue!

Fed and watered we headed for Brock. The door opened, out stepped Bob Harris uttering:

"I was very impressed with your dowsing last night". I demurred, pointing at Joy.

"I've one map left of the locality where I think Atlantis is. Would you like it and see what you can find out?" I demurred again.

"Why not Joy?"

"No, you'll get more mileage with Sally" Joy responded and then disappeared.

Bob was looking for a point where there had been a pillar!

OBELISK

The previous week I couldn't think of the word, let alone spell it.

"Its Crystal" I said and then Bob mentioned Copper.

The previous day an inner voice had told me to buy a Copper kettle! I'd found a dented, dirty, electrically operated affair with a split spout! Common sense prevailed, I didn't buy! Some years later however I found a little dented one which I did and that gleams happily in my fireplace – when clean!

Friday morning, thinking I had no time for a bath, I apparently did and wondered about the Copper! I'd homed into the Angel of Water, for I was using the prayers of the Essenes (7) thinking it might help as Copper has an affinity with it. The result; wonderful molten Copper leaves poured into my forehead. Copper had again and again cropped up in Michael Watson's lecture. I asked Bob if there was a connection?

"Yes, it was the metal of the Atlanteans, it's still used to tile the roofs of Faro."

My next questions:

"Is there a connection between Faro and the Adriatic?"

That had been popping up as I used the Essene prayer to the Angel of Water on Thursdays mornings.(5)

"Yes, there'd been a battle between the Romans and the Atlanteans there" and Bob advised I should read 'Critius' by Plato for further info! (I haven't).

We parted, me wondering what on earth I should be able to discover for Bob Harris. Was it coincidence that Joy and I shared the same maiden name – Harris!

The speakers over the weekend covered a variety of topics, some I understood, some I didn't. Julian Kenyon spoke as a scientist and Michael Watson as a physicist. I learnt that in the world of science there was a growing belief that dowsing is the only means of making contact with what some call the Ether, the Life force, that which pervades everything, that which is sub atomic, the Scalar Field, which I thought was a pretty sobering thought. Sunday morning, elegant Edward Fawcett with furled umbrella as his pointer, gave an amazing presentation on 'Dowsing Pre' History'.

In the car park Sunday afternoon, Major General Cooper enquired about the cake.

"It's going to be a big 'un, isn't it?"

"Well , No" , I'd replied.

And so ended my first Congress of Dowsers, resulting in many people saying I was very psychic and asking:

"Have you had special training?"

"No, it has just come along, step by step".

"In that case your time is now" an elderly gentleman remarked, as I took him as well to the Station. I envied his travel style. One small attaché case!

Finally home, I had a lovely warm welcome from my husband. He was watching T.V. That brought me down to earth!

BACK HOME

Monday morning I returned to bed with breakfast – cereal – and wrote my diary. When I got to the cake I decided I really couldn't do a small one.

Pythagoras said he'd help with angles , a diamond shape I didn't think would be easy. I don't know whether he was around when I eventually worked it out, for it took about three hours before I came up with what I wanted but as I wrote this he says he was!

Then I felt like snuggling down under the bedclothes, but I didn't. I just continued sitting there quietly. After a little while I knew the time was right to dowse the map, so fetched it. No thoughts popped in saying I shouldn't, but it did occur to me that the time was right to use the new Pendulum.

Well this was Monday morning, named after the moon, Angel of Life day, I should have been doing the housework, it didn't turn out like that! There I was in bed, map in front, Pendulum to hand. I didn't know where to start, or what to do, so I slowly passed the map between my hands, to see if I could sense anything. Nothing much happened. I then held the Crystal Pendulum all over it, nothing much happened!

I decided to be more positive.

"I want to find the site of the obelisk". I found it! Bob Harris had written his name and address on the map. The A in Harris was actually pointing at it! I then put the question.

' Had there been another obelisk in the Adriatic? The Pendulum indicated 'Yes'. I asked what they had powered. Ships. Anything else?

There was a 'No' to land, but lots of 'Yes Buts' and 'No Buts' kept coming, until I got it right. SPACESHIPS! (Yes Buts and No Buts are two further signals a Pendulum may describe) and thus you can have a really interesting conversation.

I discovered the obelisks, lined with a seam of Copper, had sent their energy to Venus who proceeded to bounce it back to the spaceship. When I'd taken part in the high powered Crystal meditation at Ruby's, a little pink spaceship had crossed my brow. At the time I'd thought I hadn't achieved very much, compared with the others, but it was an example of how information can be given for use at a later date. So that was that, the past. Then I turned my attention to the present, looked carefully at the map, found a Pentagram.

Pentagrams attract and hold heat (8) so I mentally filled it with eight inches of molten Copper, with Colonel Bell pouring from his Copper kettle.

Crystals

I'd learnt about crystals on the second course with Ruby Tonks and then began collecting and using them for health, for just as in the foregoing story of not taking care, I'd dowsed some without asking May I, Can I, for I didn't know then about that!

Brenda Tills (Hawkins) had a large florist shop in Brown St, in the centre of Salisbury, and taught me a lot about Cancer. In 1986 she had bought some crystals and soon after finding I could dowse, she asked me to dowse them.

It was a very silly thing to do, for I could have absorbed their energies for then I hadn't learnt about asking questions. Brenda died soon after and her crystals were given to a friend, who then felt ill. They hadn't been cleansed.

Brenda's mother had phoned asking what she should do. Luckily I'd met in Salisbury somebody who did know about crystals and told her to get in touch.

Now back to Monday morning. I erected an eighty foot Crystal obelisk, surmounted with a double cross to keep evil away. Then I thought that maybe the obelisk should contain rutile, found in rutilated Quartz. I couldn't remember what it was but I knew it was important. Uranium came to mind, the Pendulum swung 'Yes', but I knew rutile wasn't that. Rutile is Titanium named after Titan (9) 'one of the giants of Greek mythology; the sun, son of one these giants'.

Rutile is from the Latin, rutilus, yellow/red (10) but is also called Venus Hair, after the threads of Titanium contained in it, or Fleche d'Amour, Arrow of Love (4). Isn't that lovely. When seen in a piece of clear Quartz it is very beautiful, just like Golden hair.

It was time to get up, I 'd homed into Golden yellow trousers hanging on the bedroom door. Titanium may be that colour, and also Uranium compounds, used for glazing ceramics. (11).

I thought there could appear to be a link between Father and Son, for in mythology Uranus is God of the sky, sun and rain, and the father of Cronus and the Titans.

In the Planet Suite by Gustav Holst, Uranus, bears the nickname, 'The Magician'. (12) In the Middle Ages Magicians used the Pentagram(13) The Planet has five moons. (4). Are they connected to the Pentagram, are they the reason my Pendulum swung "Yes" when I said the name Uranus? Uranium is a source of power, its isotopes used in atomic energy. (11) Titanium was used in Concord, in spacecraft, it was found on the moon in the Sea of Tranquillity but its also used in the medical and dental profession and I have some in my mouth!

ROCK CRYSTAL

Some believe this to be the most magical stone of all. The ancient Greeks believed it was an invention of the Gods for they found it on Mt. Olympus (6). It can grow to the height of a small telegraph pole and enhances healing energy when used with other stones and crystals.

PENTAGRAM

A Pentagram has five sides, is a symbol of protection.(11). It holds heat. Once I put one around a flower bed to stop squirrels eating my crocus. I saw one bound down the garden to the bed and then jump backwards! T.C. Lethbridge wrote he'd tried to mentally check on a friend one night. He couldn't, he'd seen her bed surrounded by flames! He told her, she said she'd placed the bed in the Pentagram for protection. (1)

In the Isles of Scilly following the ban on burning the fields, they lost the Christmas market, because the Narcissi started flowering later. Eventually they discovered old records about the pentagram, put it round the fields, and regained the market. (8).

In the era of the Greeks and Romans, five was the number for Venus for Venus years are completed in groups of five, and for Apollo, God of Light, for he had five qualities. Pythagoras believed it was the union of heaven and earth, two – female, three – male.(2).

The following day I made another connection, with Jupiter, Father of Venus, who was for the Romans the Goddess of Love (14). The planet would do the bouncing in the future. I reunited them, for in Alchemy Venus is Copper, Jupiter, tin (15) and tin absorbs moisture. That's why cakes are stored in them. I think you could say that Jupiter is drying his daughter after her rising from the ocean, he's got a nice towel around her!

Bronze

Five thousand years ago in the Near East Ancient Man discovered that if you put Copper and tin together you could make Bronze. We didn't discover that in Britain until two thousand B.C. Bronze is used for casting bells - I laughed reading that but then so is Brass, both could be connected one to Colonel Bell and the other to Major General Cooper, for he was Top Brass!

Now I didn't know all that when I came downstairs to find out more about jolly old Titanium and Uranium. As I entered the kitchen to put the kettle on, I found myself singing very loudly a song often sung at the end of the year,

'Ring our Wild Bells Across the Sky, The world is dying, let him die' (16)

I roared with laughter, now I knew why I'd sung it quietly on and off during the previous week. Now I was fortissimo. I grabbed two Brass bells, Brass consists of Copper and Zinc, and proceeded to do an 'Evelyn Glenny'. On Sunday evening my Husband wanted to watch her, asked if I mind missing the 'House of Eliott'. I didn't, we switched, but Evelyn's music had not been his cup of tea but mine!

Encyclopedia came next, opened at Pilgrims Way. Sunday I'd driven slowly, peacefully down a bit, winding down after the excitement of the weekend. I'd played a couple of tapes. 'Healing Force' (17) soothing, lent by a new friend. One side for cars, t' other for sleeping; I'd used that in my little cell. Soothed enough, I'd switched to the wonderful 'Green Jack by 'Jehanne Mehta's (18)', whom I'd met and heard more than once at Sylvia Ezen's.

The time was right for this work. For the first time, the dowsers decided to stand for two minutes at the end of the Congress, for some knew that when dowsers get together the energy of a place is increased. Where we had stayed appeared to need help, the left hand didn't appear to know what the right was adoing.

We had envisaged energy forming a beacon of light and I saw a column. I was dressed in pale turquoise, the colour of weathered Copper. Later in the week I'd found myself putting a column of light inside me! I then discovered the Epistle for St. Matthews day, September 21st,-

'caused his light to shine with us to give light of revelation,

the revelation of the Glory of God in the face of Jesus Christ'

2 Corinthians 4. 6. (19)

It was the time for making pillars of light.

The revelations of the Encyclopedia over, I had a bath. I homed into the pillar, for I noticed the light reflected off the chain holding the plug went in a straight line right up between my legs! I was fascinated, I couldn't believe it.

Bath over, nice and dry, I then did something I never do. Oiled my body with Olive Oil, containing a tiny piece of Rose Quartz! I then grabbed a clean deep emerald green towel and naked exited the house, you will be pleased to know, not through the front door, nor through the kitchen door, but through the French doors at the back and thus crossed over a mess left, the previous week, by guess who? Yes, Husband.

He'd started removing putty and paint from around the window and not cleaned up! I hadn't been motivated either. Now I knew why. It symbolized a beach of ivory coloured sand, ninety-nine per cent Rock Crystal! (4)

It was mid-day. I placed the towel across the path, laid on my stomach, head south, feet north, and let the sun do his magic. Suddenly I bent knees and elbows, pointed hands and feet upward, lifted stomach off the ground, looked down, saw my cross hanging between my boobs. Then I'd heard:

"Your work is finished".What work I wondered!

The Old Vicarage

Five minutes later, dressed in the Golden trousers, the phone rang. It was Gavina Guest, who'd bought The Old Vicarage. The sale had included Colonel Bell and Mrs. Bell's Library of Books.

In 1992, Cuckfield celebrated for a week the 900th birthday of the Parish Church, Holy Trinity. Five hundred sat down in the High Street for a delicious lunch devised by Katie Stewart.

I decided to give a talk about Colonel Bell in The Old Vicarage, and asked the then owners for their permission. I'd put out a plea for any information about him.

CUCKFIELD 900

Memories of Colonel A. H. Bell – Founder of

The British Society of Dowsers

I am arranging a short talk and demonstration on the subject of dowsing for Tuesday 9 June 1992. I thought it would be nice to include any anecdotes, photographs and such like to broaden the spectrum of this man's achievements. For those of you new to Cuckfield, Col. Bell lived at The Old Rectory. Please contact me if you would like to contribute in any way to this occasion, which will be at 3 P.M. in his old home by kind permission of Mr. and Mrs. Gibson.'

This had resulted in a strange happening. On 20th May I'd gone to Haywards Heath for a meeting, planning to afterwards pop to Quality Fruits. I hadn't. It was so hot to save her a long walk I'd taken Pam White home, a friend from the days when I'd been the Area Organiser for the Playgroups and Marilynne Elliott had been my assistant.

Pam home, I'd then parked outside Quality Fruits. My 'shop' had been quick but then I'd been held up by an elderly couple taking an inordinately long time at the till. I was in a hurry, I decided it must be for a reason. It was. Finally leaving, there was Gavina entering, saying:

"Sally, I heard yesterday you want info about Colonel Bell. I have his Library of Dowsing books, but unfortunately they are in Kent! You know he was a very spiritual person and into the realms of the unseen!"

That week in 1992 was very special. Plus the street party, there were Pimms parties every evening, a Flower Festival in Holy Trinity. Whit Sunday, 7th June, a performance of Haydn's oratorio 'The Creation'. Unknown to me, our 4th grandchild, Hayley, was being born then!

Cake cutting: Sally Williams, Revd. Duane Alvord, Jill Castle

Monday we went to see her. Tuesday I gave my talk which I recorded. Wednesday, Hayley's Dad acquired a much sought after position as a Senior Registrar. The following Sunday in the garden of The Old Vicarage, the Holy Trinity cake was cut. Two sections went over the Atlantic to Chevy Chase, Washington, D.C.!

Why there? A lovely group had come over from St. John's, to participate in our celebrations. I gave them the tower and strange as may seem, my cousin, Valerie Scott, lived further down the same long road; they took the entrance porch for her! When I visited in 1999, the pictures of that cake opened the door for me for a very warm welcome.

In July, Gavina had phoned requesting a special birthday cake, a camera, and mentioned her hair had literally stood on end listening to my tape, and thought:-

"She's just like me!"

"You're pretty psychic" I said

I recounted the incidents of my weekend, what had just occurred and the books I'd bought. On hearing 'The Breath of God' (20) she knew it was required for her meditation group. I had to wait about a year until I could read it!

> "You see, there is only one thing behind the appearance
>
> of many things, and that is the energy – the breath –
>
> of Life Itself.....Growing gives rise to the understanding
>
> that all experience is nothing but the Breath of God."
>
> Swami Chetanananda (20)

But I'd already parted in the car park with another, a big thick tome regarding the Essenes. That went home with Joy, never to be seen again by me, for a few days later I gave it to her with my love! It had a profound effect upon her - she became confirmed in the C of E.

The Essene were 'a mysterious brotherhood who lived during the last two or three centuries B.C. and the first century A.D.' ..were agriculturalists and healers and had a ritual of daily prayer to the Angels, (7) some of which I mention in the next chapter. I was told about them in 1991, I began the prayers night and morning and they had a profound effect. Within three weeks the Gods and Goddesses entered my life, but this is not what this book is about. There is a belief that Jesus was an Essene.

1. E.S.P. Time and Distance. T.C. Lethbridge
2. An Illustrated Encyclopaedia of Traditional Symbols, J. C. Cooper, Thames and Hudson, ISBN 0-500-27125-9
3. Touch for Health, John F Thie, De Vorss & Co ISBN 0-87516-180-4
4. The Healing Power of Crystals, Magda Palmer, Rider, ISBN 0-7126-1778-7
5. Katherine, Anya Seton, p. 78, Coronet Books, ISBN 0 340 157011
6. Doors of the Mind, Michael Bentine ISBN 978-0246118455
7. The Teaching of the Essenes from Enoch to the Dead Sea Scrolls, Edmond Bordeaux Szekely, The C.W. Daniel Company Ltd. ISBN 0 85207 141 8
8. Solar Energy and Dowsing In the Isles of Scilly for Gardeners and Farmers. A.P. & E.V. Tabraham, St. Mary's, Isles of Scilly."
9. Chambers Family Dictionary. 1981
10. Minerals, Octopus Books, ISBN 0-7064-3929-5
11. Hutchinson's New 20th Century Encyclopedia
12. Holst, Planets, Op 32 (1916) Innovative Music Productions Ltd. Notes: Robert Dearling.
13. Signs and Symbols in Christian Art. George Ferguson, Oxford University Press, 1916
14. Brewers Dictionary of Phrase & Fable, Cassel, 'New Edition'
15. The Nature of Substance, Rudolf Hauschka, Rudolf Steiner Press, ISBN 0 85440 424 4
16. Ring Out Wild Bells.
17. Healing Force, New World, Paradise Farm, Westhall, Halesworth,

Suffolk IP19 *RH.

18. Green Jack. Songs by Jehanne Mehta. White Lodge, 47, Bisley Old Road, Stroud, Glos. GL5 1LY

19. The New English Bible, Oxford University Press, Cambridge University Press. 1970

20. The Breath of God, Swami Chetanananda, Rudra Press ISBN 0-915801-05-1

7. College of Ripon and St. John, York, 1993

The Diamond Jubilee International Congress
July 15 – 19 1993
University College of Ripon & St. John, York.

THE SCOPE OF DOWSING

'Finding Divine Inspiration' headed the Sunday Telegraph report (1) but mine would have been: 'Tale of Cinderella' This is a very long tale covering many topics, some of which you may wish to skip, so do .

As agreed at Sparsholt, I'd made the Diamond cake for feeding the three hundred. Special boxes were required to house it and these were made by my young friend, Duncan Arnold. I mention this, because the Arnolds are of Scots descent. I felt the box played a part in whatever happened whilst I was there.

The Cake

I worked the proportions out by using an old seed box which fitted the oven! When I showed it to Duncan he swore he would never eat any more cake if made in such a box! I assured him I wouldn't but please would he make a similar sized one. I then made two cakes which I cut diagonally and thus formed a diamond! Cakes always used to be made in wooden boxes, for wood is a good conductor of heat.

I then required a huge board, thirty-six inches from point to point. When I came to placing the fondant icing on the cake, husband was enrolled to help heave it over. There was no room for the cake in the kitchen, so into the dining-room it went and remained, for it was simply too heavy to move again. In due course it was decorated with the logo of the B.S.D. designed by Michael Rust. That wasn't easy; the light wasn't as good as in the kitchen.

On completion I'd found that the forked twig was not aligned to the top of the diamond. I'd taken such care to get the circle in the centre. It was only when Id turned the cake around, the light shining upon it, that I saw the mistake. I was furious with myself.

"Don't worry" my husband said, "no-one will notice" but after lunch I found myself seeking a knife and removing it, praying my skills would enable me to repair the damage. We learn by our mistakes.

We had agreed to place four large candles at the points of the diamond, not on the cake but on the board. The candles I knew had to accompany me to York and I found a perfect leather cylindrical case to put them in. Deirdre and Michael were merely 'The Carriers' of the 'Big 'un'! After the cake's departure, I'd placed the candles in a diamond pattern on the dining-room table, I *knew* they were being prepared.

The Journey

A few weeks before I had a dream. I was standing at a Bus Stop, the buses just passed me by. I looked up, it was a Request Stop. I discovered I had lots of luggage. That dream prompted me to write to the B.S.D. enquiring whether I could be lucky enough to be given a lift. No reply. Three weeks to go I applied my mind to other modes of transport. Trains. Then I reflected I hadn't travelled anywhere by train carrying a suitcase since before I was married. I really wondered whether I would get from A to B. However I enquired, found out how to do it, then the lift materialized.

That Friday morning I found myself in the company of a large blonde lady, Angela for angels, who'd offered lifts on her booking form, plus a petite brunette, Marjorie. As we travelled I couldn't help remembering a similar sort of journey ten years before.

Then I was going to demonstrate on the QE2. Marilynne Elliott, dark, curvaceous, very attractive, was once again, my assistant. Sitting at a bar, as she'd chattered to someone on the other side of me, I'd felt a shrimp, hiding under my lamp, but I knew in due course my light would be fully switched on for all to see!

To get on that cruise there was one stipulation. I had to make a model of that ship, it could have been made of cake, apparently a butcher had made one of meat but I'd decided to make a proper model, for one of my son's was a Navel Architect. He'd drawn her to scale, and though it was not apparent, there were decks inside. I'd made two, one was presented to the Captain and the other I still have.

In York I was going to be the one who was photographed beside the cake. I intended saying a few words as to why I had made it! I did and to my astonishment at the closing ceremony heard them quoted by the President, Sir Charles Jessel. "That Dowsing had changed my life". And to set the record straight, the cake appeared in the next Journal but I didn't. I had to wait ten years for that to occur! I mention this for as my weekend unfolded I found many similarities between the two events.

We went to York via the M.25 and the Dartford Tunnel. Angela when she saw the bridge groaned, saying:

"I'm not going over that!".

She didn't have to, for that takes the southbound traffic. I'd already altered in my minds eye the energies going round the M.25. Why was that? From my view point we were travelling ANTICLOCKWISE. I think it was my viewpoint which was being taken into consideration. My physical energy was being wound down, and the spiritual wound up. This might have accounted for some of the distress Angela felt; she had intended going the other way!

On departure, my husband reminded me to look out for Alconbury, the American Air Force base with which he'd been involved. Angela had invested me with the responsibility of navigator. I had just put my head into the map, when I caught out the side of my eye a sign for the A.1 and yelled:

"Hey we go left here"

We were by the striped bit in the road.

"Don't think we do" replied Angela but she dutifully complied, then announced we were heading in the wrong direction! I felt awful.

"Don't worry" said my inner voice "You'll see" After a short while we came to a small gap in the road where we could turn on to the north bound lane. A few yards up I saw Alconbury. My hand fizzed, energy was passing through.

If we had not turned off at that point we would not have gone past it, for the AS.11 merged with the A.1 further up. It was something to do with an energy line passing through the Church, the male North/South line. I think the Male Axis energy ran through Alconbury Church, right down to the east of Brighton. Alconbury was where the US Air Force planned to hold spy planes and to hold them a massive concrete structure was built. This could have interfered with the line and my fizzing hand reconnected the energy. After this the storms hit us. . .

We arrived in York exhausted. Angela decanted Marjorie, Me, and the luggage. Marjorie went to register, I was left holding candles and guarding luggage! Deirdre spotted me, thus candles were passed over.

I went to register in Temple Hall and there was Jack Temple sitting on the table 'the U.K.'s leading practitioner of clinical Ecology' as per the Sunday Telegraph. I greeted him with a:

"Hi Jack"

"Hello Sally" he'd replied and we discovered we were in the same block.

Twice as I went up the stairs, he was finishing phone calls, and he kindly gave me 50p for mine! I couldn't get over his generosity, he wasn't known for it. We'd become friends when I'd suffered from pre-Cancer of the cervix and he had actually got to the bottom of it.

I'd suffered on and off for 13 years. In 1989 I'd had a second coning of the cervix by Laser at The Royal Northern Hospital. A week or two later I hadn't felt well again and that was when Jack had discovered the underlying cause which had then been accepted by my Consultant.

Now to my clothes and jewellery, so important in my life. This year I wasn't late for the President's reception, I wore a blue and white jersey diagonally striped dress plus Elephant ear-rings. Their first outing, blessed by my dear daughter-in-law Bev. Elephants sitting on top of a sphere; the world?

I was hailed by dear Will Hazell, he who'd taken me off to the bar at Sparsholt.

"Come and join us"

I didn't but later sat with him for the President's Address and the first lecture. I met others, Joy appeared, we went in to dinner together. It was very hot and I left after the meal for fresh air, and thus made the acquaintance of the Scottish dowsers. They were planning a party for the visiting celebrities, after the Celebration Dinner on Saturday.

Next morning I was on edge to get to grips with Labyrinths and Transformative Pathways with Richard feather Anderson. Chairman – Michael Bentine, co-chairmen of the Congress with the American Christopher Bird. Venue: Temple Hall. I'd learnt the difference between a Maze and a Labyrinth. The latter has a single path and a Maze dead ends!

Coffee break. Joy appeared in great distress. She'd lost her glasses and her specially made Crystal Pendulum.

"Which is more important?" I'd enquired.

"Her Pendulum of course" said someone.

"Don't worry," I said, "In my handbag I have one for you."

"I can't" she'd replied, but I said:

"You can".

This Pendulum I'd called Colonel Bell.

Before Christmas at Hatchards in Piccadilly, I'd bought the Pendulum Kit (2) which included one. I'd known it had to go to York. Now I knew why! Then she announced:-

"Last weekend in Wales I met a grand-daughter of one of Colonel Bell's wife's sister's!"

That settled it. Incidentally the Pendulum Kit by Sig Lonegren sold more than a million copies in fifteen languages (2) and that info came from Duncan's Aunt, Claire Sinclair in Toronto in 2004!

All and sundry dowsed for hers but as far as I know, nobody found it. Incidentally I did know how sad it was to lose a Pendulum, especially a Crystal, but I'd learnt that if one does it maybe for a purpose.

Mid-morning, coffee time, I smelt delicious coffee and I bent over someone's cup, dowsed it, and discovered I could have half a cup! Whoopee, for I hadn't drunk any for a long time. As I drank, I met David Beale.

Some year's later, on a course with Patrick MacManaway, I discovered that for me to drink coffee didn't weaken me – we were muscle testing and everybody else found their muscles weaken. Why did I get a different result? Coffee protected me if I was going to be a channel of healing.

I'd first met David on a Jack Temple course. Then he had growled at me:

"Good thing some of us have our Third Eye open" when Jack had announced it should be closed! (The Third Eye is situated just above the eyebrows in the centre above the nose.) We chatted, went back together for the second half of Labyrinths. It was wonderful learning how they could be drawn. How they form a spiral. One configuration was the shape of the Pyramid complete with capstone. They represented the Tree of Life.

Suddenly I'd felt motivated to hold his hand! Oh dear, all those men – and women – who got propositioned by me! Energies flowed, I wasn't allowed to enquire for whom or why. At one point his hand vibrated, later he asked why.

"To increase your own vibrations" I'd replied.

I said Mike Shaw's always did, the wonderful healer who'd lived in Tunbridge Wells, who you may remember dowsed my house in 1987 and found it geopathically stressed.

David's healing completed, he kissed my hand.

Then it was the turn of Michael Bentine. For half an hour a capacity audience rolled in their seats with laughter. He spoke of his connections with Peru, he was the grandson of a Vice President. I remembered my connections, I had Peruvian cousins, I nearly went when seventeen, what stopped me was the language, I can't speak Spanish! I had a wonderful Peruvian broach, "Gods Bird" which protected me and I had Peruvian plants flowering merrily in a new flower bed, but their scent was disappointing!

"Do your ribs hurt from laughing" asked my companion.

"Yes". It reminded me once more of that trip on the QE2 when we had laughed and laughed for a whole week. Our ribs had ached for a couple of days afterwards. We'd sat with the entertainers, one being Bernie Clifton. He had made us laugh and laugh, so much so that other diners said they tried to hear our conversation, that our laughter had made their holiday.

At the end of the half hour with Mr. Bentine I opened my mouth – I knew I wasn't saying much at that Congress but this I felt was important. I thanked him for writing 'Doors of the Mind' for it had opened mine to the possibilities of the paranormal. To my astonishment I had now experienced such things. Consequently a few people asked me the title of that book.(3)

Pyrites, Fools Gold,

Before breakfast, in the bathroom picking up my clothes, I'd been careless enough to drop twice a piece of Pyrites, Fools Gold, which had then broken. That stone had been all the way to Canada, with Peter McKie, the husband of

Kit Mouat, who'd founded Cancer Contact in Cuckfield, giving him energy. Now it was in four bits! I'd popped them in my pocket and there and then I gave the largest piece to David to hold. He had a tremendous reaction, had never experienced anything like it in his life.

Still reeling from the laughter, we talked standing by a wall, I put my hands upon his shoulders, yes there in Temple Hall, people passing by. Energies flowed. To me my hands felt warm but he experienced great cold in his back. He was quite overcome.

David had some new Pendulums, Copper, Brass and Stainless Steel. In the middle of lunch he came with them, asked me to choose one. Within two hours of giving Colonel Bell away, I had a larger and heavier one, known as an Abbé Mermet, after the amazing French dowser who had over a thousand Pendulums.

The Mermet Pendulum can hold a sample. I was thrilled and in went the smallest piece of Pyrites. That this had taken place with David I'm sure had been well thought of in advance.

Some weeks before I'd found in a drawer a bottle of his Water Violet Remedy. Not knowing why, I'd placed it on the windowsill in my healing room. Then suddenly I'd decided it should be in the kitchen, and I should take a few drops. It's for quiet people when healing is taking place. I hadn't had much. Was the upshot that healing flowing into him and the tremendous reaction to holding the stone?

I'd dressed that morning in a sand or pale Gold outfit, which was relevant. I'd learnt that Gold was the colour which connects the cosmos to the earth. A birthday present from dear Elaine had been a bottle of Aura Soma ' Vision of Splendour'. Her choice had me roar with laughter. Aura Soma are balancing oils and this was Golden Yellow over Clear. I'd taken it with me and on my return it had lost its colour!

That was Saturday morning. There were all sorts of wonderful workshops in the afternoon but I played truant. York Minster was my magnet. Friday evening I'd been told:-

"You must go to the foundations, they are mind blowing".

They'd met the ancients there!

York Minster

Three o'clock, was my time for the rendezvous. Setting off, I went up a dead end, the back entrances to shops, one Hope antiques. I couldn't turn round, I had to walk to the end, touch a blue garage door, and then turn round. I thought of the Maze.

Wending my way I eventually found the Minster, passed a couple playing Bach on the pavement and had instructions in my head:

"Give them 50p". I did.

At the entrance to the Minster were listed the Sunday Services. My choice would have been the choral at 10 A.M. but I felt mine would be the 8.45 A.M.

Then I entered the Minster, through a small door, within a much larger one. As I walked up the south transept a Priest mounted a pulpit and called for Silence. It was 3 o'clock on the dot. He announced:

"Please stand or sit whilst we pray for the World". I sat, felt myself swaying with pulsating energies.

Then I made my way to the Foundations, paid the entrance fee of £1.50, decided on the larger of the identical leaflet – for those with poor sight – mumbling something about leaving my glasses behind! Then my eyes alighted upon the Roman and Saxon remains but also the modern blocks of concrete stabbed with stainless steel pins. Which was for me?

"Saxon".

A child's headstone and my internal voice informed:

"You were that child".

(Re writing this in 2004 my legs tingled at that. When that occurs it's confirming the truth). Now there I was in the great Christian Minster of York and many Christians do not believe in reincarnation; they claim there is no reference to it in the Bible. Well there is, though all mention of it and karma were removed in AD553 by those attending the Ecumenical Church Council in Constantinople. Why? The Emperor's wife, Theodora, wished it. I learnt this reading 'The Truth Vibrations' by David Icke (4) However a little bit escaped.

Matthew 17 v.10-13

'The disciples put a question to him. Why then do our teachers say that Elijah must come first? He replied   Yes Elijah will come and set everything right. But I tell you that Elijah has already come, and they failed to recognise him, and worked their will upon him; in the same way the Son of Man is to suffer at their hands. The disciples understood that he meant John the Baptist.

This was foretold in Malachi 4. v 5.

'I will send you the prophet Elijah before the great and terrible day of the Lord comes'.(5)

But I do and I am a Christian and the following information satisfies me.

In 'The Direct Path' by Andrew Harvey (6 p.40) there is a very good explanation, believed by Buddhists, told him by a lady called Shanti.

"When you die, you will meet a great white light which is God. If you live a good life, you will have the courage to dive into this light and choose it and become one with it and you will be free forever in God. ....Everyone meets the holy being they believe in. If you are a Christian you meet Jesus; if you are a Buddhist you meet Buddha."

Shanti met Krishna, he said You could stay with me here forever but I want you to go down and be a healer and tell everyone about what you have seen so that they can have faith.

I want you to teach people about the truth of reincarnation and so I will arrange for you to meet the people you knew in your last life and have everything you say checked and believed"

"And then Krishna explained to me how the system of rebirth works. You come into this world with two Souls, one inside the other. The outer one is the one that you will evolve and develop in this life; the inner one will go on and on travelling until you reach final union with God. The outer one, Krishna told me, will die at the end of this life; everything you learn about God will however penetrate the inner one and so help it grow in wisdom and understanding on its journey".

Buddhists however do not call them Souls, but tigle, "drops".

"In Tibetan Buddhism we say that everyone comes into this life from another with two 'tigle', two 'drops', one enfolded in the other.

The larger one is called 'the lifetime indestructible drop' and the inner one 'the eternal indestructible drop. The larger one develops during a particular life but dies at death; the small one transmigrates from life to life until enlightenment'.

Now back to my story! I went on my way, saw the well, and a little voice said:

"Go to the Lady Chapel".

I couldn't, it was roped off for Evensong. I should have loved to have stayed but I knew it was time to go. I did and as I did found myself listening to a Guide speaking about the East and West Windows. The former, the greatest expanse of medieval glass in the world.

I completed a circle returning to the College, peering in shop windows as I went. One, I was allowed to stare in, a bric-a-brac, but not allowed to enter, but eventually I came to another.

"You can go in if you like". My voice informed.

It was a beautiful china shop. I looked carefully. By the till was a glass topped display box holding jewellery! I peered, a necklace of bright coloured glass caught my eye. I asked the assistant to get it out; she'd been busy talking to the owners. It wasn't right. I looked again, two more, one dull Bronze, the other of palest pink clear glass, the largest ones containing strands of blue and yellow, rather like a Marble – Art Deco. It had been the assistant's! I bought it, and exited through the back exit. My trip to the blue garage door had paid off.

Later that year it came to light as to why I'd bought that necklace. It was a past life. I'd been Queen Etheldreda who'd married twice. Aged twenty in A.D. 652, she'd tied the knot with an older man, Tonbert, Prince of the Fenmen . Part of her marriage settlement had been the Isle of Ely. It was also stipulated she would not consummate the marriage, for she considered herself a Bride of Christ. Tonbert died after three years. A few years later she was persuaded to marry the son of the King of York but she still wouldn't consummate the marriage. She gave her dowry of Hexham to her favourite Bishop Wilfrid.

In 1996 when on the island of Iona, I discovered why but that is a few stories hence. She'd had a fondness for bits around the neck, lace and beads and Audrey and thence tawdry stem from her! When she became a nun, she stopped adorning her neck!

Now back to me, it was teatime, I was hungry, I wanted a bun or cake but I couldn't find a shop - I wasn't meant to, buns and cakes were in Temple Hall. Hunger assuaged I was faced with a choice of two lectures, one about dowsing in Russia but I chose the other by two Austrian Doctors about 'The Laws that Govern Natural Energy Transfer' using a Basalt Pendulum. I wanted to know about that because Sylvia Ezen, alias the author Sylvia Francke had mentioned its wonders.

Banquet

Then it was time to prepare. At Winchester I'd been told to bring my best bib and tucker, so I did. A green dress with Art

Nouveau buttons and buckle, nephrite Jade ear-rings, a broach for fixing my badge and as I set off a passing man said:

"You looked glamorous!"

I wondered whom I might find to chat with or share a drink. No-one. I waited patiently for a gap to appear at the bar. Eventually the President and Secretary moved to let me through! I didn't think much of that. I had a Bloody Mary!

Joy appeared. We were piped into the dining hall and given long stemmed carnations. A lovely idea. Then I realised Joy had a man in tow, she wasn't needing me this year!

Where to sit? Joy was heading for distant parts but I'd been told to sit near the cake. I stopped and walked down the aisle in front, then stopped at a table where I knew someone. A table for eight, the end seat already bagged, so I sat down next to an elderly gentleman. Sitting there I thought;

"I must photo my cake".

The four candles were burning brightly!

That done, I sat down again. A lady now sat upon the bagged seat, so I enquired where she came from.

"Lockerbie". My Heart stopped with shock.

"Lockerbie?"

"Yes". I said nothing.

On the 1 July, having a nap after lunch, I'd seen in the region of my Third Eye a

Golden object which clarified into the shape of a plane. I'd communed with myself,

"Did I have to go on one? No,"

"Did I have to go to an Airport? No"

"Lockerbie".

I discovered that when in York, a healing had to be performed for that dreadful air crash. Then I'd homed into a small window in our sitting room full of wonderful patterns. I'd sketched it. I knew it was important. Three crosses made from Hexagonals. The sides of the cross were each a Pentagram.

I'd dowsed who should help me. Maureen Williams, whom I'd met a few weeks before at Anthea's, Duncan's mother. She only had the bedroom next to mine!

The previous Thursday I'd asked Elaine whether she had anything to do for me whilst I was in York. Elaine is a wonderful healer and dowser, who'd introduced me to absent healing.

This is a method of healing used when the recipient is not present, considered to be more powerful than when the recipient is! Healers use the term, 'Putting it in the Post' Amazing results can occur and we had worked together much over the years. Now her help was required at the end of the banquet at nine P.M.

As I'd fixed my pink carnation, 'Lockerbie' said:

"Have mine, you were obviously in the know, it doesn't go with my dress".

I'd slipped mine into the brooch, she then carefully arranged her flower behind. Then I'd collected all the broken stems and stuck them in the centre of the blue and white table decoration. It looked like a rising column of energy! I'd also placed two coloured pieces of glass upon the table, one blue, one green.

The Banquet had started with Toasts and then the President, Sir Charles Jessel cut the cake. I was called forth and presented with a bouquet. I'd asked if I might say a few words. I did, and said:

"I have been a cake decorator for many years, on All Souls Day 1990 I learnt that the Founder of the British Society of Dowsers had lived in the village where I come from. This is my tribute to him for 'Dowsing has changed my life'.

Squeezing back to my seat a man at the next table jumped up, and in a loud

The two Chairmen, Michael Bentine and Christopher Bird, with Professor Dubrov.

foreign voice exclaimed :

"Ah Sallee", lifted my hand and kissed it.

Much confused and full of emotion I sat down. I had no idea who he was. If

I had chosen the other lecture, 'Development of Dowsing in Russia and The C.I.S' I would have. He was Prof. Alexander Dubrov, the 'highlight' of the event, according to the Sunday Telegraph. I would have learnt that there were four Colleges of Dowsing in Russia. After Graduating their Sciences graduates went there to obtain scientific knowledge!

Dowsing makes the unseen or unknown, known! Through their dowsing the Russians saved themselves millions of roubles at a time when they were strapped for cash. That is how they obtained so much knowledge but not now, for in 2002 I met eminent Russians at a gathering organised by Dr. Julian Kenyon. The computer is now their tool.

My 'speech' over, it was time to enjoy 'A Dowsers' Feast', Yorkshire Style. First came the Yorkshire pudding then the Roast Beef – delicious. Towards the end 'Lockerbie' turned and asked:

"What is your line?".

Everyone always wants to know that. I didn't give my usual reply, but in a light way something to the effect that I never knew what would be my next thing, what God demanded of me, to which she'd replied,

"Much more exciting".

Then it seemed right to mention the plane.

She told me of the trauma, how people felt, how they had been recompensed, how the money was useful. The hill farmers were having such a bad time, everyone had been scarred for many years to come. Then I'd realised it wasn't for the dead but the living I'd come to heal. She'd suddenly turned and taken my hand. The energy flowed in, I'd turned to the elderly deaf man beside me and asked:

"What's the time?" He'd replied,

"nine ten".

Later checking with Elaine, that was the time she'd tuned in.

"I'm afraid I was a bit late".

Mind blowing, I'd felt shattered. (My legs tingled at that again in 2004)

Dinner over, everyone disappeared, no-one invited me for a drink or to join them. I felt like Cinderella, a rather tipsy one. I'd imbibed liberally red wine, nobody had been quaffing that. I knew that energies and healing flowed through me far better when I am well oiled! I returned to my bedroom, popped bouquet into the basin, sat on my bed and reflected!

History was repeating itself. The same thing had happened on the QE 2. The Captain had held a party on the night I'd presented him with the icing model.

The Lecturer in the adjoining cabin had had an invitation, but then he knew the captain and I didn't. I'd felt put out, made a bit of a scene; I'd been overwrought and tired. This time I reflected on the Scots and their party, I'd learnt my lesson, it was time for some healing.

I heard Maureen return, I knocked on the wall. She'd returned to change. Someone had spilt water all down her and for an hour she'd sat in a wet dress! That's how God's purpose got worked out.

I prepared the room and then we set about the healing of Lockerbie. I used the large leaflet of the Minster foundation (the small one would have been useless) and placed upon it the drawing of the window. She put protection around me. Kneeling on a lovely tweed blanket, holding the Brass Pendulum, I spoke the necessary words, then cleansed with orange light.

When people are naturally drawn together it can mean they had had dealings in past lives. We had. Since she'd returned to her flat nasty things had been happening, pictures falling down. Someone had dealt with that but I felt there was something else. There was – murder! I'd murdered her. We put that right. That done I felt motivated to give her one of my carnations for she didn't have one.

"Oh thank you, I didn't get one, I got in too late".

Then she quietly asked,

"Do you see Auras?"

"No, do you?"

"Yes". Sometimes they are white. When you give Healing yours is white". This was the second time she'd seen me at work. Then she left.

Then, I saw the Smoked Salmon sandwiches I'd made the day before. I felt I'd like some salmon, fished it out, poured some Elderflower Cordial, sipped it and wondered why I hadn't thought to give her one.

I looked out the window, the name Abigail floated in. Abigail? Why, Who? Was it the dog I once knew, was it the daughter of my God-daughter Sarah? No. Was it the child buried in the Minster? No."

I mentally filed it for later investigation. The voice said:

"You'll sleep well". I did.

Tuesday night, I'd remembered. Abigail means 'Father of Joy'. Next morning I'd phoned, saying:

"I think your father needs you." Her answer:

"Oh, I thought I'd settled him down before I'd left" I still didn't know if the dear man was alive or dead!

Sunday - Labyrinth

I woke up in time for a quick swim and a quick breakfast. With no talking, I'd get to the 8.45 service. Setting off I forgot pants and bra, I'd have to return naked under the towelling bathrobe. Lovely swim and I chatted to Bob Sephton. He was the one who told me you should only ask the question once.

He said it was vital to keep your mind active on retirement, many of his friends were no longer on planet earth. That gave me consolation. My husband was certainly doing that. Exiting pool, I had such a quick shower I didn't rid myself of all the chlorine. I set off for my room but I didn't get there! I was heading for a Labyrinth

A Labyrinth had been marked out with blue rope on the sacred turf of the quadrangle of the College of Ripon and St. John! No-one was there, I walked in, then found myself running and as I ran my arms were going into the air, horizontal, one clutching the bath towel and swimsuit. I realised what I was. A plane!

Getting to the centre, the white centre, I dived to the ground, touched it with my forehead. There were bits of heather and Tartan ribbon there. Then I arose and my arms went up like wings again and I flew out. The title of the second Lecture had been Labyrinths are Transformative Pathways! Yes, most certainly.

Rushing back to my room, with no time for a bath to rid myself of the chlorine, I popped on a home-made colourful skirt, known as stained glass, named by someone when I wore it on a pilgrimage to Oberammergau in 1990. I'd trimmed a cheap top with the skirt material so it looked all of apiece and far more 'up market'! A useful tip for anyone who likes making skirts. Buy a plain cheap top and trim with the skirt material.

I thought that skirt was most appropriate for York Minster and its huge stained glass window. The outfit was completed with Jade ear-rings and brooch, the remaining carnation. and the new glass beads

Then to breakfast. I would have chosen tinned grapefruit, there was none, but there were prunes! That after all was a good idea, for the water of York was bunging me up. Prunes, orange and some of my millet flakes turned out to be very tasty.

I had twenty minutes to get to the Minster and walked the much shorter opposite way. I spied a stone shop, I spied an obelisk in shades of ginger. I thought:

"Could I have it?" "No".

In any case the shop was closed, but it was open from 10 A.M. until 5 P.M. every day including Sunday! I would just have to miss it. At the Minster I admired the recently replaced tracery in the great West Window.

The Service was at the east end under another wonderful window, the size of a Tennis court. Then the puzzle of where to sit? Quite a few already sat on the right side, then my inner voice said:

"Front Row Left".

At that time, if left to my own inclination, I was inclined to sit on the right side of a Church. I knelt down and was motivated to build in front of me the obelisk! Something told me all my sins had been forgiven. Then the Service began..

We stood for some bits where I would normally have knelt. I go to a Communion Service every Friday morning, so I kept an eye on the Server on the left hand side to make sure I didn't boob. The altar rail was in front, I thought the Communion would take a long time, there was only room for four to kneel or stand but when it commenced I discovered those on the right didn't go up to the front rail but walked up the side, so I did likewise on the left and there I was kneeling next to the Server!

To my great astonishment I discovered in York they did things differently, gave the Communion from the left, anti clockwise, not starting from the right, as I have always known. I was deeply moved, somehow it was very significant that I was the first participant in that Communion. Well it was all to do with that Past Life of Etheldreda. Royalty would have taken precedence, but I have digressed a little.

One prays for all and sundry during a Communion service. Anywhere in the world could have been chosen but for that Sunday the 'powers that be' deemed that the whole of the Church of England should pray for the Christian community of PAPUA NEW GUINEA. I was shocked to the core.

Each year on the May bank holiday the village of Cuckfield celebrates with a Cuckoo Fayre. At the Library's second-hand book stall I'd been gob smacked. Amongst a row of old books there was one new one, 'The Proving Grounds' by Benedict Allen.' A Journey Through the Interior of New Guinea and Australia'. (7) From the dust jacket had peered the face of a Warrior with tusks through his nose!

Apparently, Julia Roberts said "nobody using the Edith Paine village library would be interested in that book" but I was! We had a son 'down under' and never knew where he might go! The Library has now passed into history, it was the first room in the Queens Hall, which is now the office of the Parish

Council.

As soon as I was home, I'd started reading, and read and read. The whole thing was totally riveting and now here in York Minster we were praying for the Papua New Guineans. It had come again. I didn't hear Chichester!

Towards the end of the service I realised I was probably in the Lady Chapel! By then I'd built a line of energy to the Lady Chapel of Holy Trinity Church, Cuckfield. It was after that I'd noticed a figure of Our Lady holding the infant Christ. So the message of the day before had come to be, I'd gone to the Lady Chapel.

At the completion of the Service I didn't moved, I wasn't allowed to talk to anyone, so I'd watched the bits and pieces put away, and the ropes re-fixed to stop visitors going near the altar. When completed and the sacristan departed, I got up and unfixed them!

I walked reverently to that great altar, touched the blue stone in the centre of the crucifix, touched the blue tassel hanging from below the sacred oil lamp, then I re-fixed the rope across the aisle.

Looking around, I came to where candles could be lit. I lit three and tried to put them in a triangle. Then I remembered the mistake I'd made on the dowser's cake.

This time I checked, moved one candle to another branch, then the alignment was correct. I looked up, realised my triangle was surmounted by the large candle above. It seemed perfect.

It was nearly time to go, a young sacristan showed me out, he was having to seal the chapel off for the next service. As I saw the great nave beginning to fill, I knew why I had not gone to that service. My place had been in the Lady Chapel. My love of singing in Cathedrals was not for me that day, I had to return to the Congress.

The sun was shining, I was drawn to a path through a little park. I'd missed it the day before. I looked at the memorial to the fallen, I saw a plaque on a wall to a young astronomer, I took a photo. The priest who walked by at that moment told me there were more exciting things to photo than that but I wanted it as a record of the stars that boy, John Goodricke, had discovered. If I hadn't I wouldn't be able to quote it to you now!

Typing this on Lady Day 2004, I wondered where the photo was, I wanted the name of a book but that was in another room. I was lazy, thought it would

From a window in Treasurer's House near this tablet, the young deaf and dumb astronomer JOHN GOODRICKE 1764-1786 who was elected a Fellow of the Royal Society at the age of 21, observed the periodicy of the star ALGOL and discovered the variation of δ CEPHEI and other stars thus laying the foundation of modern measurements of the Universe.

be listed in Omraam Mikhaël Aïvanhov 'Man's two natures, human and divine', – it wasn't but inside was the photo! Was that divine intervention?!

I walked around the Minster again, heard singing emanating from the opposite Church. I went in through a side door, exited through the back! I loved hearing the hymn, then I returned the way I'd come, but on the other side of the road. It was in the sun. Then I saw the Stone shop, it was Open but it wasn't ten. I crossed over!

By the time I'd returned to the College I was the owner of an obelisk! The year before I'd made one, this time I'd bought one! I was back in time for coffee and sitting in the quad I waited for the bookshop to open. I knew I had to order all the writing on Labyrinths, then dowsed if there was anything else. 'Yes'. I eventually found a small Golden yellow book with a faceted Crystal upon the front, The Symbolic Language of Geometrical Figures (8).

Next I spied Jaquie, a friend from the 1992 Congress, then she'd received healing. On Friday evening we'd walked into the President's Address together but then I didn't sit with her, having asked if I could! She'd understandably been rather rude.

This time it was quite different. She was full of praise, no doubt due to the Cake! I joined her coffee group, then realised I'd left the obelisk behind. I found it, showed it to them and then Maureen appeared, dressed in clothes to match and off to Temple Hall with her it went!

I set off across the quad for the lecture given by German Professor Dr. Hans-Dieter Betz, to discover how the dowsing field works. It was Scientists trying to prove something!

After the break I returned to hear Doctor Mainey speak about the Ether. He had a hard time with the Chairman interrupting. At the end, in my innocence, I said I thought he should contact Dr. Julian Kenyon. This lead to the gentleman ON MY RIGHT saying;

"I didn't know you knew him".

Who was this man? Wing Commander Beaden, a one time Vice President of the B.S.D. On the recommendation of Julian I had been to see him many years before to learn about dealing with Geopathic Stress. He'd showed me banging angle Iron into the centre of a line, actually broke up the rays. When I'd told him of the good results I'd obtained, he'd decided I couldn't be doing much harm!

He'd also showed me a glass sphere in which certain crystals had been placed, for harmonising homes. I expected my Pendulum to whiz over it but it hadn't, just slowly swung over the object. He had also asked me how I viewed my Pendulum and I had replied that it was my best friend. I was thoroughly reprimanded, I had to realise the Pendulum was an instrument, a scientific one at that, used for measurement.

Once more fate had brought us together. He showed me his latest object for dealing with problems in houses, truly beautiful to look at, clear with crystals and a Maltese cross, named I think the Sea of Tranquillity. I'd taken my very best hankie which had a huge lace boarder, I thought in the shape of that cross, which I think I'd bought in Malta. I'd then agreed to buy the sphere, I seem to remember it was about £40. I'd then been asked whether I would like it after lunch or tea. Very firmly I'd said:

"After Tea". We parted, me for lunch.

As I'd walked to the Minster I'd seen a lady in blue walking towards me, recognised her as one of our lot. Jenny Edwards. I guessed she'd been to the previous service. She had. Had she been sent to prepare the way for me? At lunch choosing food, we saw each other again.

"Did you enjoy the service?" she'd asked.

"Yes" I'd replied and I mentioned Papua, I mentioned the energy line but she hadn't thought to do that. Well maybe there was no reason for her to make a link, maybe there was for me.

Energy lines between places, especially Churches, seemed to be one of the things which Elaine and I were required to do; one of our lines of business at that time! You may well ask, why we did it. Well to be honest I didn't know! If we'd thought of it, we could have dowsed to find out why, but we didn't and I don't intend to now in 2010. It was something we did then. Others, wiser than me, may well have the answer.

Where to sit? Carrying a Scrumpy Jack – a delicious cider which I'd never tried – I saw the good Scots Doctor who'd helped restore me to normality at Sparsholt. I wanted to know if he felt any different. I'd had his card in my healing room since Christmas. I thought he looked brighter.

I sat down, then looked up. Opposite was Professor Alexander Dubrov who'd kissed my hand, he mentioned it. Wow and then he said words to the effect that I was like a moving star!

I felt he should have my pink carnation and asked:

"Please will you take this back to Russia to the oldest Church where you live." It was Moscow.

"The Kremlin" came the reply. I was dumbstruck.

My Pink Carnation, which had been to York Minster, was going to that centre which struck fear into the hearts of men –The Kremlin. In three days he would be there.

What happened next? I realised I was sitting diagonally opposite Doctor Mainey. I discovered he knew Dr. Kenyon, had even once thought of buying his Practice but their motivation in life and how patients should be treated were rather different. I understood what he meant.

Then I felt motivated, nay, I heard the words:

"Give him the obelisk".

"Oh no" I thought, "I've only just got it".

In fact it had just returned, for Maureen had appeared saying she'd lost it!

"Don't worry, it will turn up, after all its not going to disappear" I'd replied.

It was still under her chair!

"I have to give this to you" I said to Dr. Mainey.

He looked at it, held it, could see by my face my anguish and said:

"Would you be terribly offended if I gave it back to you?"

"No" I'd replied but it was the second time within a week I'd tried to give something away.

My guardians after lunch were Joy and Bob, they saved me from buying the Sea of Tranquillity, they felt it was not right and certainly not right for me.

Then we went off to the closing illuminating talk by the other co-chairman, the famous American dowser, Chris Bird, in which he'd said we learnt from our mistakes. Then came the President's Closing Address. Suddenly, to my astonishment, I heard my name mentioned, my words quoted. Bob poked me, saying:

"That's you". Well I knew that was me but I never expected to hear myself being mentioned in the President's Closing Address!

I was in a fix all through the afternoon as to how I was going to refuse the Sea of Tranquillity. I shouldn't have worried. I got a cup of tea, wandered outside, looked at the rear of his car. I tried to make the sign of the cross over it, I could only manage the vertical. No way could I make the horizontal. Then in my handbag I came upon a picture of the Tibetan Dilgo Khyentse Rinpoche, discoverer of the spiritual treasures of Padmasambhava (7) and how that came about you will learn later in this story.

I turned around, chatted to someone I didn't know, Wing Commander Beadon returned, said how pleased he was to have met me again, sorry he hadn't recognised me, chatted to the other lady whom he knew, went on his way. He had forgotten our arrangement! Thank God.

People were to-ing and fro-ing, saying their goodbyes. I wasn't, I was staying till Monday. I sat in the peaceful quad looking at the people milling around the Labyrinth. I knew I could not and should not go near it. I sat there, contemplating, thinking and Chris Bird sat down beside me. I was so in awe, I was tongue tied, I didn't know what to say! He went on his way.

Drinking hot water I decided what to do. I folded the paper containing the details of the Sea of Tranquillity, placed the obelisk upon it and decided to bury it.

Later I reflected. I'd been on a high from the Minster, I hadn't closed my Chakras down to a suitable level. To do that I see the expanded cones shortening and thus I'd allowed other forces to penetrate. I'd just read how something similar had happened to Benedict Allen. Suddenly Aborigines had materialised, saved him from fighting when he'd faced aggression from other Aborigines in Australia. (7).

Setting off to bury the leaflet I'd passed Primary Education. The door was open. In I went. Why? My daughter-in-law Ros, had trained at that College and would no doubt have used that room, a classroom filled with flowers and paintings. On the wall there was a verse of All Things Bright and Beautiful. I sang it at the top of my voice! The acoustics were good.

Then I buried the stuff under a beautiful apricot rose. Within me I felt the Wing Commander was doing his best to help humanity and I couldn't take the hard and fast line of my guardians.

I realised why when Angela started talking about Souls and their age. That's what she did sitting in the Quad, she could tell their age! She spent her time observing such things. Apparently there were not many old Souls present at that Congress. Mine, she said, was older than Jack Temple's. Was that the reason why once I had wondered if I was cleverer than him? Depending on the age of one's soul will depend on the light which one sees, the methods that one can employ in healing.

As Jack had said at Tekels Park,

"Some people can do it with their minds, Sally is one, others cannot".

What this means is the level on which the healing is being achieved. My two guardians had worked out why this object was not good. It was pushing the problem upwards onto another level, a level of which Wing Commander Beadon was not aware.

Back home I saw a piece of paper with crosses, photostated years before. My hankie was NOT a Maltese Cross but a Cross Pattée, quite, quite different. Just shows how observant one must be.

I'd thought:

"Its got that cross, I've brought one with me, so it must be for me" but I hadn't, I'd brought another on my hanky!

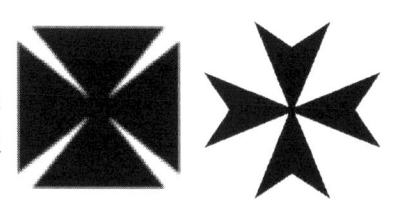

After the burial amongst the peach roses I'd had a bath, then began packing. What would I still need before the final journey? That evening – white! A choice between trousers or pleated skirt – far kinder to my waist. I decided on a long T Shirt embroidered with Silver shells and creatures and the legend:

SEA SEASHELL

SEAVIEW

SEAHORSE

That was appropriate, I was attending the seminar drawing Labyrinths.

Dinner was chaos. Again I didn't know where to sit. I plummeted where I stood. I was between three suited men and a shirted, not the same sort, on my right and then a couple came and sat on the other side. They knew the suits.

"Oh God" I thought to myself, "what am I doing here!" I made contact with shirt then BSD staff joined him. There I sat, wondering what to say and to whom. Again I was sitting at the table with the Professor. I asked him for his card and said I'd send him a cake.

"When it arrives I will send you a telegram, saying Love Alex." he said. I did send a small Christmas cake and received a lovely letter.

The three suits continued to talk their language. Then the one opposite started talking to the couple next to him. Suit on my left then turned to me, an Indian in fuels. What could I contribute to that? Nothing! So I did the standard question. What had started him dowsing.

Illness, illness connected to ALUMINIUM. Homoeopathic Lycopodium 6 or 30 was recommended to remove it! Well that cleared that one away, that's why I'd sat next to him. I'd had problems with Aluminium, in fact I still do, I'm allergic to it, I cannot touch Aluminium foil. However food packed in it doesn't seem to affect me.

Then he enquired what my line was! I mentioned I had no scientific knowledge. Once more the answer had been:

"that's much the best way". He told me to buy Boerickes Materia Medica (10) so that's how that wonderful Homoeopathic tome came into my life.

Then I realised the girl at the end knew about the Basalt Pendulum. I asked shirt and B.S.D. if they would mind moving up. I really wanted to know more about it. I learnt their son had nearly died, they'd met Jasper Carrot at some fair, he'd sent them to Jack Temple!

Next I heard the name of the man who'd been sitting opposite. Dr. Cyril Smith! I'd written to him when a sceptical son wondered how on earth the use of Sapphires could promote chastity!

On purpose I'd left out ' The Healing Power of Crystals, (13) wondering if it would interest him! He'd glanced down the Glossary of Stones in Healing, spotted Chastity (promotion of) - Sapphire. He'd exploded, asking:

"What do you do with it, do you stick it up?"

Dr Smith's reply had been it could be something to do with pheromones, I didn't know what they were and my dictionaries were no use. However in the Penguin Encyclopedia, third edition 2006, I learnt it is a chemical substance secreted to the outside by an animal which has a specific effect on another member of the same species. Priming pheromones cause a change in the physiology of the recipient, such as an effect on reproductive hormones.

Dr. Smith felt this would be the effect of wearing a Sapphire, the traditional engagement stone, to keep a girl virgo intactus until the wedding night!

During that weekend I'd kept hearing his name, but nothing had clicked in my brain! I'd missed his seminar! I'd missed my opportunity, I threw up my hands in horror, but it was all meant to be.

Labyrinth session over, thirsty, I was in the company of a very attractive Canadian, who recognised me by my Silver white hair! Approaching the bar, both with dry mouths and not quite knowing how to refresh our palates, she let drop that she had also homed into the scene of the child sacrifice in Bath, when we were at Sparsholt. She had also wanted to do something, but her group of dowsers were settled on their course of action. As I had healed it, she had seen it change. That was a wonderful revelation and validation for me.

Sitting together, me with another Scrumpy Jack, I told her of my morning experience in the Labyrinth. We'd learnt that at the next session we were expected to relate our personal experiences. No way was I doing that, which she appreciated, but thanked me for telling her

For some unknown reason I opened my handbag, pulled out the ticket I'd kept from a recent visit to Highgate cemetery. I'd wanted to see the tomb of Carl Marx. At that very moment Bob Harris, the man who'd asked me to dowse the site of Atlantis, materialised at my side, saying:

"There's a Ley Line from there to Cleopatra's Needle, which goes to the House of Commons as well".

"Oh God" I said, "I was up Big Ben earlier this year. " (my legs tingled at that as I typed this in 2004).

He laughed, saying to my fair companion:

"This lady goes very high, she wrote and told me she'd ended up sunbathing in the nude".

Then they departed. Since then Bob has also gone very high. In 2005 and 2008 he was voted Master Builder for Energy Efficiency by the Federation of Master Builders (F.M.B.) and has his own company entitled Earthdome Ltd. He uses Wood Pellets for heating his constructions.

But back to 1993, I now had the opportunity to look for Dr. Smith and found him talking with two men. I joined them and popped my question, he departed.

Then we talked about Gods and Goddesses, that they came to help us mortals, but one man felt they also required our help! The Gods and Goddesses entered my life in 1991, and their prayers were needed come Monday morning.

That night going to bed I picked up 'The Teachings of the Essenes from Enoch to the Dead Sea Scrolls' which Joy had just given me (12) A little thank you for the Pendulum and the large Essene book I'd given her as we left Sparsholt. I couldn't say I'd welcomed her gift gladly, after all I already had a copy. Couldn't she have found something else?

No, it was meant to be for it fell open at page 78.

Essene Prayers

"With the coming of day I embrace my Mother, with the coming of night, I join my Father and with the outgoing of evening and morning I will breathe Their Law and I will not interrupt these Communions until the end of time".

(From The manual of Discipline of the Dead Sea Scrolls.)

But first there was a prologue to the Communions and the Essene solemnly and reverently repeated the following:

"I enter the Eternal and Infinite Garden with reverence to the Heavenly Father, the Earthly Mother and Great Masters, reverence to the holy, pure and saving Teaching, reverence to the Brotherhood of the Elect."

I would say the above but omit the last line as I didn't know who they were! In 2009 I met members of Essene Network International who thought I should join. I haven't! YET! When their Prayer Sheet came I discovered they had changed the format of the introductory prayer, to an easier one!:-

"Let us enter the eternal and infinite Garden of Mystery, our Spirits in Oneness with the Heavenly Father; our bodies in Oneness with the Earthly Mother; and our hearts and minds in Oneness with each other and with all of creation". (13)

Back to Sunday night in 1993, this was the nudge I needed. I prayed to the Angel of Work but communication with that one I always found very hard.

I went to sleep, awoke about five o'clock, rain was pouring down on York. I tossed and turned reviewing much of what had happened. Sleep refused to return. At about five forty-five I decided it was time to pray to Monday morning's angel, Angel of Life:

"Angel of Life, enter my limbs and give strength to my whole body"

I then had to contemplate on trees and feel myself absorbing vital forces from trees and forests. p.43 I pondered which tree to think about and then enlightenment dawned. The Tree of Life, symbolised by that Labyrinth in the corner of the Quad!

A Wet Walk!

I realised what I had to do; get up and walk seven times that Labyrinth in the rain! Oh no! Then what should I wear? My ancient blue bikini with a lemon towel.

Six fifteen I set off, holding a little blue stone, given in September 1991 by the Broadstairs Chairman of the National Federation of Spiritual Healers. For the first and only time in my life I'd gone to the Healing Arts Exhibition at the Horticultural Halls, London. To my astonishment, over a cup of tea, I'd suddenly found myself helping her and for that she'd given me the Crystal!

'Lockerbie' had dismissed this as useless, along with the green stone, when at the banquet I'd placed them on the table. I hadn't argued, I knew one was man made but I didn't think the other was dyed

No consideration had been given to the colour; what that could do on some level. Seeing the blue stone, reinforced for me, what I had to wear. I matched the blue string of the Labyrinth!

At some point sitting with Angela in the Quad we had observed many entering the Labyrinth and she'd given me a wise warning. One should go alone so as not to be contaminated by those around.

As I was about to step outside, certain words came. I stopped. I needed a bit of protection, so I mentally wrapped myself in a long blue cloak, emblazoned with crosses, front and back, sides, over head and under feet. Then into the rain. A long blue cloak is recommended by the Federation of Spiritual Healers for protection.

I did walk the Labyrinth seven times, sometimes bowing in the centre, sometimes outside. At one stage the blue stone got left, sometimes I picked up stray pink petals lying around from other peoples carnations, sometimes I felt myself striding as though in the Army. I'd flung the towel off soon after entering. Eventually it was over. Soaked, I placed a stray carnation petal amongst a carnation someone had fitted to the entrance pole. I wondered what daughter-in-law Ros would have said if she'd seen me!

People had been very busy in that Labyrinth, leaving all sorts of things, but it had to be washed and purified by rain before I could enter for my purification, for finding the white centre. That is how Richard feather Anderson had coloured his drawing.

Labyrinths

Each circle of the Labyrinth represented the colour of the spectrum corresponding to light waves vibrating at a certain frequency, which become higher and higher as the colour approaches the violet end of the spectrum. The wavelengths of the different colours thus form a continuous series, ranging from the longest (red) to the shortest (violet).

As light vibrates symmetrically around its line of propagation, the chain formed by the successive vibrations is in the form of a conical spiral......which also represents the centre of the circle.....it is at this point that spiritual peace is to be found. It is not the peace of immobility and stagnation but a state of extremely intense vibration in which the most sublime activities can be undertaken. It is in this peace that the spirit can manifest itself to the full.(8 p.49)

I found this in The Symbolic Language of Geometrical Figures, which I'd dowsed I had to buy. Above the violet is white light and that is why Richard felt the very centre manifested that. When looked at like that, one realises the full significance of what the Labyrinth symbolises. It is not surprising people experience transformation. Joy after her trip was knocked OTT by her Mother, afterwards she nearly collapsed in the dining-room. So let that be a warning, take care.

Well I had walked my Tree of Life! Picking up the towel, as I'd trotted back to my room I passed three people wrapped in weatherproofs, sheltering in a corridor. Whether they were our lot or not I do not know, neither what they thought of me, but the male had a little grin!

A Hot Bath

I'd had enough cold water, so had a hot bath and contemplated not my navel but what I'd just endured! Then I realised the overflow was just like mine at home and was reflected in the bath water! The chain linked the two, just as a picture in Richards feather Andersons diagram, showing that the two worlds were linked, Man being the Link. There it was symbolised in my bath. Never before had I seen the two.

I thought about those I'd already met, those I would still like to meet and what to do with that bouquet. I felt strongly I didn't want to take it home. Someone entered the bathroom along side. There was a gap between the ceiling and the wall to allow air to circulate, I heard a sigh. I plucked up my courage, called:

"Good morning, are you going home today?"

"No, we're staying and travelling about Yorkshire for a while " came the reply.

"I have a bouquet with me, do you think you could scatter it wherever you go?"

"Yes" and said where she would be at 9.15.

Packing & Departure

As I completed the packing before 9 A.M. I had a shiver of excitement. I was going home to my beloved. I wanted to phone him, but I didn't have time. I tried to find my lipstick and realised I was being held up.

A little voice within said:-

"Occupant of next room was the recipient for the flowers!". Hearing her key in the lock, I popped my head out, saying:-

"Are you...

"Yes",

"Here are the flowers". She was Mary Ison, one of the Dowsing teachers, and she thanked me for the cake. Well that got rid of the flowers – such an ungrateful creature was I.

Next, I wondered how on earth to make contact with Angela, where should I put my case whilst breakfasting. I was on the top floor, three flights down to the ground, and rooms had to be cleared by nine thirty.

I carefully descended the stairs, then exiting heard words to the effect that I was now going to cut the ties and break the bonds. Oh. Was I going to leave the Dowsers?

Just as I rounded the corner of Temple Hall there was Angela, sitting in the passenger seat of a strange car. She shouted:

"Put it in the back".

She gave me her keys for her car, so I could put the rest in, and once more I marvelled at how my problems were solved.

That last breakfast I sat with the couple I'd talked with the previous evening. I wanted to know more about the stream at the end of their garden; it was good for healing M.E. They hoped children would come and stay in the cottages they let and bathe in the river. Hurrying out I said:

"Oh, you haven't given me your address?" She turned to her husband,

"Have you got a card?"

He fished in his pocket, produced his business one. D.W. Roberts, F.R.I.C.S., Chartered Quantity Surveyor - just like my husband!

"Has he any work? " they asked,

"No".

Nor had he, another victim of that recession.; wasn't the world small! Uncluttered, I sailed on my way to learn more about the Basalt Pendulum with the two Austrian scientists of ecosystems, Dr. Gernot Grafe and Dr. Maria Felsenreich.

They had studied the life bearing properties of water and found it the supreme transforming agent for energies entering the planet from the cosmos. A man mentioned the Sea of Tranquillity, as being another way of healing. Joy dug me in the ribs;

"Aren't you going to say something?"

"No". I replied.

If she wanted to she could.

What I'm trying to say is that one method appears to be right for some people, and if it appears to do the trick, well and good. They may only be concerned with the purely physical . If that clears up, to their minds they are healed, there suffering is over and that also applies to the physical world.

The Austrians had found by using the Basalt Pendulum and mixtures of crushed rocks, that polluted water and land could be revitalised. Then Dr.

Maria Felsenreich said she had used prayer and that it had worked for five weeks but then reverted. Then I dropped my little bomb.

"Maybe you should have prayed to the Earth Mother".

Shock registered all over the face of the good Austrian scientist. That would never do!

I thanked the Austrians, workshop completed, for allowing me to attend for their workshop had begun on Sunday evening

Then off I went for a coffee in the lounge of the President's Reception. Richard feather Anderson was beside me and I told him I'd walked the Labyrinth in the rain. Somewhere along the line I also met the lovely Canadian, and told her.

"Well at least you weren't quite in the nude" she'd laughingly replied.

I didn't see anyone else to chat with. I stood wondering, feeling I was standing there for a purpose, almost like an animal sniffing for scent. Coffee finished, I set off for where I was meeting Angela. She couldn't go without me and she'd intended doing the Basalt workshop but she'd never materialized!

I headed for Reception, the entrance to Temple Hall and turning a corner there appeared round the opposite corner Tom Butler in a Golden pullover. We fell into each others arms, emotion flooded through, energy, it was staggering.

"What is your name" he said. "You were such a dazzling light as you came round the corner".

I replied, "You have my name!"

Then he remembered, it was on his desk! Shaken, we parted and continued on our respective routes. Together we had made a pillar of Golden light, for I had donned my Golden trousers and that was why the Aura Soma 'Vision of Splendour' lost its colour!

I found Joy, we had a good-bye hug, found patient Angela, who'd only been waiting half an hour, then discovered we were only two, Marjorie having departed Sunday night!

It was a good journey home, sunshine nearly all the way, returning down the M.1 thus making a circle which I think is a very good way to travel. We stopped at a Little Chef for sustenance, Angela gave me a Rose Quartz Pendulum she'd made and I managed to leave my Crystal on the table, which I luckily remembered before leaving.

I thought we'd be back at five, she thought four thirty. She was right, I was wrong, my insistent voice was the wrong one. It balanced the negative thoughts she had when we entered York. She was convinced we were on the wrong road, and I'd just hoped and prayed we weren't. It's nice that nobody can be right the whole time, it puts life into perspective and stops one getting big headed. However I did wish there weren't two voices. I had been told why and what they represented which I have regretfully forgotten!

It wasn't long before my husband arrived with The Sunday Telegraph containing an article about the International Congress. It was lovely seeing the picture of the quad in colour, the quad that only that morning had seen me walking in the rain.

It was Jenny Edwards who'd been snapped with her rods, whom I'd met as she returned from the Cathedral. Ten years later, International Congress, Manchester, the picture came with her.

It was then that I learnt that the man who'd kissed my hand was there 'as the highlight' and Joy also got a mention but she said she hadn't said what was printed!

This bore out why I went through a particularly nasty spell one morning, years before, when I realised I shouldn't allow myself to get into the hands of the Press.

Back home I was pretty shattered, all I wanted to do was sit quietly but my husband was full of news! What the papers were saying. The MCC still not allowing women in the Pavilion at Lords!

Finding divine inspiration

by Joe Saumarez Smith

"I CHOOSE everything by dowsing," declares Mary Ann Thirsk, "what to wear when I go out for the evening, what vegetables to buy at the local stores, even which vitamin supplements I should take in the morning."

She has made the trip from America to attend the International Dowsing Congress, held this weekend in York. More than 300 dowsers have paid £200 to celebrate the diamond jubilee of the British Society of Dowsers and are attending courses on everything from Water Finding for Novices to Labyrinths as Transformative Pathways. A guest speaker from Russia, Professor Alexander Dubrov, who has investigated dowsing for 20 years, is here as the highlight.

"We're not all nutters," says Michael Guest, secretary of the West Midland Dowsers, "but there's a slippery slope. You tend to start with finding water lines and then you start using it to make yes/no decisions in everyday life and then you wonder about its medical applications. People make a good living out of dowsing and if they can do that there must be something in it."

He introduces Edward Bush, the vice president of the Canadian Society of Questers, who, having retired from his job as a civil engineer, now dowses across the American continent. His reticence about his success — "I act as a consultant to various mineral and oil explorers, usually individuals because it's harder to justify my charges in company accounts" — is not shared by Barbara Prisbe, a dowser from Oregon, who tells of Bush's finds.

"He's an extremely good dowser. He had two wildcat oil strikes in Kansas last year. Now that's pretty impressive."

In the university quad, a course on finding a vein and methods of marking is taking place. Forty people carrying forked sticks and pendulums stalk the grass. Every few seconds there is a twitch from one of them as they cross water or power lines.

"Concentrate your mind on what you're trying to find," instructs Edwin Taylor, "because you can only find what you're looking for."

A couple of university students appear from a doorway, obviously just out of bed, and stare bemused at the sight that greets them.

At the afternoon's coffee break the talk is all about dowsing's curative powers. "Friends come to me and say they feel ill but when they go to the doctor nothing can be found wrong", says Joy Austin. "So I use my pendulum to dowse what's wrong and I tell them to go back and say 'please look again in the kidney areas' and that's where the tumour or whatever will be."

At the next table Jack Temple, described in awestruck tones as "the UK's leading practitioner of clinical ecology", is seeing a patient. "Your eyes last had perfect vision 1,2,3...," he counts as his pendulum swings, "...21, 22 years ago and the deficiency that causes glaucoma is of level 1,2,3,4 in your right eye and 1,2 in your left." He produces a book of Gauguin postcards and tells her to stare at one. Meanwhile he removes a bottle from a cardboard box and pours a drop on her hand. "Do the same thing every day and your eyesight will slowly improve," he insists. She is uncertain whether the treatment will work and adds: "I don't even have glaucoma in my left eye." I'm later warned by several "water only" dowsers that those who claim medical results are "the sort of people who bring our name into disrepute".

In the evening, Michael Bentine, one of the congress's co-chairmen, is enjoying celebrity status. A practising dowser for 16 years he describes it as "essential" that dowsing enjoys greater recognition.

Peter Carter Ruck, the other "famous dowser", was unable to make the weekend.

All together: dowsing students are told to 'concentrate on what you're looking for' Photograph: Asadour Guzelian

I wasn't ready to return to this world. He started getting supper and then continued with the news about the head of MI5. I couldn't take it and yelled:

"Sit Down". I could take no more. I knew why. I'd received healing, my energies were all upset.

I needed the obelisk. Upstairs I put it at the centre of a table, then felt at peace. Supper over I needed weak tea, Orange Pekoe, it matched the obelisk. I took both outside, sat down under the veranda, realized the obelisk required a Christening. I named it Ruby, after the mother of a baby just born in Pakistan, for my stone was a Pakistani! Ruby is the dear daughter-in-law of my first friend in Cuckfield, Evonne Gubbin.

Next I walked around the garden, talking to the plants. At a clump of blue agapanthus I realized they were the same colour as my swimming outfit, and the Labyrinth. I told them:

"Yes, we know, we were there with you" they'd replied!

I was astonished, I'd never had that happen before. The bed wherein that clump grew was once a circle for once there had been a blue upright swimming pool a gift from Marilynne Elliott when she had a pukka one built. When no longer required, I'd merged the empty ground into the adjoining flower bed. Then the 'Powers that Be' requested a Silver Birch – Betula papyrifera – the Canoe or Paper Birch, be planted there!

The Birch has some amazing properties; fertility; light; protection against witches and drives out evil spirits, hence the birching of felons and lunatics. It is the Cosmic Tree of Shamans, they had to climb seven or nine notches up it's trunk, symbolizing the ascent through the planetary spheres to the Supreme Spirit. (18)

Much goes on which I do not understand. Things get buried there, stones put there, special Norfolk stones, round white ones, much else as the years passed. Everything has energy, everything has an Aura, everything has a part to play in our lives. Some we may understand, some we won't.

If we comply with what God wants, if we can be his agents, then healing which has to be done, can be, by agents unseen and unknown but they also need tools supplied by us!

Late Monday evening I'd phoned Joy to make sure she'd got home all right.

"We've just been taking Aluminium out, it was in the water".

Joy had her own spring water – York came as a nasty shock. I told her of Lycopodium in case her method was insufficient. It drew my attention to the fact that I should take it out. I had one tablet every other day for three days, so the Indian gentleman had been very helpful.

Tuesday, bath water running, I sensed something foamy was required. Then I got it. Seaweed and Arnica by Neals Yard, to de pollute me from the heavy metals of the road, the petrol fumes which dear Angela had kept complaining about.

My little voice instructed.

"Put a full cap in".

I complied and on Wednesday used half a cap, Thursday, just a little. Hopefully it did the trick. I also washed my hair with Neals Yard Seaweed shampoo. I still do this after travelling for Seaweed removes heavy metals.

Then I'd dressed in a purple outfit. I'd been wearing a green/purple ruby/zoisite pendant, bought after my pilgrimage to the Passion Play at Oberammergau in 1990. I'd seen it in the window of a Goldschmit, known it was a 'must have'. It's a very powerful combination, though I didn't realize that at the time. It 'can create altered states of consciousness and can serve as a vehicle for reaching and utilizing talents and abilities of the mind. All of the psychic abilities can be stimulated and amplified by use of these consolidated energies. In addition it provides for amplification of the entire energy field of the body. (14 p.708 Melody) (There's lots more beside that snippet!)

I'd removed the cross I was wearing and hung it on a crucifix. I was still pretty shattered, but setting off by bike to buy eggs, I noticed the clip on the handlebars holding the brakes and gear lever, it had number twenty-two.

"Well" I thought, "I've ridden this bike hundreds of times but I've never noticed that. Must be a reason – after all its a good number".

'Numbers are cosmic energies and 22 is a Master number. Be a master builder, in other words co-create the life you want. So hold a very positive vision for your future or just your next step'. (Diana Cooper - Cygnus Revue, issue 8, 2009). Well cricketers were in tune when they made the length between the stumps 22 yards (?)!

That night doing some exercises, I found I was facing down the landing, looking at the lampshade. Suddenly I realised I was looking at the face of a Red Indian child – the lampshade had stemmed from a child's bedroom. My husband had recently put it there. I was overwhelmed by emotion. I suddenly realised my Father had come back to me, had come back to guard me for evermore.

I had had to be alone in York. It was a pilgrimage, a pilgrimage which included walking a Labyrinth. I had intended doing this in 1992 at Chartres but on the eve of departure that was cancelled. Chartres was not my place to pilgrimage, but York.

I had to acknowledge that during the seven years I had been a dowser something had happened, that allowed myself to be in the right place at the right time. Whether it was intuition, whether one equates that with psychic aspects or not, I do not know. Energies are certainly raised when dowsers meet, this is known, things happen which might not otherwise.

However I hadn't gone quite alone. In January I'd ordered from the Library 'The Tibetan Book of Living and Dying'.(9) Three weeks before York, it arrived, but then I'd been too busy to read.

On Tuesday 13 July I had to return the book but then it had opened at the picture of H.H. Dilgo Khyentse Rinpoche; I learnt he was going to help me and I'd realised I had to have his photo, and that's how that was in my HANDBAG! Well he did help, didn't he!

Now on the morning of my return I'd looked at that wonderful face. But why on earth did I have it? In 1993 I'd discovered Padmasambhava was my Ascended Master. I'd been shocked to the core, for Padmasambhava was the father of Tibetan Buddhism and a great saint.(9)

H.H. Dilgo Khyentse Rinpoche (1910-1991) was acknowledged a peerless master of the Dzoghen teachings, discovered the spiritual treasures of Padmasambhava and master of many important lamas, including H.H. The Dalai Lama but I know nothing of those teachings.(9)

Gall Bladder

Waking on Wednesday, I thought about the Soul level of my Gall Bladder, which a few weeks before had tested weak. I'd worked on it and meant to get Joy to test it. Now this morning I asked a few questions. It was pre Lemurian!

I did not know how we were made then but whatever energy then symbolised the Gall Bladder, it had received a great blow. Well it was over eighteen million years ago. I could have been a Lemur, for that is thought to be the origin of the name. (15) It was Wednesday, I prayed to the Sun Angel and filled it with Gold light and then entered the bath. I'd done the Gall Bladder, then how about the spleen.

Spleen

A speaker on Aromatherapy had said it needed basil. It was post Lemurian, I had become a completely human type, an Atlantean! I sent Basil to those who had damaged it and lying on my tummy I gave a great gasp in that lovely foamy Arnica Seaweed bath. It reminded me of the Aura. which I filled with white light and despatched to the spleen. Then I'd knelt, looked down and discovered I was completely naked! No cross and thought:

"We come into the world with nothing, we leave it likewise."

I proceeded to put on a strange lot of garments and as the day proceeded they got even stranger. I felt it might be a special feast, was it Beltane? I thought of looking in the prayer book but never had time. I felt I was beginning to get sensitive to such energies.

First, on went an old red/white patterned skirt, size 16 not worn for years, homed into before leaving for York. White top from Saturday morning, the strangest old tights. They definitely symbolised lines of energy in the coarse, almost fishing net, weave. I wasn't warm, later went on a red top, even later I got colder, put a thick sweater in between. Yes it was July, not the middle of winter!

I decided to clean the house and chatted away to the Silver grey AEG, I was telling it all about the Congress.

"Does it answer back?" enquired husband.

"No, but it blocks out all other extraneous noise!"

I continued and so Cinders came back from the ball and once more tried to get to grips with reality!

It was when I got to the loo and I was recounting the buying of the Bloody Mary that I burst out laughing. BLOODY MARY, no wonder a Russian had kissed my hand.

"Probably smelt the Vodka on your breath" teased husband, forgetting Vodka doesn't smell. Somewhere along the line I did the washing, so that night I set about the ironing.

THE CARDS

Suddenly in the middle I thought of the Professor. "I must find his card, it would be dreadful to lose it. Putting down the Iron, I searched my purse and came across several cards, his, Tom Butler's from our first meeting, and a man I'd sat next to at the last session, who'd given it saying:

"If you have any helpful info would you please send it to me, I might be able to test it for you".

I'd told Angela on our way home:

"He's trying to pick your brains" she'd said.

Next day I felt so strongly motivated that I actually burnt that card under the

Silver Birch. It reminded me of another Canadian who'd wanted the same thing on the QE2. I realised then he would make money out of my knowledge, I didn't let him, he said he'd write – he didn't!

Taking the cards from my purse, I noticed my left hand beginning to burn and I wondered for which cards? I decided the Professor's and Tom's. I took them back with me, placed them on the photo of Dilgo Khyentse Rinpoche, which just happened to be lying in front! Then I knew they were going under my pillow!

I went on with the ironing. Phone rang – it was Tom wanting to know if I had got home safely. Then he commented that the York local paper should have had a heading:

'Couple burnt hole in the ground!'

"Well, Well, Well". I said.

His rejoinder –

"What about the future?"

I had no comment but said I'd just found his card and mentioned the Professor. He'd dowsed him, found much the matter and offered to put something right. It clicked, that was why I had the two cards together. He could monitor him and see if anything improved. He said he'd rather monitor me!

I came back to the ironing wondering where he fitted into the jigsaw puzzle of previous lives. What he would say to this I had not the slightest idea. Then stapling unceremoniously the three gentlemen together I placed them under my pillow!

Much to my relief they were only there for a couple of nights and then their residence was my healing table, above which hung a cross of Canterbury and a calendar of Chichester Cathedral. That was Wednesday.

Thursday was for cake decorating. After lunch I'd taken a cup of Motherwort outside. I wanted to sunbathe. I took off a pink baggy cotton (surgeons) outfit, that's what husband called it, but I couldn't take off the indigo shirt. Before that could happen I had to face the sun and make a line of energy to the Kremlin. Was it being prepared for the arrival of the pink carnation? (my legs tingled at that typing in 2004). That done I was allowed to completely undress, drink my tea and wait for it ..... have half a cup of Urine! The rest went to the Silver Birch! I did get up to some strange things!

Radio Three was out of action as far as I was concerned. England's performance at cricket was simply too ghastly to listen to, so I turned to Radio Five. After several hours of being told to go down to my local garage and buy something called a Wammee, I could stand it no longer. In desperation just at five o'clock I tuned to Radio 2 to hear the announcer announce:

"Today is the twenty-second of July which is the Feast Day of Mary Magdalene! All was revealed. That was why I'd homed into twenty-two on my bicycle. Susan Haskins had written her book 'Mary Magdalene', published that day by Harper Collins.(16)

Over the past few weeks I'd given thought to that lady. I'd thought if she was so loved by Jesus surely she must have been an apostle. I gathered she was, she'd been the first Apostle to the Apostles. She hadn't been a prostitute. That had been Mary of Egypt but due to confusion over the name, she became Patron Saint of Sinners.

I have a 'hot spot' in my kitchen – it's an energy centre – where I sit whilst cake decorating! I thought about it all, I wondered where Tom fitted into the picture – Jesus shot into my mind, the man, not the Christ, the man that some say went to live in India after the 'Ascension' into heaven.

I was so shocked, I abandoned the cake decorating, fled to what had been a blooming Golden flowered Seneco Greyii. No wonder we'd been in Golden clothes that morning! The Seneco needed a thorough pruning, so placing a mask over my face, thus hopefully preventing a lot dusty dirt or spores entering me, I got myself thoroughly grounded.

Friday with a donation of £10 in my pocket, I cycled into Haywards Heath and spied a book sale and there was 'The Reluctant Jester' (17) by Michael Bentine. They'd been on sale in York, I could have bought a signed copy, I hadn't but now I had and saved money.

Initiation and The Sephirotic Tree of Life

So that Monday morning in the rain I'd walked 'my Tree of Life', the date 19 - 7 - 1993, added together made three. Three, 'the need to communicate and become involved in the pure joy of living' (18)

Monday – Moon Day - It was also the day of the New Moon! I didn't realise that until the 9th October on checking dates. No wonder so much happened, for energy is much greater then.

Back home and at the right time I began reading my little Golden book, 'The Symbolic Language of Geometrical Figures' (8) Getting to the end I became fascinated by the diagram of the Sephirotic Tree of Life.(p.133)

I'd already seen a picture of this in my book of Symbols.(19) An ancient sage holding the tree of the Sephiroth as the 'Portal of light, the doorway of the Tetragrammation through which the Just will enter". (14) The ten spheres were in Hebrew but in the yellow book they were in English (8)

There were two words which I didn't know. In Qabalism (spelt with a C or K) Sephiroth means the ten principal aspects of God born within us. Tetragrammation means 'Jehovah or other sacred word written in four letters. (8) I became transfixed by the top three which formed a triangle.- Kether, Chokmah and Binah. What did they mean?

Well the Lord seems to make sure knowledge comes my way. I'd just met some neighbours and we'd exchanged news.

"How are you, still busy, still dowsing?" "Yes, what about you?"

Almost hesitantly they said they were studying in their spare time the Cabbalah and Astrology.

"Mean anything to you?"

"Yes, they've come my way" I'd replied.

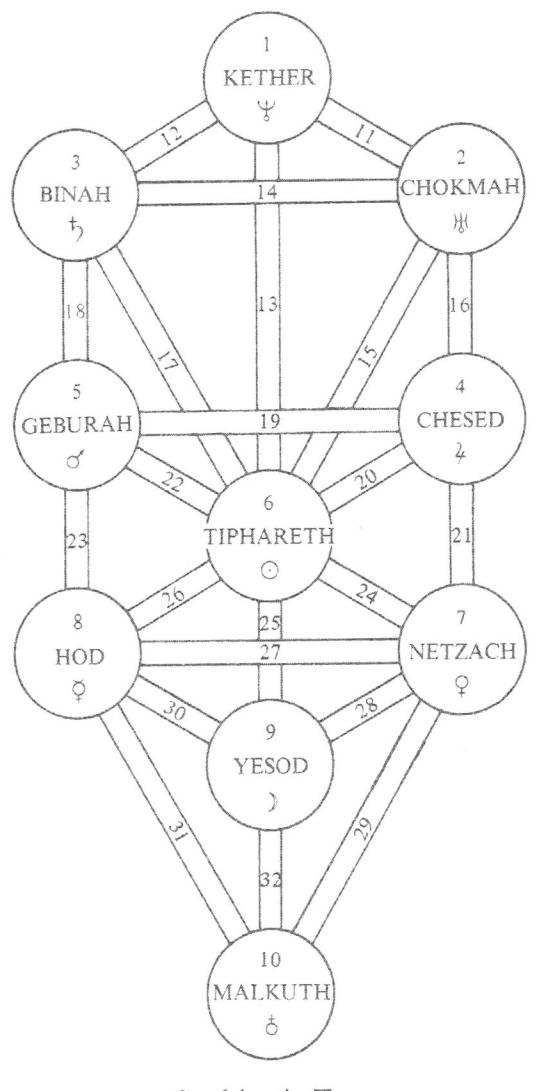

Sephirotic Tree

I went home full of glee, no need for a course or the Library. When the time was right, I put a note through their door, saying HELP please, and thus at the right time I borrowed 'The Fruits of the Tree of Life' by Omraam Mikhaël Aïvanhov, (20), the author of 'The Symbolic Language of Geometrical Figures', my little yellow book.

I didn't want any other author, Omraam was the man for me. I could relate to him and found answers to many things which had puzzled me. Please don't throw up your hands in horror for it was made clear at the start many feel studying such things may put one in league with the devil! No-one should study it in depth before being well prepared, for as in everything in life, good or bad may come your way. This was 1993 and since then many books have been written about the Cabbalah.

All cultures down the ages have believed in a Tree of Life in various forms but modern man seems to a vast extent to have lost touch. In Cabbalistic terms there are ten faces of God, with five aspects, spirit, soul, Archangels, Angels and Planets. Each fruit can be cut into layers with different meanings and knowledge. Growing in spirituality one's energies become refined, one begins to walk the Tree, (or if you prefer,) eat from it, in a different way.

The base of the tree, No. 10, Malkuth represents Planet Earth, Man, representing the Cross. At the top No.1, Kether, God the Father. In between are eight other fruits of God, No.2 Wisdom, No.3 Intelligence, the second aspect equating to the Soul.

Man has cut himself off, ten is no longer linked to nine, Yesod, The Foundation, of which the Chief Archangel is Gabriel who has the 'Power of God'. [20]

If we've managed to break the link, no wonder we are in such a mess, but look deeper, into oneself, then the link may be mended. Frightening Beings may appear. On beginning this path sometime in the late nineteen eighties they did to me on lying down to sleep, I thanked them for coming and sent them away with love and light, and thus I passed the test but at that time I didn't know what was happening.

If threatening ugly people come rushing at you when going to sleep, it is the 9th Sephirah, Yesod, Guardian of the Threshold. If my "Heart had not been pure or I'd lacked the light" I would have been defeated and not progressed along the path. (p35 Omraam's Tree of Life) If one is strong enough to pass the test one is able to contact the Angels, it is also the region of the moon. Rudolf Steiner also mentioned this in I think Rosicrucian Esotericism.

Thus do I see how my various intuitive gifts were revealed once I'd started on the inner road of the initiate.

Some years before my dear friend Seanaid Collins invited me to meet Sylvia Ezen and Janet Tintern, and to my surprise I found myself telling *them* stories, apparently they were stories of initiation and apparently when you get to Binah, No. 3, on the feminine side, the initiate enters a very narrow gateway. So I'd got to Binah wherein lies the fifty gates of Understanding. One multiplies the five aspects by the Ten faces of God.

It doesn't mean one knows everything but it means one can have entry to deepen one's knowledge. I'd been an Initiate on a Great Journey of Discovery which anyone can do. The Chief Archangel for Man, is Uriel or Sadalfon which means:

GOD IS MY LIGHT

Each Sephorith is a different aspect of man, we are all born with the Tree but apparently we have got severed for the tenth one is MAN, Malketh, and he has broken his links to heaven but my link was restored in the autumn of 1988.

By the time the initiate has walked his path he will have passed through the previous seven Sephiroth or balls of light, touching, delving to a lesser or greater extent all that they represent. At that point one may sit back I think and Contemplate God. That is what that Archangel, Tsaphkeil represents, the Soul Aspect of Binah, Intelligence. The Angels which administer it to us are the Thrones. I had a revelation about this on 12 March 2004, I had reached this point!

More about Labyrinths

As one walks this path one takes seven right and seven left turns, one is climbing upwards, reversing the descent of light to matter, a zigzag of seven left and seven right turns, as in a flash of lightening. This is exactly what one is doing when walking or running a Labyrinth. At York the Labyrinth had seven paths, that is why the Labyrinth maybe equated to the Tree of Life. However not all Labyrinths are made of seven paths, some may be nine, twelve, whatever.

Now what I wanted to know at the Congress was why some are made with a left entrance and others a right. Richard feather Anderson didn't know. He thought there was none. I didn't agree. I'm sure the Ancients knew why they were making them. Was it to do with whether they wanted these to be used in MOONLIGHT or SUNLIGHT, that these aspects might be concentrated on Planet Earth?

The seven major Chakras are linked to the seven path Labyrinth. Is it any surprise to learn that the entrance is the third Chakra, the yellow, that which is linked to the Solar Plexus. Above the navel in women, below in men, near where the umbilical cord was cut. Since 1993 many books on Labyrinths have been written and the earliest depicted Labyrinth is in an Egyptian Pyramid

Pink!

In 1988 my pre Cancer of the cervix had reared its ugly head again. Someone suggested I had healing and the healer recommended was Carole Anne Thornton. At our second meeting she told me I would feel tired and should wear pink and enquired if I had a pink nightie, I didn't, or pink sheets, I didn't, so she suggested I wore pink somewhere for it is the colour of self love and I needed a lot! Trying to comply I'd pinked my toenails and bought pink hankies.

That evening, having had healing from Carole, getting supper, as I went to welcome my husband with a kiss, I sent a milk bottle flying. I cleared up some of the mess, then we ate. After supper my husband swept the rest into a dustpan, and drained the milk through my best nylon sieve, not to sieve the milk but to separate it from the glass. I thought it a brilliant way of clearing that mess but I didn't cry and I had been told I should.

That night in bed I wrapped myself mentally in pink cotton wool, as suggested by Carole. I woke in the night and started cosseting myself with pink cotton wool balls. Then I thought to lay inside them a Mother of Pearl shell. There it was all shimmering.

Then I had the thought:

"I know what I am, I am a little pearl and I am very fragile with a very fragile bruised Heart and I am sitting in this Mother of Pearl shell and that is why I have to be wrapped in soft pink cotton. I have to be wrapped up in the soft pink cotton wool so I do not break" And there I lay in my nice warm cosy bed thinking and visualising this thought over and over again. It was wonderful.

Next morning I had a late shower, used a complete tank of hot water. I washed my hair, visualised all the drops of the water covered in Mother of Pearl washing away all my hurts. Standing there I swayed from side to side, rather as you would rock a baby.

When dry I felt clean inside and out. I imagined myself as a little plant which needed careful nurturing and these thoughts continued all over the weekend.

On next seeing Carole she was astounded in the difference from one week to the next and asked what I had done. I told her about the pearl. She said no way could I have thought that up; my Mother had sent it!

I think my trip to York was very worthwhile. My new Pendulum was promoted. Colonel Bell, became Brigadier General and he'd swung in a very happy and strong manner. After all the B.S.D. Committee then contained a couple of Generals! Brigadier General now adorns the cover of this book, and he's very delighted at that.

1. Sunday Telegraph,
2. The Pendulum Kit, Fireside, Simon and Schuster In. ISBN 0-671-69140-6.
3. Doors of the Mind, Michael Bentine ISBN 978-0246118455
4. The Truth Vibrations, David Icke, The Aquarian Press, ISBN 1-85538-136-2
5. New English Bible, Oxford, Cambridge.

6. The Direct Path, Andrew Harvey, Rider, ISBN 07126 7095-52 5.

7. The Proving Grounds, Benedict Allen, Harper Collins, ISBN 0-246-13633-2

8. The Symbolic Language of Geometrical Figures, Omraam Mikhaël Aïvanhov, Editions Prosveta, ISBN 2-85566-366-0

9. The Tibetan Book of Living and Dying, Sogyal Rinpoche, Rider, ISBN 0-7126-5437-2

10. Boericke's Materia Medica with Repertory, Jain Publishers.

11. The Healing Power of Crystals, p.149, Magda Palmer, Rider, ISBN 0-7126-1778-7

12. The Teaching of the Essenes from Enoch to the Dead Sea Scrolls, Edmond Bordeaux Szekely, The C.W. Daniel Company Ltd. ISBN 0 85207 141 8

13. Essene Network International, The Membership Secretary, 525 Lexington Building, Bow Quarter, Fairfield Road, London, E3 2UF

14. Love is in the Earth, Melody, An Earth Love Book, ISBN 0962819034

15. The Initiation of the World, Vera Stanley Alder, Rider, ISBN 0 09 089700 5

16. Mary Magdalene, Susan Haskin, Harper Collins,

17. The Reluctant Jester, Michael Bentine, Bantam Press, ISBN 0-593-02042-1

18. Numerology and The Divine Triangle, Faith Javane and Dusty Bunker, Whitford Press, ISBN 0-914918-10-9

19. An Illustrated Encyclopaedia of Traditional Symbols, J.C. Cooper, Thames and Hudson, ISBN 0-500-27125-9

20. The Fruits of the Tree of Life, Omraam Mikhaël Aïvanhov, ISBN 2-85566-467- 5

8. Royal Agricultural College, Cirencester, 1994

The last weekend in September I went to my third Congress at The Royal Agricultural College, Cirencester, Gloucestershire. Built in 1845, the first such college in the world, the rest followed – they did then!

The year had whizzed by. On leaving York I'd wondered if I would be at the next Congress, had thought NOT but Fate decided otherwise! How could I have doubted? Was it another aspect of the word *fool*, for after York I'd discovered I'd been a Fool, a Jester.

The first week of September my husband and I had returned to north Cornwall, Merlin country, and walked the North Cornish Coastal paths. One glorious morning we were accosted by a chatty lady, who proceeded to tell us how often she had been in those parts and where she stayed.

I'd retorted we'd been going to Cornwall since 1954, three years before we were married! Then something prompted me to ask where she came from.

"Near Cirencester, near Malmesbury" she'd replied.

"Oh, I'm going to Cirencester at the end of the month, please could I have your address".

Due to her, in the afternoon we visited the resting place of Sir John Betjeman, Poet Laureate. That night the telly had a programme about Malmesbury, made by him in the sixties. Coincidence? As I'd watched I'd enquired within:

"Do I have to go there?"

"Yes".

Nearer the day I'd discovered why and the time; 12 o'clock precisely. Elaine was also roped in, having to home in to me there. She was also travelling.

Twelve o'clock precisely, where was I? Approaching the bridge over the

River Kennet at Newbury. I'd experienced first hand why a By-pass was so desperately needed. That didn't worry the Powers that Be. I'd found myself making a noise and to my amusement the brakes of a large lorry going in the opposite direction joined in, echoing.

As I'd got later and later, I'd wondered why I had been so adverse to going on the Motorway. I'd known for weeks I wasn't but if I had I should have taken even longer! A crash had occurred which delayed people for three hours. I did my whole journey in three and half. Finally I arrived and there was a parking space!

Malmesbury is the oldest Borough in England, set high on a rocky promontory, a Saxon fortified hill-top town from about 600 A.D.(1) As I'd

driven up narrow roads I'd spied a river. When I'd 'done' the Abbey, my parking time up, I'd found the way to the river and had a lovely walk along it's banks. A few weeks earlier I thought they might have been ablaze with pink rose-bay Willow herb but now I'm not so sure, it might have been purple loose strife, so if I've got it wrong, please forgive me..

Then I'd come to a lane marked Holloway. Holloway Road, London, at The Royal Northern Hospital, was where I'd had Laser treatment in 1989. When I was little, there had been a haberdashery shop, Touts, somewhere down that long road and the Touts were friends of my Mother – they used to spend Christmas Day with us and Mr. Tout would always go to sleep during the Royal speech! It was a fascinating shop for a little girl for it had one of those overhead wire systems for sending the money.

Driving out of Malmesbury I noticed the turning for Tetbury and immediately chose to go there! I knew I had time for a detour and I wanted to go because the Tout's son had moved there with his wife They'd sent us a wedding present of a Silver sugar sifter and we had once visited them and I wondered if they still lived there.

Driving down the winding road, on the horizon was a large finger of God (2), a Church spire. I zoomed into Tetbury, squeezed up a narrow lane exiting right beside the Church; Parking was easy – opposite. Leaving the car I again noted that finger pointing upwards.

I didn't walk straight to the Church, for on the opposite corner was a Jewellers! I wasn't in the market for jewels, especially hand crafted ones, but something made me look. Suddenly I saw a Fire Opal set in Gold and pearls, it was signalling. Three weeks before I'd bought a fire Opal in matrix from Merlin's Cave in Tintagel and found it very powerful.

Laughing, I crossed the road and entered a most beautiful early Georgian Church, all decorated in cream. So light with a beautiful large east window, so different from the heavy grey stone interior, with no window, at Malmesbury. That building had been foreshortened many centuries before. Both took me completely by surprise. That Finger of God is the fourth highest in our land! Tetbury was a very rich area and still is, liked by some of the Royals.

"Hello".

The greeting came from a lovely lady guarding the bookstall, her last afternoon. We had a long conversation, concluded by her saying I should tell the Jeweller about my Fire Opal, how I used it for healing.

Pugin

Then she mentioned Pugin, that he had designed the Royal Agricultural College. I didn't know about him, I was none the wiser, but thanked her. When I began travelling 'down under' I kept coming across him! If you have a tour of The Palace of Westminster, as I have in 2010, you will learn that almost all the interior decoration, the vast to the minutest, was his design, including the Golden throne Her Majesty sits upon to deliver the Queens Speech. But enough of Pugin, God's Roman Catholic Architect.

I set off for the Jeweller, enquired of our friends, met with a blank. Two years later, I suddenly had a phone call from their daughter-in-law, she'd found my address in her late Mother's address book. It had been my Mother who'd kept in touch, it was all so strange. I knew in 1997 I would be going that way again, for the B.S.D. Congress would again be in Cirencester.

When I did, on the dining-room table was a pewter sugar bowl, identical to one I had, which had belonged to my mother. She must have given it to them, no doubt complete with teapot and milk jug. It was a very strange feeling. I also discovered that the road I'd zoomed up in 1994, could now only be zoomed down!

But back to 1994, I then found my way to Cirencester and the route took me past the head of the River Thames. A really good feeling for the Londoner that I am. Finally, cold, tired, hungry but exhilarated, I'd arrived, arrived wearing my new Dash outfit, a long navy knitted jacket and trousers of the same colour, which have been faithful friends to me ever since!

The first person I met was Jenny Edwards. As we talked, Jack Temple strolled up. He was making a Labyrinth and a measurement of seventy-two was an important item.

"That's a special number but I can't remember why." I'd replied.

"Is it" they'd chorused.

"Yes". I wouldn't have known that if I hadn't walked the Labyrinth at York. On my return I'd decided to learn more about it.

'Seventy-two is the synthesis of all the powers of the Sacred Name of God, Yod He Vau He. The seventy-two powers are represented by seventy-two Planetary Spirits which are constantly at work in the Universe'. (3) No wonder it was used in the Labyrinth.

Time was running out. I was running out. I was cold and shaky. That's when Joy appeared, plugged me into her special Reiki energy department. She'd become a Master since York. That done, I'd returned to my room in J.C. Block, not Jesus Christ, but that's what I'd called it.

It was perfect, through the window I looked out towards the entrance, could see people coming and going. I hadn't booked en suite. I was conserving money. The shower and loo were right next door. Showered, eaten seeds and carrots, dressed in red pleated skirt, navy top, re-energised, I'd departed for the President's Reception.

"Sherry or orange". I thought neither agreed with me but opted for Sherry. Dear David Beale, giver of the Brass Pendulum, told me what to do if I got a migraine. Stroke upwards from the bridge of the nose to the crown of the head seven times. A useful hint which happily I didn't require!

Reception over we drifted 'follow-my-leader' fashion across a dark area through big oak doors to the dining room. Dinner was followed by the President's Opening Address plus first Lecture, all completed just after nine-thirty. People were heading for bed, but I wasn't ready for that!

What to do? Still feeling shaky inside, shivery, even after being treated to red wine by Marjorie, Angela's other passenger to York, I wandered slowly in the dark, found myself under an arch and homed into a turret on the skyline, to which I'd nodded and saluted.

Then I found the bar, beside it – Will Hazell – who'd offered me that drink at my very first Congress. He didn't fail me now, I had a brandy, and then knew I had to move on. I met a practitioner of Radionics, about which I knew little. Linda E. Fellows and her partner Anthony M. Scofield, ran Meridian Associates, a Health Support Group in Folkestone. I learnt several practitioners were ill and that she also needed help.

In due course I dowsed their home and discovered the building of the Channel Tunnel had affected the Elemental Iron in the ground. I'd mentally healed this on my return with the aid of Chiron and Merlin standing in front of the Avebury Stones, Linda duly reported that their home then felt much better!

Chiron in Greek mythology is the son of Kronos by a sea nymph. A Centaur, he was the tutor of Jason and Achilles among others. (4)

But now it was time for bed, midnight, but I didn't sleep much, I worked. Lying there I pondered what energy the Radionics people used. Eventually 'Kether' floated in and I thought:

"Oh, I think that's at the top of the Tree of Life".

Four A.M. I extracted the plan I'd made during my studies, I'd known I'd need it, but for what I hadn't.

Kether. The Soul Aspect, God the Father, Metatron, 'He who stands by the Throne', the Archangel, topmost on the Sephirotic Tree of Life.(3) Could that be the reason for the illness. Those practitioner's vibrations had not reached a high or fine enough level? Why was that energy of such concern to me, that I had to stay awake for half the remaining night?

In August I had a quick trip to Norfolk to see William and Mim Topliss-Green. One morning meditating in bed, praying to the Angel of Air, I'd mentally made a purifying system. I'd seen it activated, told dear Mim.

"Did YOU MAKE IT?" she'd asked.

"I don't imagine so", I'd replied.

"THEN WHO DID?"

"I'll dowse," I'd replied and she put the questions.

"GOD?",

"Yes" went the Pendulum.

"What was the energy used?" Pendulum indicated I didn't know, but she did.

"Radionics?" to which the Pendulum swung;

"Yes".

Now in Cirencester, on waking, I assessed my day's activities, prayed that Colonel Bell would guide me *to do and say* whatever was required. At Malmesbury Abbey I'd picked up a keyring with a green stone set on a cross. No price tag, the last one, I'd haggled! Saturday morning I knew why and for whom and popped it into my handbag.

Breakfast time, I discovered the main door we had gone through the previous evening lay on the far side of Pugin's Gothic quad. Entering I discovered, as I chose my breakfast from the self service counter, I was heading for a queue coming from the other direction! I'd barged it head-on. Covered in confusion, I'd muttered to a passing male:

"I always do things back to front", who'd retorted:

"Well at least you're consistent".

When confronted with a large dining-room, I don't always know where to sit. I didn't. I stood still, surveyed the scene, sensed, like an animal, once again where I should go. The vibration of Ginger brought me to my next acquaintance, Jim Crossland.

I'd bought ginger in Malmesbury, then left it behind! As we'd talked I knew this man needed help. I gave him my address. He made contact. I was shocked at how far I had come in the past few years. The knowledge I acquired, the depths to which my psychic powers had gone.

It had been a relief to him to find someone who understood what he was talking about! And the strange thing was, as the months passed, I was always led to open a bottle of red wine – be well oiled – and then the phone would suddenly ring and he was on the end. It happened time and time again.

At breakfast I was a bit on edge, I'd been asked to chair the second seminar of the morning. I'd never met Lady Dulverton, didn't know whether she was young or old or what. All I knew was the title of her lecture: 'Treating the whole person at all levels'.

I'd rushed from breakfast, hurried to the Lecture Theatre. Halfway there I'd realised I'd left my notepad. I started to rush back, then common sense prevailed or was it Colonel Bell? Notepad could wait, her Ladyship couldn't, my lips required lipstick, I dived into the tiny cloakroom, toilet 'engaged'. I faced the mirror to beautify, then the occupant emerged – Joy. I gasped, reached for the packeted Malmesbury cross:

"Here this is for you with my love". That's all we said the whole weekend. Our paths never crossed again until we hugged each other goodbye.

Then, at last, I met her Ladyship, a minute's talk. First seminar over, it was our turn. A first for both of us. I'd thought about what to say, how I didn't want ME getting into the intro. To my horror I heard myself saying:

"I am also a healer *a World Healer, sometimes we get it right and sometimes we get it wrong!*" Oh Colonel Bell what had he made me say! Was it surprising that I was never asked to 'Chair' again!

Later he was proved right. Her Ladyship wasn't on as high a level as others on her dowsing workshop, for in the afternoon she'd informed dear David and (Beth) Elizabeth Beale their dowsing was incorrect. Monday morning David phoned in great distress. It was then that I discovered people dowse on different levels and that he and I were on the same level.

It's a hard path we tread as dowsers, we have to be very wary of what we are doing. It is only by our mistakes that we learn. Her Ladyship spoke well, she'd practised well, knew to the minute how long her talk would last and she had studied much. At the end she needed a brandy, the best I could produce was The Bach Flower Rescue Remedy! We never met again! But if this 'mistake' had not occurred, David and I would not have learnt about dowsing the question.

'Am I dowsing on the same level as..........)

Coffee time, mid-morning, I could relax, look forward to the rest of the day. What was on the menu? Much, but my choice was Sig Lonegren and Avebury. He'd written Spiritual Dowsing (4) which in 1988 Elaine's husband, had given me, which strangely he'd bought at Avebury. The book had made a great impression on me, and through it I had learnt that most people dowse on level 5 but some may dowse on either level 6 or 7 and that dowsing can lead to spirituality. Then I'd bought The Pendulum Kit (5)

I'd wondered what Sig would be like. Well, he was a softly spoken giant, huge belly, tied back hair, American accent, a beautiful way of speaking. His topic – Sacred Space in New England, Old and New.

After lunch he was leading a workshop at Avebury. I wasn't missing that.

"Meet in the main car park at 2.00 P.M. Volunteer car drivers required". I volunteered, knowing my Silver Scirocco had to go as well.

Avebury was virgin territory to me. I'd often been told :

"You should go".

At long last I was. I knew nothing about it. I'd read nothing, didn't know what to expect. All I did know was that I should be in the company of a man who did and I was very excited at the prospect. A neighbour, Bernadette, had said:

"I wonder what will happen to you there, what you will sense".

A visit to Avebury

At dinner, Friday evening, I'd offered Marjorie a lift. A 'thank you' for the red wine, but at the last minute she'd popped into a bright red open topped sports car! How I laughed.

I had two passengers whom I'd never met. Nearly last to leave, we were certainly last to arrive, we'd missed a turning. Red sports car had suddenly zoomed off to the right. We checked the map, went straight on and it was all meant to be.

We drove through the town of Marlborough. That morning I'd learnt in the College grounds there was 'Merlin's Mound', a miniature Silbury Hill. Then we'd driven past the huge man-made Silbury.

At various points along the route, various sounds emanated from me, healing sounds, so I'd warned my passengers, for I never knew when they would erupt.

Arriving at the car park we'd been greeted with the sports car, dark head bobbing up down, setting off again. We didn't follow. We decanted, walked quite a way down a footpath. As we did I felt energies passing through my hands. We'd arrived.

There it was, standing huge grey stones, sarsens, a great ditch, circular mounds. Looking to the horizon a great avenue, marked by stones. I badly wanted to walk down it but there wasn't time.

We caught up with the main party, fifty or so, dowsing equipment at the ready. I didn't want to dowse. I felt in limbo, not part of it. To satisfy our leaders I complied, just once, to prove I could find an energy line. Two workshops had joined forces. Two Leaders!

Avebury was first discovered whilst fox hunting on 7 January, 1649, by John Aubrey.(6). 'Avebury does as much exceed in greatness the so renowned Stonheng as a Cathedral doeth a parish Church. These downes look as if they were sowen with great stones, very thick, and in a dusky evening, they look like a flock of sheep (and that's why they are also known as grey wethers!). One might fancy it to have been the scene where giants fought with huge stones against the Gods'. (7)

A century later many had been removed.

Sir John Betjeman, 300 years on, described it as a haunting place to see at all times and in all weathers but most impressive of all on a still moonlit night, when it seems to be peopled with ghosts and the old Church and cottages of the village seem quite new and insignificant..' (7)

It wasn't night, but a beautiful autumnal Saturday afternoon, nor any old time of the year. It was the week of the Autumn Equinox and the feast of St. Michael and All Angels, 1st October 1994, 1+10+1994 = 34=7, the most mystical number. What a day to visit the most ancient spiritual site in the United Kingdom.

That week in the Baltic the ro-ro ship Estonia had sunk. Suddenly Sig announced he wanted a healing for it. We formed a large circle.

"Anyone can add what they wish", he'd informed.

Bosnia, Ireland, were mentioned but what had popped out of me? *Canterbury!* I couldn't think why. We joined hands, silent as the great Sarsen stones. Then the silence broke. A human voice sounded a note, it went on a long, long time, which someone on the other side echoed!

I was flabbergasted, the sound had erupted from me.

"Who made that bootiful sound" asked Sig. I stood next but two to him.

"I did" I quietly said.

"You've done it before?".

"Yes".

I had but never in public. I'd known I had to do a healing with Elaine but I'd forgotten and those words I'd been led to say that morning, had come into play. I was a World Healer!

That was the second echo of the weekend, Echo the beautiful nymph who'd lost her voice due to her desire to have the last word. A lesson to us all maybe to shut up in time. The first, you will remember, had been performed by the lorry as I'd approached the bridge over the River Kennet which also runs through Avebury, which I didn't know then or it's name.

If I felt in limbo on arrival, can you imagine how I felt after my first public performance? Shattered, knocked sideways. I felt drawn to a particularly large megalith and hugged it.

Next stop the Sanctuary. Once an impressive place but no longer due to plundering man. We were last, I'd felt 'detached'. There had once been seven rings, the inner and outer of stone, the rest wood. I found myself pacing carefully to a particular spot near the centre. I couldn't hear clearly what it was all about. I did know that inside me a scream wished to issue forth. I didn't let it.

Before we left, one of my passengers, Annie Stevenson, centre liaison officer for the N.F.S.H. (National Federation of Spiritual Healers) and I were agents of healing to Mother Earth.

Sig's workshop over, Annie, crafty lady, knew her work wasn't and suggested we should make the most of being there.

"You haven't seen the most sacred spot of all, the Cove. We could have a cup of tea".

I certainly wished to make the most of that visit and I needed a pee.

We parked in the centre of the village, the sun was setting, there was no time for tea or pee. We crossed the road, headed for two huge stones. One weighed more than sixty tons, once there'd been a third. There was also an obelisk symbolising the womb and phallus, but the guide book remained silent on that! (2).

I wanted to walk, found myself pacing again and I paced to the other side of the huge mound. I attended to my needs, anointed the soil, ascended the mound, strode right round what was left and felt wonderful in new boots supplied by Marks and Sparks. I then crossed the road, and continued on the mound until it petered out.

Then I went to where in the 1930's Alexander Keiller, heir to the Dundee marmalade business, restored twelve of the original eighteen grey wethers to their rightful place. I found myself weaving in and out, in and out. I sensed there was someone else doing the opposite and that it was Merlin. The weaving ended at the massive Swindon stone, erected 4000 years ago, one of the few megaliths never to have fallen or been moved. I gave it a hug, a blessing and goodness knows what else.

Sometime, in history, locals attributed those huge stones to the 'Magick of Merlin'. No wonder I'd felt he was walking with me. Magic or not, geologists think those great stones were once part of a huge continuous sheet of sandstone, Silica and Flint.

It was time to leave, I found my companions who'd also had a fascinating time. By the time we returned it was dark. I drove round the many, many, roundabouts skirting Swindon. I didn't want to come across another for a very long time but that afternoon we'd certainly been on a magic roundabout.

I just had time to change for dinner, have a Guinness, meet up with Tom Butler, not seen since York. I wanted to talk about the revelation that had occurred on my return. He took it in his stride, as we ate vegetarian dinners and then departed.

I returned to the Tithe Barn, venue of the previous evening. I didn't want a drink but I did want to talk to someone. That didn't take long. I wandered off in the direction of my Friday companions, those involved with Radionics. I wanted to pass on my findings and did. Then Annie and her friend joined me and we had a fascinating time, including a healing for me! The cylindrical leather case, which had carried the candles to York, also returned.

Time for bed. I got as far as the Quad, then remembered the leather case, retrieved it, and beat a tattoo all the way back. It was lovely. I chuckled, Colonel Bell was saying goodnight to his troops. I was rewarded, had a very good night's sleep. I'd eaten carefully, and a kind man had put protection under me and my bed. He'd confirmed what I was beginning to suspect. My Hydrogen problem attracted some form of energy, with which he was acquainted but I wasn't.

It was raining Sunday morning. I quickly packed, slung two bags over my arms and hurried to the Scirocco. Very different from .the first Congress when I'd bits and pieces everywhere! I then returned for my camera, said farewell to the room and set off to study Pugin's Gothic Quad.

Lifting my eyes to the tower, I'd suddenly seen the bell high above the main entrance. I laughed. At that moment a man I didn't know offered to snap me.

"Yes please."

It had even stopped raining. Then, for the first time, I felt I could enter through the small side door and queue correctly for breakfast! My timing was perfect! I rudely thumped the small rucksack upon the massive back of Sig. I didn't care that he was conversing. I wasn't missing the chance of telling him what 'Spiritual Dowsing' had meant to me. I'd wished to tell him ever since I'd known he'd be there.

Breakfast over there was time for the bookshop. This year I knew I would be spending money, the reverse of York. I'd garnered a small pile, dowsed if it was complete, it was and collected a half price beautiful 'Pi in the Sky' (8) so leaving Access card, I'd rushed to the next lecture.

'Stone Circles, A Pre Historic Enigma? By the end I didn't ever want to hear again about them! However, when Long Meg in Cumbria was mentioned, I felt she needed help. On holiday with our sons in 1977 or 78 we'd come across her on a walk.

"Horrid old girl" said Kate Fortlage when I mentioned her but I was immediately rewarded. I wanted tin.

"Ask Donovan Wilkins, he's got some", said Kate, the famous Cornish dowser often seen on T.V. There he was right behind me, the next lecturer! Coincidence? Why did I want tin. To try and heal the pain in my back, it didn't. And what was that pain due to – the metal from bra hooks which I eventually got rid of it by using the extraction pills of Jack Temple.

I got round to dowsing this when rewriting. Why had I taken it? It was to do with the lungs. Stannum (Tin). Biochemistry (9) and Boericke,(10) state it is a MUST for the lungs – in Homoeopathic form – but mine had been in its natural state. Somewhere I'd collected poison which it removed.

Too late for coffee, I rushed for the books. A queue, so I decided to have another look. There was a pile of books on Labyrinths, I felt compelled to buy one and looking up saw the author. It was Sig.

The previous year, I'd noted I had to buy a book for Elaine and this was it, the same author, almost the same place where her husband had bought Spiritual Dowsing, I was returning the energies she'd given me, but I didn't think to ask Sig to sign it.

He looked at my badge.

"I have a sister name Sallee, in Celtic it means Willow".

"I've never been able to buy a Willow for my garden" I'd replied. "My dowsing has always been ' NO'"

"Maybe you were blocked".

"Maybe I'm the Willow".

"Maybe!"

There was no time to develop the theme, I'd reached the head of the queue. I was going to be late for the final talk, 'Strange Experiences of a Cornish Dowser by Donovan Wilkins',

He'd just started. I slipped into an empty row by the door, thus was in an excellent position for Colonel Bell's finale. Donovan had a piece of Flint with incredible healing energy. That was my queue. Turning my head to address the assembled company, from the bottom of the amphitheatre (that's what it felt like) I'd announced:-

"I come from the place where Colonel Bell lived, once it was a Flint Factory. I've used Flint, I've gone to bed with it. It became extremely hot" at which a male responded:

"Hope you don't electrocute yourself".

The place erupted in laughter. What better way to have your final say!

The Message of the Willow

It went very deep, the message, for it may symbolise sadness, weeping or wailing. The Japanese Ainu believed the spine of the first man was made from it. (2) I dowsed that was important. Willow bends, gives way, springs back, survives. Trees like pine and oak resist storm, break.

According to Claire Sinclair,

"Orientals believe it symbolises life's trials because it bends with the wind as opposed to the unyielding oak. Our trials lessen if we have flexible minds."

A cricketer has to be flexible. Hitting that ball all over the place, the wood used is Willow. I'd been introduced to cricket from the beginning of my life, performed head over heals on the sacred turf of Lords! My Father had been a playing member of the MCC, and I knew he was with me on that trip, but I hadn't known in what guise. I did after that, his cricketing self!

Then I'd told Elaine about the Willow:

"Aspirin is derived from Willow, it's given for Arthritis, Arthritis is stiffening". In Homoeopathy Black Willow is good for the lower back. Need I go on?

St. Catherine is associated with Avebury. To show him the Cove, Charles II had been led by John Aubrey through the inn-yard of the Catherine Wheel Inn. The dining end of the inn was built from fragments of a single megalith but closed in the eighteenth century through lack of trade'. (7)

On Friday 7 October, holding a collection box in aid of St. Catherine's Hospice, suddenly the widow of Philip Thompson-Walker, Betty, appeared. He'd lent me his dowsing books in 1989, and one, 'Dowsing' by W.H. Trinder had led me to Map Dowsing and learning one could place plain paper beside a map and continue dowsing the area which wasn't shown.

I'd dowsed their home, discovered harmful radiations on two separate shelves of a bookcase, particular books. These had belonged to his Father in London and were 'a set'. He could quite believe they were harmful, his Mother had been ill in that home.

This is an example how objects absorb harmful radiations and carry them wherever they go, until cleansed. This can be done by prayer, asking a Pendulum to cleanse by letting it swing in various directions, using white light, Crystal light, yellow light and no doubt you may know of other ways. But after the cleansing, one then checks with a Pendulum if it has been successful.

Now this Friday morning, Betty enquired:

"Are you still making cakes, I want a very little one to take to Paris to celebrate my son's 50th birthday?"

"Yes".

"Would you like my husband's books?"

"Yes".

Fifty. I'd make a five sided cake. That's when I discovered the angles of a pentagon were 72 degrees. No wonder it is such a powerful symbol. On delivering the cake and collecting the books, there was an extra one – Water Divining (11) which reminded me that the best twig to use was made of Willow! And so more books on dowsing came to join those given by Gavina .

Two weeks later, walking in a beautiful park with our little grandchildren, Becky and Hayley, I'd suddenly seen a huge Willow and nodded thrice. I knew that tree was 'mine'. I also knew where I'd first been a Willow. By the river at Malmesbury; I'd felt completely at peace there.

A strange thing happened the day after I'd finished retyping this story. My husband returned from our allotment bearing a beautiful circle of woven Willow, a base for a wreath, found on Gordon Stewart's bonfire heap. He'd no idea I'd typed this story. It was so perfect, I asked him to place it on a wall – it's still there.

Now back to Mr. Pugin. In 2007 Rosemary Hill wrote 'God's Architect' Pugin & the Building of Romantic Britain' (13) I decided to learn about him but in that mammoth tome I could find no mention of the Royal Agricultural College, but plenty of other interesting stuff!

1. Malmesbury Booklet
2. An Illustrated Encyclopaedia of Traditional Symbols, J.C. Cooper, Thames and Hudson, ISBN 0-500-27125-9
3. Hutchinson Encyclopedia 195 Edition, ISBN 1-85986-018-4
4. The Fruits of the Tree of Life, Omraam Mikhaël Aïvanhov, ISBN 2-85566-467-5
5. Spiritual Dowsing, Sig Lonegren, Gothic Image Publications, ISBN 0-906362-7

6. The Pendulum Kit, Sig Lonegren

7. ISBN 978-0-713-99499-5 The Stone Circles of the British Isle, Aubrey Burl, Yale University Press, ISBN 0-300-02398-7

8. Footprints through Avebury, Michael Pitts, Stones Print.

9. Pi in the Sky, Michael Poynder, Rider, ISBN 0-7126-5312-0

10. Biochemistry, Eric F.W. Powell, C.W. Daniel, ISBN 0 85032 098 4

11. Boericke's Materia Medica, B. Jain Publishers, New Delhi 11-0055 10.

12. Water Divining, S.N. Pike, Research Publications, 1945.

13. God's Architect, Pugin & the Building of Romantic Britain, Rosemary Hill, ISBN 978-0-713-99499-5

9. The Birth of the Sussex Dowsers 1995

On the 31st January 1995 the A.G.M. of the B.S.D. was at The Medical Society of London, 11, Chandos Street, Cavendish Square, where the original committee of the B.S.D. held their meetings. Michael Rust on one occasion said to me:

"I have just seen the chair Col. Bell sat in!"

In 1992 when I joined the B.S.D. the meetings were held in Burlington House, Piccadilly, but then, I believe due to cost, they returned to their original venue.

Heather Willings was at the meeting and we decided to travel back to Victoria Station together. At Oxford Street there were road works, so we decided to continue walking, me saying I knew the way to get to Piccadilly, but somehow we took a wrong turning! We were in Park Lane and almost got a bus going in the opposite direction! What Heather thought of that I don't know!

As we'd walked we'd discussed the thought of starting a Sussex dowsing group. I felt Col. Bell wished it but I didn't feel I had the energy to do it or that I lived in the right place.

In April I received a letter from Heather.

'Dear Sally,

We don't expect you to travel 40 miles – but I thought you might be interested to see how the group is progressing.

Hope all is going well,

Love Heather.

They'd held their second meeting in May, so that's how the thriving Sussex Dowsers came into being. Heather died in 2009 but had left Chichester and the Dowsers many years before. She didn't even wish to come to the tenth anniversary celebration lunch, but I was invited and I did.

Distance or no distance, I began going to meetings. When they went on their first Field Trip, I map dowsed from home. Map dowsing, using a Pendulum, is another aspect of dowsing which can be very accurate. Many professional dowsers do this when seeking minerals or oils or artefacts – it saves them time when they get on site but also pinpoints say at sea, where drilling should take place. From his Obituary I learnt that Major General Scott-Elliot was a great exponent of this.

In 2000, The Sussex Dowsers came to Cuckfield on a Field Trip, so thank you Heather for getting on with the job, we are indebted to you.

In 1997 at the invitation of Heather, I spoke on my trip to Iona in 1996, entitled:

'The Pendulum and the Pilgrimage'. 'With her Pendulum as guide she found colour rays flowing through the Abbey, past lives and a landscape rich in holiness. Sally has been dowsing for over ten years and uses prayer and symbolism in her healing work. Her journey to Iona was a memorable experience.'

Well, has that whetted your appetite to read in due course my adventures on that magical isle?

In 2008, I spoke on my epic trip to Egypt, travelling by myself with a wheelchair with a right leg extension for company! I had fractured my right knee patella and when I did it, I *knew* it was for a purpose. I had already booked my own private tour with Audley, whom I thoroughly recommend. So does The Guardian and The Observer and Wanderlust Magazine.

I *knew* I had to be in Egypt on a certain day, at a certain place and that there would be no point in going at some other time. When I got there I discovered the Goddess involved had a table of sacrifice outside her sanctuary, and the sacrifice was a right leg!

Inside I knew I was bringing down an energy from above, that there was an alignment of five stars in the heavens, The energy was peace and when Sandy

McKenzie, Chairman of Sussex Dowsers, looked on the Internet to see what was going on at that time, there was an alignment, and the centre planet, was Chiron the Wounded Healer in the Right Leg! Spooky! But my epic trip to Egypt will be in my next book!.

If you have read the story of my first visit to The Royal Agricultural College, Cirencester, (Chapter 6) you will know I suddenly said I was a 'Healer and a World Healer! The trip to Egypt was for that.

10. Free Will 1995

Two years after the York International Congress, the B.S.D. were once again there for the Annual Congress but this story is not about that. It's about what happened afterwards, which made me wonder whether we have Free Will or not? We may appear to do so but if we are in tune with ourselves, and all there is, then true Free Will seems to disappear.

Once again it had been Seanaid, who suddenly seeing me in the greengrocers, said:-

"Sally you must come to lunch and meet two people who have come to live in Cuckfield Judy Porter and Tina Breene."

That was how I met Judy who now prefers to be known as Jude, who was the highly acclaimed T.V. Set designer Judy Steele. Tina later wanted to be known as Christina, and she is a highly acclaimed charismatic psychologist. In 1999 the pair founded The Triangle Healing Centre in Cuckfield, which sadly closed its doors in 2009.

Why Tina Became Christina

She was given her name at birth & it was shortened to Tina when she was 6 months old in Germany by her German nanny.

It was when she was going on a pilgrimage and had to give the names on her passport for the a visa in Turkey she'd thought she'd be asked why she was denying the Christ in her name ...and of course she wasn't – but she had started asking herself.

Another pilgrimage and an interesting series of prompts trying her full name resulted in Germany, when exactly 50 years and 6 months, she returned to it. By doing this she was able to take on the true power of her full name

Back to the lunch. It was memorable. One reason being I'd cycled completely dressed in a flowing pleated white skirt and top, with I think a Gold belt, and they wondered who on earth had come to meet them!

Jude and Tina were often away together, I became jealous, until I realised I had much in my life which they didn't. Having learnt that salutary lesson, when I said to Jude:-

"I'm going UP to York but I don't know HOW I'm getting there", she'd replied:

"I'll drive you" and her next question had been:-

"DO you think I should become a dowser?"

"Yes", I'd replied.

Why? At the bottom of her garden were not the faeries but the garden of Colonel Bell. So it was settled. Jude then said she wanted me to think of it as a short holiday break, go afterwards anywhere I wished. God's idea of a holiday, at least for me, was to work me, work me and then work me some more, but that is by the by.

Where did I want to go? I thought of Hexham, to see the place Etheldreda had given to Wilfrid. Then I looked at the map. I'd thought Hexham was by the sea, the sea was what I fancied. It wasn't, it was inland up in Northumbria, to the left of Newcastle and I'd been there. No, definitely not Hexham. Then I thought of where Etheldreda had fled, again far up the coast. No not there. I sat back, pondered, Scarborough floated in.

"Scarborough, that's where we're going after York" I later informed Jude.

We set off after Sunday lunch. The Congress had been busy, networking, meeting new people, we were in the midst of a heat wave. I went to the Minster for the 8.45 A.M. service with three J's; Jude, Jenny, Joy! Another new friend was Elizabeth Sullivan, who'd built in her garden a huge Labyrinth from redundant kerb stones, each chosen by dowsing.

Just before Sunday lunch I'd spied Michael Cook, who'd unexpectedly become the speaker on Friday evening. His subject was, 'Aromatherapy' which I was interested in. I was looking for a special book, I wanted to know if he could recommend one. He could and did. In spite of the heat, he'd unearthed

'The Garden of Eden', from under a pile of stuff in the back of his very large car. It was by his partner, Jill Bruce.(1)

After lunch we set off for Scarborough and we both visualised a B & B overlooking the sea but before reaching there, we were taken to the sea down a stony track. This ended at cliffs with a row of parked caravans and no sea to be seen due to a thick SEA MIST!

No Scarborough for us that day, inland we went. and whilst Jude was getting petrol, I had a quick look at The Garden of Eden.

We set off again and then I commanded Jude to "turn left" down Church Road. She couldn't comply, so again I commanded, "next turning on the left, 'turn left'". She'd complied – still Church Road! By this time I knew we should have our longed for cup of tea in a Vicarage or Rectory garden, so all the way round, we looked for such a place with a B & B sign attached. Nothing.

Driving from York, Jude talked of her time ten year's before when working in that area for Yorkshire Television, of the hotel where she'd stayed. That was

where we ended up! Wrangham House Hotel, Stonegate, Hunmanby, North Yorkshire YO14 0NS. A beautiful, elegant, probably Georgian, brick house, once a Rectory!The hotel was small, empty, but not the previous night, we couldn't have stayed then. Yes, we could have tea in the garden. It was peaceful, we felt we could stay for a day or two. The tea came, it was the best cup of Earl Grey I had ever tasted. Then we were shown our rooms. Six and Seven. We gasped, those had been our numbers in York. There was another gasp from Jude, on entering her room. It was the same as ten years before, even the wall paper had not changed. But mine had been refurbished in beautiful pale blue, a canopy over the bed, vastly different from the sparse student's room at York, it was fit for a Queen.

I was longing for a bath, the bathroom hadn't appealed at York. Different block to two years before but I wasn't that dirty, I'd showered each morning after my morning swim but I laughed when I saw the bath – a hip-bath! Have you ever tried to lie full out in one?

The Hotel was next to the Church. We decided to go to Evensong at 6 P.M. The Notice was not up to date, service didn't start till 6.30, but we enjoyed seeing the locals file in. I was hungry when we entered, one and half hours later, I was even hungrier, starving. A new incumbent, a long sermon!

Finally Service concluded, we thankfully returned to Wrangham House Hotel, destination the small chintzy bar and discovered a couple ordering drinks.

"We've been to Evensong", we gasped.

"So have we", they gasped back!

Drinks all round, male departed to change shorts for trousers. His companion sat down, we sat at the other end of the room, just too far apart for a friendly chat. I got up and went up to her.

"What are you doing" she'd asked. Jude replied:

"We've been to a Conference", I interjected,

"No, we've been to a Congress in York, we're dowsers and healers. Well, are we going to join you for the evening or are you going to join us, for I'm too exhausted to go on standing here?"

She came to us, saying how she'd been praying for help and healing. She'd had a terrible battle with her conscience. It was her sister's birthday, at the other end of England. She felt should have been there. Instead for once she'd put herself first and was feeling guilty.

Her husband returned, we ordered supper. Mine was very light but included the most delicious white syllabub. I was in harmony, I was dressed in white again. We had the most amazing conversation, including St. Hughes Monastery at Cowfold, Sussex.

Later Jude and I went there for a service on one of my birthdays. Extraordinary experience, the ancient Roman Catholic rite, all in Latin and we just hoped and prayed two C of E's weren't spotted!.

At bedtime Jude and her husband departed, Liz and I were left alone. Healing flowed through me, she saw Jesus. And that was how Liz Sayers came into my life and is still part of it.

Monday morning I'd dressed in pink and white, an outfit I'd made before going to York. It struck me that it looked like the white and pink sugar substance I would no doubt have bought in Scarborough – Rock.

We had the most wonderful full English breakfast, beautiful, so much we didn't need lunch. Then we were off to Beverly, where Jude had a friend, she'd kept talking of Beverly on leaving York, but that name just kept reminding me of a daughter-in-law! We explored the Minster, saw her friend, and I returned with a lily from his garden!

We'd booked for dinner. The dining-room had once been the Library of the Rectory. The first course arrived with a limp and tired piece of Lime Green parsley. I knew it was important, and to Jude's surprise, I'd placed it under my chair.

At the end of dinner, before leaving, I mentally removed some of the books that would once have lined those walls, to the walls of our dining room! I thought knowledge might come my way!

There was no-one to talk to that night, so I went to my beautiful bedroom with 'The Garden of Eden'. At three A.M. I woke up and the book opened at:-

LIME

Astrology: Mars

Chakra: Heart/Throat

Etheric Bodies: 2/3

Colour: Dark Red

Organ: Circulation System

Tree of Life: Geburah

Number 8

PHYSICAL

Improves the circulation system greatly. Can remove chlorine from body, also arsenic. Will heal cuts readily. Removes parasites from the tissues.

MENTAL

Has an affinity with LIBRARIES (my caps) and collating. Can mobilise money in your direction. An oil for the tycoon.

SPIRITUAL

I see a very small elf, who is helping the oil assimilate information on computers. It seems to be ingesting data panels. It is evolving to deal with complex issues to do with computing, which we have not yet even contemplated.

Well I know it didn't open at Parsley but it was a strange happening at 3 A.M.!

Next morning we set off again and headed for Sherwood Forest of Robin Hood fame. We went via Clumber Park where there is the most wonderful avenue of LIME TREES, the longest in Europe!

Finally, exhausted, we arrived at Southwell Minster, the most rural and untouched Minster/Cathedral in England, with apparently NO shortage of money. We were staying for a one night stand at another B & B, kindly booked after the Congress by Jenny Edwards.

It was The Old Forge listed in 'Staying Off the Beaten Track'. Before leaving home I'd known we'd stay somewhere listed in that book. I'd left an old copy on the bed!

Bliss, I had a large bathroom and large bath! I had a large swig of 'Tear drop' crème de Menthe Liqueur, which I'd been motivated to buy and take with me! That set me up when we got there. Next morning I placed some in the bath before setting off for Communion which, if my memory serves me right, was held in a delightful tiny round chapel.

Why crème de Menthe? Peppermint. At the end of the day I knew why.

Packed again, we headed for Loughborough University, I knew we had to go there. All along on that trip I knew that sooner or later I would see the maiden name of my grandmother Rose Hubbard - France. I'd looked for it on the gravestones at Southwell Minster. Finally it was there on a lecture hall at the university!

We'd bluffed our way past the Security Guard and Jude went into the Info block, returning with two brochures for Students - advanced and otherwise! I had been in very commanding mode as we drove around.

Then we set off for a monastery Liz's husband had mentioned. Nearing it we heard bells ringing. We had to find from whence. A peel was being rung in a tiny country Church. Campanologists on holiday. The last thing to expect on a hot Wednesday morning. Then we found the Monastery of St. Bernard, it was for Jude, it was her turn for something miraculous to happen. It did. I just sat in the car and waited.

Then we headed off for lunch, once more I became very commanding, I felt military, then we headed home.

PEPPERMINT

Astrology: Virgo

Chakra : 3rd eye is opening

(also vibrates between pelvic and Solar Plexus)

Etheric Body: 6th – radiating outwards

Colour: Green

Organ: Brain

Tree of Life: Path from Tiphareth to Chesed

Number: 2

PHYSICAL

Feels smart – together, military almost. Stomach and bladder especially urethra ulcerative colitis. Evolving to help skin Cancers especially from radiation.

MENTAL

Can help put things in order. It can be used to clear the head for intellectual pursuits. Very serious oil – stern almost – connection with UNIVERSITIES. (My caps)

SPIRITUAL

Starting to evolve – seems to be collecting military intelligence – may be used for Laser burns in future, its genetic coding is changing. Seems to have a way of containing fluid in the cells. Maybe be used in conjunction with plastic surgery in some way.

The oil feels stressed as it searches in an increasingly toxic environment for its own genetic coding to fulfil the task it has been given – it seems stuck as to what to do next (circa 1992)

(1994) Has now evolved enough to be finding its way into hospitals where it will be used for burns from warfare, especially Napalm substances.

Anti-bacterial properties have intensified, preparing for a battle with fly bites – evolving in preparation for fast evolution of mosquitoes.

So it had been Colonel Bell bossing me and thence us, around!

A few days later Jude sent a card:

My dear Sally,

Just in case you feel you have missed out after our extraordinary adventure.

SCARBOROUGH EVENING.

An Historic British Poster reproduced from the original held at the National Railway Museum York (we went there) c.1915, 'Cheap Tickets Issued. Full particulars at N.E.R. Booking Offices.

Buxom Edwardian 'ladies' with their beaux out on the Esplanade. Yes, I think we were guided to the right place!

P.S. Jill Bruce still has a few copies of The Garden of Eden. Jill Bruce

Aromatherapy, Kings Court, Bridge Street, Walsall, West Midlands, WS1 1JA

1.The Garden of Eden, Jill Bruce, Magdalena Press,
ISBN 0-9523695-0-8

11. Lincoln 1995

Faith, Hope and Charity

The Blue Door

A door symbolizes hope, initiation.(1) When knocking or ringing the bell, we hope it will be opened, or we hope the key will unlock it. Sometimes the knock isn't answered, sometimes the key doesn't work. When the latter occurs, what does one do? Panic, yell for help, throw a stone, contemplate a cold night on a hard doorstep. Well all these things happened to me in a space of four days. On reflection I decided it MEANT something.

In September 1995, Jude and I were off again, this time to Lincoln, for a B.S.D. course 'Learning to Dowse', please don't laugh, though Deirdre and Michael Rust did when I arrived. Apparently they couldn't believe it was me who'd enrolled

We'd swapped roles, I drove, I thought it would be good for my confidence. Jude felt she should learn to dowse, for you may remember her garden abutted that of Col. Bell's. I'd never used rods and it had come to me that I should. I'd even had special ones made after meeting Allen J. Heiss, an American, at York, who had wonderful telescopic ones.

End result – I never did get to grips with the rods due to circumstances beyond my control and I never ever got to grips with my special ones, though others found them wonderful. Jude rarely has been able to dowse, only when the need was very great, then the Pendulum worked! But that is no reflection on the tuition. It is us.

The venue? Edward King House, within the precincts of Lincoln Cathedral. According to Jude it had the best views from any loos in Europe. Gazing through them one looked upon the wonders of that huge Cathedral astride the top of the hill, beached like a huge liner. At night, floodlit with amber light, it was a truly awe inspiring sight.

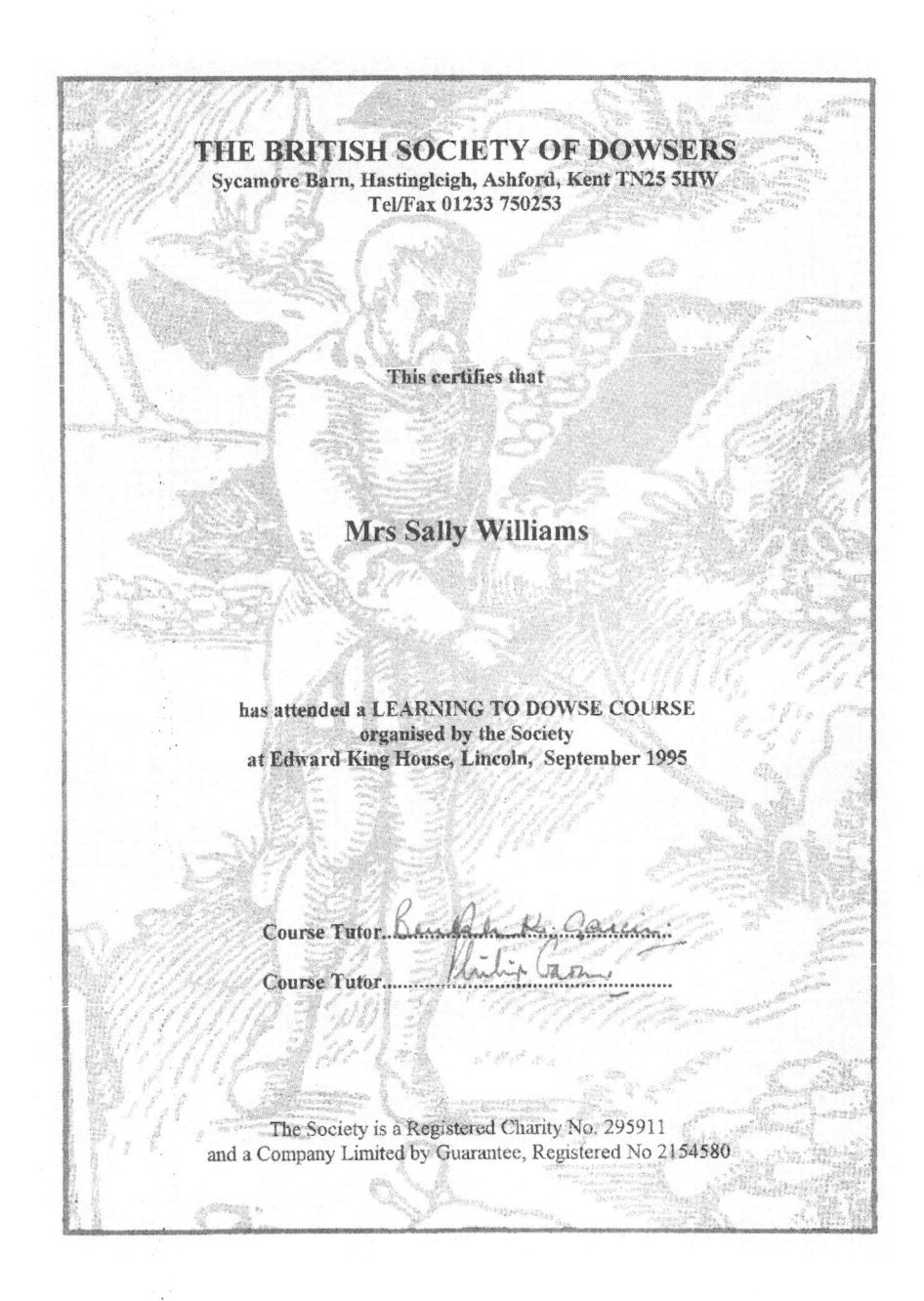

> **THE BRITISH SOCIETY OF DOWSERS**
> Sycamore Barn, Hastingleigh, Ashford, Kent TN25 5HW
> Tel/Fax 01233 750253
>
> This certifies that
>
> **Mrs Sally Williams**
>
> has attended a LEARNING TO DOWSE COURSE
> organised by the Society
> at Edward King House, Lincoln, September 1995
>
> Course Tutor...
> Course Tutor...
>
> The Society is a Registered Charity No. 295911
> and a Company Limited by Guarantee, Registered No 2154580

Friday night I slept well. I had dowsed the room, as we'd been taught using bent coat-hangers and moved the bed. Then to my surprise, discovered I was having an early start with a scented lavender bath, in order to see the

Cathedral in the early morning light and receive Communion.

Setting off down three flights of stairs, I got lost. I was in a passage leading to the back garden, seen from my bedroom window.

I opened the door thinking there would be a way out from the garden – there wasn't! Returning, the door was locked. Then the austere figure of Father Alex appeared and said I should have put the door on the latch! Well how was I to know, I'd never been there before. They might have put a notice up. That was the first time!

I went to the Service, the congregation, including me,was just three. I stayed until the candles were blown out, then chatted with the verger and learnt about the problems of the Cathedral;

"Not us, it's the clergy who can't agree on anything".

That week the Escape Society had hung up their Colours in Lincoln Cathedral, there they were propped up in the corner, until the powers that be could agree whether to hang them with other colours on the right side or hang them on the left!

Then the Verger told me what I should do!

"You should go on the Roof Tour"

"What's that?" I'd enquired.

"Well at 11 A.M. and 2 P.M. twelve people can walk above the Cathedral between the roof and the high arches, you have to book".

Oh no, surely God wasn't wanting me to do that, me with my fear of heights! *But I'd been told I should do it.* I remembered once a nice verger in Ely telling me to see the Lady Chapel. That had been very worth while. Here was another, he booked me in, not knowing my name, and I have No. 1 ticket to prove it.

Luckily for me, some of the walk outside was sealed off. I saw the window dedicated to Joseph Banks, who named so many species of plants in Australia and New Zealand but I didn't know then I would be travelling there and seeing some. I saw the Lincoln Imp – Jude's childhood nickname, for Lincoln was her birthplace. After my trip to the roof, I'd returned to ground rather trembly and shaken, but it had been worth it. Walking above the huge arches was something I would never forget, they looked like huge Elephant trunks.

Then it was out to Lunch with a an old friend of Jude's, who'd said:

"See the Loganberry Tree?"

I'd immediately fallen onto the hard stony path, hurt my knee, but thought, 'It's not loganberry, it's a mulberry". I remembered the mulberry where my Mother had lived in West Pallant House, Chichester, but it went long ago, for part of that lovely garden is now a car park.

I was picked up by sturdy hands. I realised why I had fallen. I hadn't shut myself down from the trip to the roof space, when God was working his purpose out. I promptly did. There are various way of doing this. One way is asking one's Chakras close to an appropriate level. I visualise this happening by the cones foreshortening.

Thus I started missing 'Learning to Dowse'. I missed most of the course. I ended up being a channel of healing to all and sundry and through that I made two new friends, Pam Clark, who helped many people with M.E. and Keith Williams.

It was ten twenty when I was allowed to stop, for at the end of the evening lecture, Keith asked if I could give him healing, so we set off and sat down in a large room. The healing had been very deep, which included me seeing before finally arriving a road in Lincoln we'd driven down. I'd gazed at it, noted its shape, the same shape of a shadow I'd seen on the bathroom wall before leaving home. I'd seen the road from the roof of the Cathedral, had enquired from the excellent guide where it went; a hill, and then onwards. In the room was a picture of a man and Keith looked just like him, I couldn't believe it. Healing concluded, he'd said:

"I'm going for a pint, would you like to come".

"Why not," had been my rather terse rejoinder.

So, there I was at ten twenty, being invited out for a nightcap with a total stranger. I couldn't go out in Gold slippers. Stiff knee or not, I ascended the three flights, then had the fun of descending again, one stair at a time with the staircase in darkness. LIGHTS OUT. I felt I was escaping from the dormitory or was it a convent? No-one knew I was going. All I had with me were my keys to King Edward House, not even a handbag.

We went to the White Hart. I'd homed in to that on the way to the Wig and Mitre, our excellent lunch venue. Keith asked me about myself.

"We have three sons" and so did he.

I downed a pint of Guinness, then we returned. I wanted to stay outside, gaze at the towering golden building above, he didn't. The large door closed.

Gazing over, I tried to place my little key in the lock. It would not, it refused. No way would it go in. What was I to do? I prayed to the Angel of Locks to come to my aid. No way was I ringing the bell at 11.15 P.M. I didn't want to meet Father Alex again; be classed a Scarlet Woman. I couldn't throw stones at any windows, all so high and bedrooms were at the back. I didn't even have a key for my car. NOTHING HAPPENED.

I walked to the kitchen entrance, it was locked. I walked back and tried again. This time I succeeded but still the door would not give over. I said another prayer, it was heard, the huge door slowly opened. Giggling, I ascended the stairs, remembering to turn out some of the lights.

My whole day seemed as though it had been a dream. The various activities, which if I'd known I was going to do, would have stopped me going! I didn't sleep well, due to my burps. Lincoln appeared to need a great deal of Hydrogen!

Sunday morning I went to Communion again. Wonderful sitting under the huge roof with a good congregation. Later, to the amusement of the others, who observed I had not been much in attendance, Michael Rust, asked me to give the vote of thanks to the tutors, Philip and Beulah Garcin.

Lunch over, Jude and I set off for the next part of our adventure, some of which is related in the next story.

Four days later Haywards Heath Tangent had an outing to the Ambulance Training Section at Southlands Hospital, Shoreham, to learn resuscitation, blowing into those so attractive plastic dummies.

On arrival I needed the loo, wash basins came first, the 'Ladies' through another door. I entered the first one, did the necessary, then to my horror the door wouldn't open. It wasn't the lock, the lock thing was also the handle and one couldn't get a good grip. The door was jammed at the top, due to new paint! I gave a little yell. Well no-one was going to hear me through three doors. What was I going to do?

I knelt down, discovered there was a gap at the bottom of the door, pulled with all my might. Eventually the top came loose and I escaped.

"Would you have noticed if I hadn't appeared" I enquired of my friends. I was assured they wouldn't have left me behind.

"It's going to happen again, I've already been locked out once this week." Then I remembered this was the third time, I'd been locked out twice at Lincoln!

Friday I wore a blue top, grey skirt, well mended dotted white tights, not tights I would usually wear. Husband called them sexy. In the afternoon, during a short rest, I had a good look at them. The dots were in the shape of a cross, there was a well mended ladder. I was also wearing a very special white blouse. I mused on the happenings, decided it was another initiation. I had passed through the Blue Door. What that meant I didn't know.

The opening of the rectum is like the opening of a door. Since before York mine had not been it's usual regular self. Now with this revelation it suddenly decided to return to normal. I was mightily relieved. So, if you find the same thing happening, olives instead of sausages, see if it is the body trying to tell you that you are approaching another door!

I needed Hope, I needed Faith, I needed Love – Charity - the love of the Angels to get me through that door at Lincoln. But I admitted to myself I'd enjoyed the whole adventure. I wasn't too old to still have fun,

24 January 2001

Saturday night 20 January 2001 I got to grips with the above and wondered how I could write I didn't know *what it meant!* I couldn't think where to look for details of blue but somewhere I knew I had *something*. Three busy days elapsed, evenings I was too weary. Wednesday the sun shone, the birthday of a grandson! I'd found as the years passed that special things seemed to occur on such days, most good, once very bad.

Standing in the kitchen, wondering how to fill in some time, I was in a vacuum. Phone rang, hairdresser saying she'd be late to cut my locks. I didn't know what to do. Then I remembered the vacuum cleaner upstairs . Up I went, into our big bedroom, immediately saying:

"I MUST DO SOMETHING TO CLEAR UP THIS MESS ON THIS BED". I picked up two rolls of wrapping paper, put them in the cupboard, looked at an open file. BLUE.

A typewritten something, by me, written God knows when. The file in question was 'Colour – My Book' written in very faded red with another required file stuck in – that's why it was on the bed. I had written:-

'My next thought was to check up on Blue. My eye caught a name on a photostated extract. 'Bartholomew'. I was off.

'The human being and all other creatures also emit light and radiation waves of their own, quite apart from those creatures which have a luminous appearance, such as glow-worms, fire-flies and deep-sea fish.

Dr. Glen Rein, a biologist from St. Bartholomew's Hospital, said in a lecture at the College of Psychic Studies (April 1983) that the human body emits many of the radio waves, including visible light (the latter partly as the Aura). Dr. Rein has worked with healers and found that healing energy and electromagnetic energy has a significant effect on enzyme activity and neurotransmission.'

Blue is the ray of the throat Chakra, can bring quiet and peace of mind. Inspiration as well. I also learnt from another compilation that there are true spiritual workers and healers who radiate blue from their throat centres. Christ healed a great deal simply by talking, by using the vibration of sound (2) which of course is linked to the throat centre.

That really surprised me but it did throw light on a conversation I'd had with Jill Butler at a Cuckfield Ladies evening, though then we were known as The Cuckfield Wives. When Diane Stenning and Joyce King started the group in 1966, it was the 'Holy Trinity Young Mothers'. I'd suggested healing A month later we met again. She astonished me by saying;

"I'm feeling better since our talk, I think some of your vibes must have worked on me". Laughingly I'd replied:

"Your welcome to more chat whenever you like".

All we had done was talk whilst tasting different delicious recipes. I certainly wasn't aware I was being used as a channel of healing. Was God and St. Luke, Patron Saint of Healers, also present for it was the Eve of Epiphany, 5th January. (I'd failed to write the year!)

I was astonished. Here was my answer. Dowsing with a tea infuser I asked which part of the above was relevant, and which year. I ploughed through all the old calendars. 1994, so whatever was coming through then, I presumed, was not applicable to the Blue Door. It wasn't.

Tea infuser still in hand I dowsed which of the above was. The shade of blue I emitted from my throat Chakra when acting as a channel of healing had been changed. Then I dowsed which shade of blue.

Prussian?' No'. I couldn't think of many, so enquired:-

"Do I know the shade?" "Yes."

Finally I got a YES to MIDNIGHT BLUE. What shade was that? Very dark but not Indigo, that was the Third Eye. I hurriedly searched my old and new Brewers. No Midnight Blue, neither the dictionary. I decided I'd have to ask someone who knew about art and thought of my neighbours, then realised my current client was an artist. At that moment the phone rang, it was her!

Having sorted out her queries, I then said:

"What Shade Is Midnight Blue"?

Nonplussed for a second, then the answer:

"Very dark, almost black, midnight blue. Ultra Marine would make it, in the tube its blue but when you add the oil it becomes very dark. True Ultra Marine in made from Lapis Lazuli, the colour of the Queen of Heaven, a heavenly sky blue".

"I'll look at the tube, it's here, yes when you unscrew the top it is very dark.".

That was it, midnight blue, ultra marine, made from Lapis Lazuli. In 1992 I'd written a story about THAT but not being part of my dowsing stories I'm afraid it's not included but with luck it will be in due course in a book on colour!

Back to the tea infuser, I'd gone through the door of Midnight Blue.

1. An Illustrated Encyclopaedia of Traditional Symbols, J.C. Cooper, Thames and Hudson, ISBN 0-500-27125-9

2. What Colour Are You, Annie Wilson and Lilla Bek, The Aquarian Press, ISBN 0-85030-616-7

12. A May Adventure

A story concerning blue, amongst other things!

On Monday 13 May 1996, I went to a house in Crawley. People were ill, the dog bounded up, he was first in the queue for healing! Afterwards, I took a little walk, spotted an electrical substation, a low oblong box. As I walked past, something said:

"Go away, you old witch!"

I didn't like being called that. At times over the years, when in the vicinity of electrical installations, I'd erupted, screamed, much to the distress of whoever I was travelling with. On one occasion my husband had said.

"Can't you give me any warning!"

Then on Thursday 23 May, Jude and I set off on another adventure, several one night stands. The first stop St. David's, Wales, at the home of her friend, Mimi Roberts. We'd arrived supper time, very tired, but with Champers, a fire, and a good supper we were soon restored. and then I went headlong into channelling healing!

Friday morning dawned, the sky, sky blue. it had been pouring with rain when we'd arrived. Before breakfast, dressed in blue and white, I had the most wonderful walk, down steep steps into the valley of the River Alun.

I passed the ruins of the Bishop's Palace, up the hill the other side, looking into the distance to what I knew not, except it looked a magical place. I was seeking something up that lane, then I saw it. A bright blue steel farm gate, opposite a pink one. I'd been homing into blue for a week, first the Church windows, then forget-me-knots, then a necklace.

Above the gate, sitting on the telegraph wire, sat seven black birds. Rooks! It was the perfect spot for me to 'Lift up the Sky'. The Chi Kung exercise I was doing..

'the form is deceptively simple, but what is significant is not the form itself, but the energy flow it induces'.(1)

After that morning I didn't do it again until July 1997, it completely went out of my head but I'm sure something happened. That Friday was 24 May 1996 which comes to 9 and in Numerology equates to selflessness and compassion, keywords include those and love, patience, endings, universality, tolerance, and selfless service. (2)

Then I'd sung:-

> 'Lift up your heads oh ye gates and be ye lift up ye everlasting
> doors so that the King of Glory may come in.(3)

I'd started singing this the previous Sunday and known it was a message. Returning down the lane, singing at the top of my voice, I remembered I was in the land of the Welsh, that bastion of song.

On my way back I walked around the Cathedral. Then to the chapel. I'd felt drawn to it as I'd walked into the valley. Clear windows, once St. Mary's College Chapel. As I climbed the steep steps, a man appeared at the top. I learnt a Craft Fair was starting at 10 A.M.. I felt I had to go.

He enquired whether I was in St. David's for the Music Festival? I didn't know there was one. I enquired if anything was being broadcast. Yes, Monday evening, Radio 3, from the Cathedral. I said we'd listen. Listen we did driving back down the M.40 and my husband was also listening, and thus we were greeted on our return.

After breakfast, I visited the Cathedral, and thence to the Craft Fair. A variety of stands greeted the eye, one with rainbow scarves which reminded me of the healing which had taken place the night before and the healee had said:

"Can you see the rainbow between us",

"No". I'd replied.

Now I pondered, did I need a £28 scarf? Definitely not, I was on a tight budget.

Then glass engraving – I looked and passed on to the wonderful Welsh wool cloaks and berets. Trying on a beret, for fun, they've never suited me, I heard a man saying:

"I'm engraving this tankard for a member of R.I.C.S. I couldn't believe it, the same profession as my husband's! I decided I'd better return.

I didn't like the tankard being engraved but I wondered if I should order one. We got talking, talking prices:

"Depends on the glass, the bells are quite expensive".

Bells, Bells, Bells.

BELLS! That did it.

"Please could I see one".

"Yes, I've only one".

Exquisitely decorated with harebells, the handle encased a spiral. I held it and then as I said:

"Show me yes" the clapper moved like a Pendulum, rang against the glass Children standing beside me were boggled eyed! To cap it all the engraver's name was the same as mine! I left on cloud nine, feeling my face grinned like a Cheshire Cat.

I left the price on. I felt my husband should remove it. He'd gone very quiet as I told him and said:

"Oh, I suppose that's another £30."

It wasn't - £19.95 on Access. Then he admitted he'd had an accident with one of my Mother's Georgian Crystal glasses!

"It *was* the chipped one", he said.

"It doesn't matter", I'd replied.

I realized that glass had broken to make room for the bell!

As I went to bed one night the following week, I looked at a clay bell beside it.

"I seem to be collecting bells" I'd thought.

At the end of that week the next one arrived, brought by Elaine's husband from Tibet, a singing bell with a wooden clapper. The bell is a symbol of the void, female principle, wisdom (4) Llamas would use that bell in conjunction with the dorje, the male principal. Dear Elaine's husband didn't think either of us needed that!

The bell was symbolically decorated in a stylized manner, lotus leaves, the face of a Goddess, 51 dorjes representing small unknowns, which sounding the bell can resolve. It is connected to the Buddha and the 'Four Noble Truths'.

1. Man suffers, because he is attached to earthly existence;
2. The causes of suffering are desire, hatred and ignorance;
3. Suffering can be relieved;
4. This can be achieved by destroying its cause.

Every person can achieve enlightenment by following the right path.' (4)

Made of Bronze containing Silver, it had come to help me with the work of healing. When the time came to use it to heal myself, I cut the ties between it and those to whom it had belonged. To do this you invoke St Michael and his sword three times. Bind them into yourself and the other person and put a cross over the top, to stop them re-growing.

One Saturday afternoon in 1994 I'd heard bells ringing from our local Church, I wrote the ending had sounded like 'Ding Dong Bell, Pussy's in the Well'.

For Whom the Bell Toll

Poor Pussy being drowned in the well. Wells are found where bells are. In other words when Churches were built there is the belief that the tower was built where there was a well, for baptisms were first performed there, then the bells went above and the 'Church' got attached later! It has been discovered that energy lines go through wells, and discovered through scientific measurement that when rung the centre of the energy line expands or is greater, and the sound transmitted up and down the line.

Benton Castle

So that's the story of the bell that Friday morning. Next stop, Benton Castle, luncheon with Elizabeth Sullivan and me walk the wonderful Labyrinth. I was following in the footsteps of Sig and Patrick MacManaway, who'd spent two days using instruments and a computer trying to fathom out what was going on. Major General Bill Cooper had asked them. I felt I was a steam engine as I ran around!

Elizabeth had prepared a Cordon Bleu meal, she was not pleased when it got delayed! I delayed it! How? Having a naked swim in her prehistoric rock pool! Joy and Jude looked on in horror and then I'd despatched Joy to Jude's car to get the new dressing gown 'upstairs' had made me buy on Tuesday! I'd wondered why I required a new one, striped in palest pink, turquoise and lilac! I hadn't argued, I just *knew* I had to buy it.

It was wonderful being in that superb place, seeing what Elizabeth had created. She was a brilliant dowser, had helped the Police in various investigations and when losing her sight had not hesitated to dowse the other patients in Moorfields Eye Hospital in London and tell the consultant what to do! She had 'clout'.

After that we had a long drive, we were spending the night with Joy, and a very memorable stay that was. We went from one extreme to the other, but life can be like that, and sometimes we just cannot cope and both our hosts had their problems, one keeping their home in perfection, the other not, and maybe I fall in between!

Next morning Joy took us first to see the ponies she bred then to Gors Fawr, an ancient megalithic stone circle where I danced like a child in and out the stones. We also stopped at The Slate Quarry at Pont Hywel Mill. I bought a beautiful circular piece and a couple of rockery plants, one of which is still growing; it's always nice to bring home something to remember a place by.

We then drove to Gloucestershire, staying in my son's empty rented flat; the family had gone away for the weekend, perfect timing for us. Next we spent another night with friends of Jude, again I was a channel of healing (C of H).

Monday morning we were leaving the area but first we went to see Jo Diamond who had Cancer. Again I was a C of H. I'd had coffee to drink. As the healing flowed, I saw for the first time a succession of different faces, faces which had once been Jo's, and a halo, and we learnt which saint she had been. Corroboration came in the form of a book, the picture of the saint with his halo, the book she had just been given by a priest!

Then it was a very long drive, no time for lunch, to see Keith Williams near Banbury, stopping on the way at wonderful Whichford Pottery. Again I was a C of H! It was after leaving Keith and his wife, driving round Banbury Cross, both exhausted, me on red wine plus nibbling bread and cheese, but Jude only on the b and c, and heading down the M.40 that I started looking at the serried ranks of marching pylons!

They called me an Old Witch again!

Blue Light

I explained I didn't like being called that, we needed to live in harmony with each other and please what could we do about it. The answer came and it was to use Blue Light, the colour of forget-me-knots.

I know I'm repeating myself, that if I am well oiled, the healing energy flowing through me, is much stronger, so there and then I put in the blue light, asking that the lines carried the colour right through the National Grid.

After that they stopped calling me an Old Witch and I also stopped reacting.

The next thing that happened was The Sussex Dowsers met on 14 July at Kingley Vale, renowned for its ancient yews. By this time I'd met in Jude's cottage, Delia Elcome, a brilliant dowser. We'd arrived late, missed the turning, missed the others, missed the briefing.

A steep climb was ahead but wonderful through the ancient woodland. We passed a man sitting on a mound; I thought he might be a dowser. We lunched on the north side, saw a lady walking below with rods. I called out, she joined us, and lunch over, we started talking about Patrick MacManaway. The solitary man called out:

"Is that the magic name of MacManaway"?

"Yes" said I.

Dan Wilson, another brilliant dowser, joined us from his mound, telling us what he had intuited. I felt something should be done about it, so the four of us returned to his mound. I found myself becoming very bossy, telling them where they had to stand, putting my arms at various angles, making sound. At the conclusion of whatever we'd done, Dan got the message:

"Didn't know anyone else could do that!"

Then I mentioned the Blue Light and the pylons and what I'd done.

Dan dowsed and said:

"You've opened the door 10%"

I hadn't a clue what he meant but we decided to open it a bit more. We were seven by then, sitting at the edge of the mound. I don't know what happened, all I do know is that at the end Dan said it was now 70%.

I wondered who or what would get it to 100% and that is how it stayed until in 1997 I met John Cuninghame at Hawkwood, Stroud, on the Patrick MacManaway course. A story yet to be read! John invented some L shaped dowsing rods which swing freely, and these can be obtained from The Centre for Implosion Research. (5)

John dowsed, discovered bits of the grid lacking blue; we didn't know what it was affecting, certainly not the electric magnetic field, which was still dowsable.

On Wednesday 13 August I phoned him to find out if he was including this in a dissertation he was giving. I'd begun to think the time might be right to talk about it at Congress.

Tuesday, I'd received an article, censored in Great Britain, 'The Scientific

Jean Watford, Dan Wilson, Delia, Gerald Clark, Sally

Proof of Survival after Death' by Michael Roll. On Wednesday, in the bath, I read that in 1933:

'Pauli predicted that there may well be particles within the atom other than the proton, electron and recently discovered neutron, that would revolutionise scientific thinking.'

Then was mentioned a sub Quantum level and I found myself wearing blue!

Later I wondered if what I had read had any bearing on the work with the Blue Light. I dowsed: 'Was it Sub Atomic'? 'No'. I returned to the article, dowsed whether it was Sub Quantum, 'Yes', it was affecting the Leptons, not the Quarks.

I have no knowledge of Physics. I rang John, told him to ring Michael Roll, he then learnt that Logie and Baird were onto this.

Then I phoned Dan, to see if he could shed light on what we had done. He put it into his computer and discovered that the radiation from the pylons might be affecting those who had been burnt in previous lives and also those who mentally feel they are a blot on the landscape.

A deep and strong blue colour (known in hospitals as Cardiac Blue) is the most tranquillising colour of all.(6) I felt that the Blue Light was for Britain, other colours might be for other countries. However, when I was in Australia in April (1997) John gave me the name of someone to contact, so that the pylons could be dealt with there.

One day dowsing with Jilly Wootton, we discovered it was the 19th Level of the Aura which is affected by pylons (and then works down to the physical). The Blue Light would gradually stop this happening. Once again in Jude's cottage I'd made a new friend. Jilly is an amazing young woman with many gifts and is a trainer and teacher in advanced psychotherapeutic techniques and hypnotherapy.

PS. I believe there are 22 dowsable levels of the Aura.

1. The Art of Chi Kung
2. Numerology and The Divine Triangle, Faith Jardine and Dusty Bunker, Whitford Press, ISBN 0-914918-10-9
3. Psalm xxiv., v.7, The Messiah, No.33, Handel.
4. Singing Bowls, Eva Rudy Jansen, Binkey Kok, ISBN 90-74597-01-7
5. Centre for Implosion Research, PO Box 38, Plymouth, PL7 5YX. Tel.01752 345552 – fax.338569. www.implosionresearch.com – www.ancientsources.com
6. The Power of Colour, Dr. Morton Walker, Avery ISBN 0895294303

13. Glasgow and Iona 1996

The venue in September, 1996, for the B.S.D. Congress was the Kelvin Conference Centre, Glasgow, thinking the Scots would welcome it, but they boycotted it, for why I do not know!

Glasgow from Sussex was a long way. I decided if I was going that far, I was going further. Further was the tiny island of Iona, off Mull on the West Coast of Scotland. I'd long been fascinated by its name which means Dove. Years before I'd asked Audrey Williams to bring me back a pebble. She hadn't. Next a birder, he hadn't, then Christina was beseeched:

"Sally, I twice tried to bring you back a pebble, I couldn't. You will have to go and get your own". So after the Congress I did!

My final trigger was that John Keats, the poet, journeyed there. After leaving Lincoln in 1995 we stayed in Norfolk with William and Mim Topliss-Green. As I'd driven to Lincoln, eating lunch at Stamford, Jude asked if I'd ever been to Walsingham. I hadn't but I'd tried to find it on the map the previous evening. The reason I hadn't was that in those days it was known as Great Walsingham, so the next day we'd set off, and a miracle occurred when a cuppa was required and Walsingham is know to be a place where miracles occur.

We entered the Sue Rider shop, Jude went off for something and I found a section devoted to second hand books. I selected a few, wondered whether they were really needed, decided not,but it was when replacing them the miracle occurred. My eyes had alighted upon 'Adonais, A Life of Keats' (1). it had belonged to a Circulating Library in Africa in the nineteen thirties!

Why did I want it? In 1994 I missed my Form's small reunion. A bit later I realised I was going near the town where an ex pupil Judy lived, so I phoned, caught up with the news and she invited me to lunch. A few weeks later, entering her little cottage, I saw a plant on the far windowsill and enquired what it was.

Pot Basil

"Oh, its Pot Basil, do you remember the poem, by Keats?"

"No, but I still have the poetry book." I'd replied.

"It's not a very nice story, she buried her lover's head under a Pot of Basil!"

My next question wasn't about poetry but horticulture!

"How do you deal with the white fly, my Basil always gets it."

"I tip the pot upside down, holding the plant in place with two wooden spoons, and dip it in water", was her answer.

With that I decided she was a practical woman!

Two night's later, very tired, having made an amazing wedding cake for one of Seanaid Collins daughter's, after delivery, I'd realised I could have created the design for the top better, it hadn't had flowers, but that mistake was due to lack of information. I hadn't asked enough questions!

I was desperately tired, wanted my bed, but I knew I had to get to grips with 'Isabella or The Pot of Basil'. As I did, my left hand got hotter and hotter and hotter, something it had never done before! Then the next poem caught my eye, 'The Eve of St. Agnes', the heroine's name Madeleine, was the same as our first grandchild. Some of it seemed familiar.

> 'A Casement tripple arch'd and diamonded
> With many coloured glass fronted the Moon.'
>
> Eve of St. Agnes

Where had I read that before? Then I remembered. The Library. I'd been sitting thinking about something and found my gaze homing into the books on the other side of the room. I felt myself being drawn to them, and finally investigated. It was 'The Enchanted Forest' (2), the story of Stansted in Sussex, near Havant and it had opened at a description of the Chapel, which had been restored. Keats, whilst staying at Bedhampton, had attended it's consecration. I'd never gone there or heard of it, though we'd lived in Havant.

Finally going to bed, I'd wondered if the history of the Keats family had anything to do with me, for having read the poem, I then read the introduction and discovered many coincidences. St. George's Hanover Square, his parents had married there and I'd been a bridesmaid.

The house in Hampstead, now known as Keats House, was where Keats vomited blood and knew he had T.B. That house is a stones throw from where I was born, where my Father vomited blood and knew he had T.B. Keats's Father, had been killed by a horse, and I've had more than one try to do the same for me!

From all this and more, I decided my Father had been John Keats. As the years unfolded so many other coincidences occurred, I discovered some friends were all part of that incarnation and they knew they were, which explains why they are now such good friends to me. So this is why I decided to go to Glasgow and then to Iona.

Where to Stay?

Where would I stay? I tried the Abbey, No Go, tried the Dowsers, No Go, even thought of missing Congress. Then Sunday I'd read a Lesson at the 8 A.M. Service. I do it once a month and what did we do, we prayed for Glasgow and surroundings!

Back home, I phoned Jude, told her my predicament..

"Sally, what you need is guidance, who can we think of who knows about Iona". I'd replied:

"Christina and her mentor" -(Peter Dawkins of Zoence). (Science of Life.)

Phoning immediately, Sarah Dawkins answered and said they stayed at the St. Columba but there was also the Argyll. No, I was staying where they went. She added the latest issue of Gatekeeper Magazine (2) contained a map of Iona and the Chakra system. You see not only do we have Chakras but Mother Earth does as well. I thanked her, immediately phoned The Columba. The two nights I required were available, but not a third. Then I'd enquired:

"Do you know of anywhere I could stay in Oban"?

"Yes, a rather eccentric hotel in Shore Street, The Kelvin" she replied.

"That will do, please could I have their number".

Within the space of about 90 minutes everything was solved. Once knowing where I'd place my head after Congress, I knew the rest would fall into place. I was going from one Kelvin to another!

The Journey

Friday 6 September I'd spent the night wondering what to wear. The weather was warmer up there than down here but friends advice had been;

"Take Warm Clothes, its freezing up there!" so it was Cirencester's Navy Dash, trainers and chest adorned with a very large wooden Pendulum.

Everything else went in two Multi Vision bags, one small, one large. Elaine's husband offered wheels, not car wheels but baggage wheels; I gave that thought, No. Another thing to carry, but those very wheels came in handy when I went to Oz and N.Z in 2007!

Due to traffic jams, I nearly missed the Thames Link to Kings Cross and I was pushed unceremoniously out of the car when husband realised I'd only four minutes; that saved him fond farewells! I grasped bags, staggered to the station, up the steps, in slid the train! Phew, that was a near one and oh my poor back!

Sunday night I'd lain on the floor and swung my legs over my head, something I was used to, but that night my back hadn't liked it. I'd crawled down the landing to get into bed and wondered whether I'd make it to Scotland. It was still very painful but I was on my way and when I reached Kings Cross Thames Link, I had to get to Euston.

Kings Cross

"Have a taxi" said husband, "or you could walk".

"Go on the Tube," said a son ,"or walk".

"What about a bus?" I'd replied.

"Wouldn't hang around that area!" said middle son – he knew, he was working there.

I didn't take any of their advice, for there was a bus approaching and the bus stop was opposite the exit, so I hopped on, waived my ticket, not expecting it to be accepted and saying:

"Euston", and the reply was:

"That's O.K."

My £56 Return Apex stated seat number J.33. I was sitting on a Master Number! What you may say is that.

In Numerology it is a number which you do not add together. As I typed this on 25 August 2009, I looked for a definition of such a Number, I could not find one! Then next morning a wonderful bit of serendipity occurred. The postman brought the latest edition of Cygnus Magazine (3) and there was my answer! Diana Cooper had written :

'A Master Number is one in which the digits are not added together. 33 is the number of the Christ consciousness and is a message from the Universe to work with the Christ light'.

It was a table seat, I smiled at the two women already ensconced opposite, not a glimmer back. I sat quietly, then the elder got up to get coffee. The train was pretty empty, suddenly I heard someone saying they were going for sixteen days to Iona! I hopped up, sat down beside her. Her name was Catherine, she lived in Sussex, but had lived on Iona for several years.

"People think they can walk it in an afternoon. It's only 3.5 miles but you can't for bogs have to be skirted. I always allow two hours to get to St. Columba's Bay".

I need a guide I thought.

"Would you like to take me there?" I'd asked.

That was the one place I did want to go to. Columba was reputed to have sailed in a coracle from Ireland there . It was also the Base Chakra. She'd readily agreed and agreed to phone to make arrangements.

I returned to seat thirty three, and gradually we began to chat; had their coffee helped?

"You must go to the Rennie Mackintosh exhibition, that's why my daughter is with me, she's an Art Student", I was told.

I don't know if I had ever heard of Rennie Mackintosh but I certainly made up for it in double quick time. Then we had a wide ranging conversation including health food shops and The Bach Flower Rescue Remedy - I realised mine wasn't in my handbag - then dowsing.

"Do you know a man called Jack Temple"

"Yes, he got to the bottom of my pre Cancer, no doubt he will be at Congress – he's had some varied press this year".

She'd seen it. Jack had opened his mouth re the Duchess of York, plus Princess Diana, so had made headlines. She had a friend who kept going to him, didn't seem to get any better. She was pleased to meet someone who had and this is what he discovered for me.

My T.B.

Jack Temple discovered the underlying cause of my pre-Cancer of the Cervix, a miasm of T.B. This stopped or held up the energy of Phosphorus. Phosphorus is a Homoeopathic remedy for T.B.

I had had a second coning of the cervix by Laser at The Royal Northern Hospital. Jack's discovery was accepted by Miss Mansell, FRCOG, Senior Registrar to Mr. A. Singer, at Islington District Colposcopy Clinic. She said when I reported his findings, that they often found an underlying cause, but how she would have treated mine I do not know.

What I did, was to use Jack's formulated Homoeopathic pills, to remove the T.B., and put in Phosphorus. I dowsed the relevant number of each, placed them on Micropore and then stuck them on where the miasm lay, the pubic bone....I didn't even know where that was, but soon discovered! As soon as I did, the peculiar feeling I'd had before receiving healing from Carole Anne Thornton, departed. To my horror after the op it had returned and that was when I wondered if the Laser treatment had failed.

In Homoeopathic circles, only a certain number of miasms are recognised but Jack used the term for anywhere there was a block of nutrients. So in my own way I'd had T.B. which unknown to me, my Mother had always worried about. This knowledge that my Father had T.B. stopped my parents having any more children. (My legs tingled when typing this in 2007)

Glasgow Central

The train was 10 minutes early. Descending to the platform I was blasted by a heat wave. There was no man standing with a green B.S.D. Board. I walked up and down, getting hotter and hotter and eventually, having allowed time for the train to have arrived, I'd dowsed.

"Have I been forgotten? 'No'. Is he here? 'No'. Should I get a taxi? Yes".

B.S.D.'s booking form had listed:

"Would you like a lift." I'd written:

'Yes from Glasgow Central Station to Kelvin Halls would be useful' but something within had felt it wouldn't materialize – I'd almost crossed it out.

The taxi was a real bone shaker, the roads weren't smooth.

"Where to".

I tried to explain, he had the radio on, windows down, boiling, I couldn't understand or hear him. Then I tried saying why I was going there.

"What's Dowsing". I couldn't go into that and weakly replied.

"I'm a Healer".

At that he said he'd got a bad wrist, had it for months, which resulted on arrival with him jumping out his cab and straight onto the back seat and grabbing my hand, plunging it onto his wrist, and he clapped his other hand on top. I suggested he turned the engine off, then placed my other hand over his and there we sat for quite a while outside the Kelvin Halls!

I asked why he hadn't seen a Doctor, didn't he believe in them and wondered if he would let me off the fare. Didn't. True Scot, but I didn't begrudge him.

Clasping bags, I struggled into the Kelvin Conference Centre and was welcomed by a charming man who said there was a cup of tea nearby. They wouldn't give me one, it was there for Branch Representatives! I went to Reception, there stood Sir Charles Jessel who'd quoted my words in his closing address in '93.

"Hello Sir Charles, I've just given healing to the taxi driver."

"Hope he waived the fare."

"No".

Lumber Region

Finally I found my room. The dowsers were having tea in the dining room, but without delicious shortbread but I'd filched some on returning to the first room gasping.

"Please can you give me some water".

Allen Heiss, welcomed me, the inspiration for my rods in '95. After that long journey, my back was dreadful. They all tried to sort out what had happened. Gave it healing. Muscle spasm seemed to be the answer.

"Why didn't you sort it out yourself" one enquired.

"I did" I'd retorted," but after eight hours travelling I and it need help!"

That over we dispersed to dress.

The Bathroom had no lock and the door didn't close, but that didn't deter me from a much needed soak!

Black Watch Tartan!

When I'd returned from Lincoln in September '95, I'd immediately made a Scottish themed Ruby Wedding Cake for Seanaid. For reasons unknown, I'd delivered it ensconced upon a Black Watch cushion tray. Now, one DOESN'T usually deliver a cake on a slippery cushioned tray! Delivery over, I went to Windowscene, which sold curtain material. To my amazement there was a roll of Black Watch Tartan!

There and then I knew if I went to Glasgow trews would be required from that material. Eleven months later I bought it! That was all. I had an old unused pattern and an old zip from a son's pair of jeans. I'd taken the pattern to Windowscene, placed it upon the material and discussed which way it went. £22! A Master Number! (Co-create the life you want. So hold a very positive vision for your future or just your next step (3)) Back home I found, if placed the other way, I had enough material for a scarf! In the winter I'd looked at Black Watch scarves, but they hadn't matched my Black Watch skirt.

I then found another pattern with narrower legs and put both together, hoping I wouldn't be taken to task for having the Tartan the wrong way up! Those trousers held, unseen to anyone, a phantom Quartz Crystal Pendulum, hanging from peach ribbon. I'd made belt loops, made them long enough for *both sides* of the waistband. When finished I realised a mistake, I'd put the loops *inside* ! I thought again, decided it was so that something could be hung unseen. A brilliant idea, I could hang keys, purses, anything. I'd definitely been led to do it.

Bath over, on went the outfit, which I hadn't even tried. White blouse, black onyx necklace and earrings, scarf pinned with Mama's Scottish broach and thus attired entered the Reception. Immediately a man homed into me, later apologising for his over friendly overture! Thought I was someone else! Then another approached, saying;

"Look she's even got the...he was referring to the broach"

Has it got the Cairngorm?

"Yes".

I was then subjected to an interrogation as to whether I stemmed from Wales, Scotland, England, all due to my Welsh surname! (Williams) It wouldn't do. I tried another tack.

"My Father was a Royal Fusilier, so was my Guardian, Sir Philip Carlebach, Knighted for his contribution to the founding of the Army Cadets".

"That's better" he'd said!

"My husband was a Royal Engineer. I dowse at home with my charm bracelet which has the badge of the Royal Corps of Signals".

That settled it, I'd proved my credentials, then Pat, his wife appeared. It was the start of a new friendship, I'd met the Davies's, Northamptonshire dowsers, who knew Joy.

But why Black Watch Tartan?

Elaine had said I'd be skinned alive if I wore it in Glasgow! I didn't! Her Tartan Book informed :-(4) 'didn't belong to a clan! The Black Watch, the very first Highland Regiment raised in 1739 – and now I believe tragically amalgamated. Their first commander, a Lowlander – no Tartan! The Tartan is a 'hunting set' based on the Royal Tartan. Known in the 18th century as the 'Government Tartan', it was the natural set to use for a Royal Regiment, and subsequently also became known as the 'Universal Tartan' (5). (I think it has truly become that!) The colours are muted so the troops couldn't be seen.(2) I'd been right when I'd felt I was wearing it for protection. I later discovered their motto. *Nemo Me Impune Lacessit.* **(No One Attacks Me with Impunity)** (5)

As the train had crossed the border into the Lowlands, something or someone said in my head.

"Welcome".

I felt it was John, 20th Earl of Crawford, their first commander! (My legs tingled as I typed that, a sure sign one is on the right track!)

The Congress.

It moved in it's usual fashion, fascinating talks, people. Me where I had to be, synchronously as always spot on, much to the distress of the President, Major General Bill Cooper, who'd said:

"Sally you're always late".

I could hear Colonel Bell saying:

"Late on parade again!"

Well I don't work on G.M.T. I work on God's time! Saturday morn, adorned in Black Watch Trews and long sleeved cheap old indigo cotton T. shirt, I'd found myself behind the wonderful Charles Holderness and tapped him on the shoulder with his Nature Study Book!

The Tale of the Nature Note Book

In 1995 the B.S.D. formed the Earth Energies Group for dowsers to pool and exchange knowledge. I joined. In March the first Newsletter arrived with a very interesting article by a Mr. Charles Holderness in Leicestershire. I wanted greater information, so grabbed the phone! Imagine my astonishment when he said he knew where I lived. He'd had a couple of terms at Holy Trinity School! When he left, his Nature Note Book left with him, it became his father's Bible!

It was a study on how crops should be grown. The Class was 3C, the boys gardened behind the Alms houses, there were seven vegetable plots, a nursery plot and several flower borders. Each plot contained two rods and was worked by two boys.

I suggested the present staff and pupils of Holy Trinity might like to see it. By return it arrived, together with his methods for dealing with harmful energies, a field as you know, I also worked in.

In passing, he mentioned by name his cousins at Whitemans Green, with whom he'd lived. Then I met Miss Tidy, who'd taught generations of children at Holy Trinity, including our sons. A most wonderful woman, living to a ripe old age and who had an amazing memory.

I told her the tale; she mentioned a Mrs. Ede, whom I knew, so I phoned her with the news and she was overjoyed. The daughter of the cousins he stayed with, lived in Haywards Heath. She phoned her, then the daughter phoned Charles. There had been no contact between those families since 1966.

The daughter then phoned me, she was so excited and said her father had been a wonderful gardener. When little, to firm the ground, he'd made her jump all over it, and then wearing his carpenters apron, the pocket filled with onions, she'd popped them into little holes. I'd never heard of stamping the ground before planting onions, so decided to do so.

So I put this story in Holy Trinity Parish Magazine, I felt it was so lovely, and hoped some on reading it might remember the handsome boy, whose nickname had been Tank.

The book started with a poem:-

> 'There's not a pair of legs so thin, there's not a head so thick,
>
> There's not a hand so weak and white, nor yet a Heart so sick,
>
> But it can find some needful job that's crying to be done,
>
> For the Garden glorifieth everyone.'

So endeth the tale of The Nature Study book, it was back in the author's hands, for sadly neither Holy Trinity School or Cuckfield Museum wished to keep it.

At 10.45 there was a presentation from the Earth Energies Group and then questions from the floor. Charles was on the panel for Earth Energies and Illness, presented by David Cowan. I was on the panel for The Physics of the Earth Energies Grid, presented by Jim Lyons with Panel members, Jim Lyons, Patrick MacManaway, John Carver! A very illustrious trio in the world of dowsing.

I concluded with the tale of how I'd acquired the beautiful huge Pendulum adorning me..

Pear Wood Pendulum

On a lovely afternoon, Sunday, 8 June, Sussex Dowsers held a meeting at Devils Dyke, the other side of the Sussex Downs opposite Brighton. Someone was using a new wooden B.S.D. Pendulum; I wondered if I required one, if so, it wasn't from the B.S.D.

I'd recently spoken to the Old Cuckfieldians about Colonel Bell. It was at the conclusion of the meeting that Miss Tidy dropped a little bombshell:

"I now know where your sons got their brains!"

I'd been flabbergasted, I'd always felt they'd got them from their Father. I was 'backward' at Henrietta Barnet Junior School, my Mother had been summoned and informed I wouldn't pass the exam for the senior school.

It was after that my education altered considerably, first one year at Sarum Hall, Swiss Cottage where I learned to love eating beetroot in white sauce, and was advised to read Arthur Ransome to improve my English! Next, Setterington, Belsize Park, but that closed after I think, a year, then Francis Holland School, Clarence Gate, with the motto:

'That Our Daughters should be as the

Polished Corners of the Temple'

A couple of years there and then to secretarial college, The Triangle, South Molton Street. I became a secretary. As so many mothers said:

"Typing will always come in useful!"

It has. So my university has been 'The University of Life'.

Now you know about my education, I will return to that evening in Cuckfield! Mr. and Mrs. Eric Ede asked if I could help them, so on Friday 21 June, Summer Solstice, Delia and I went to see them and we became friends.

A Master Wood Turner, due to the Nature Study Book, Eric had been in contact with Charles. Their conversation inspired him to make a Pendulum. As soon as I saw it, I knew I should have it. At the end of the afternoon he gave it to me and Delia ordered one!

Saturday night was Circle dancing night. I'd made a pretty skirt to wear with red gym shoes, but arrived just as the last steps were danced; I'd had a dowsing lesson from Charles. Later Allen Heiss said:

"You must do the thing which Michael Guest has!"

The Stones

He had five stones which one placed in any order. When my turn came I immediately made a cross! Allan said:

"I see it as a crucifix".

Michael had a sixth stone. No matter how I tried it would not fit happily in the pattern. The next morning I thought about it, used it for a healing within, and thanked him. I'd been shocked at the speed at which I'd placed those stones.

Back in 1988, cycling to an Armistice Day service, I'd come to realise that it didn't matter whether my pre-Cancer was healed or not, and later someone said that had been a very significant thought.

In the Cygnus Review, Issue 7, 2009. there was an article, 'CANCER IS NOT A DISEASE: IT'S A SURVIVAL MECHANISM,' based upon Andreas Moritz book of that title.

'Tumours of any kind are direct manifestation of fear... They heal spontaneously when your resistance disappears and you are able to replace this attitude with one of acceptance and, yes, love.

'When you consciously accept/embrace what or whom you resist in your life (whom or what you resist is merely a mirror image of yourself), you will not only lose the fear, but also the body's cells can return to their natural balanced growth mode. Balanced growth always results in homoeostasis or health'

So that decision had been very important. Entering Holy Trinity, I'd sat alone in the Lady Chapel, and perceived a cross being imprinted upon my back. I'd been very shocked. Over the years I'd tried to rid myself of it, I obviously hadn't.

Apart from the Scots many familiar faces were missing from that Congress, no Joy for one, but Sunday morning one had appeared.

'Jack-in-the Box' Jack Temple popped up. As I entered the dining hall he'd jumped up from his cronies, given me a huge hug! It was good to see him in such fine fettle. A truly amazing man to whom I shall always be indebted. He later said he'd never forgotten his 74th Birthday cake.

I'd retorted I'd never forgotten the stone I'd given him, a wonderful huge 8 oz piece of Labradorite in 1991! I'd only had it a month, it had cost a fiver and I'd bought it on a Crystal course with Stephanie Collins at Flint House, Lewes.

At the time he said he'd turn it into a remedy but instead he'd given it to his wife!

Sunday lunch – excellent Sole Bonne Femme - final farewells, then Charles and another and me, went off to Glasgow. He and I parked our bags in one locker at Queens Street Station which caused a problem on our return!

Granite

Before entering St. Mungo's Cathedral we sat by a really large red Granite tomb. Ten days before using a Crystal Pendulum, I'd dowsed a meridian flowing through my foot. It required Granite, I'd homed into a Granite something somewhere in Glasgow. I'd spun in the energy with the Pendulum. It was from that tomb, which turned out to be very significant by the time my journey was over.

In my healing room I'd left 'Proving of Granite, Marble & Limestone', (6) borrowed from Philip Edmonds, a local Homoeopath, who for a few years taught an informal group at Sue Ball's home in Warninglid. At the time I'd suddenly thought:

"I've got Uranium".

In the middle of the night I'd suddenly been awoken with a warning. I realised I'd mixed up Uranium and Granite. 11.55 P.M. the previous Tuesday, I'd had a drop of 1M and then the thought flooded in:

"I'm going to sleep for a long, long, time" which was repeated several times.

Approaching St. Mungo's Cathedral, Charles suddenly stopped and dowsed. It was the extent of the Cathedral's Aura or energy field. I asked permission to enter. I'd been told St. Mungo's was gloomy but we found it huge, impressive, beautiful, sunlight streaming through the modern stained glass windows.

We had a wonderful dowsing lesson. When he found negative energy, I hummed very quietly, through which it was healed and the Pendulum changed to another direction, a 'Yes' signal rather than a 'No'. Then a young man wanted to know what we were doing and he was went away enlightened!

When Charles and I returned to the station, I discovered I needed another locker. I'd kept protesting as we put our bags in that we needed two! He hadn't agreed, he should have listened! The locker could only be opened once! And that was the last time I saw lovely Charles Holderness. A few months later he suddenly died. A great loss to dowsing and all those he'd helped. He had another method of altering the flow of harmful energy through a home. He'd dowse where it entered, then put a cross over the energy line, and redirect it around the road! (And my legs tingled as I typed that.)

Journey to Oban

Before leaving Glasgow, I'd wanted to know where I would lay my head on returning from Iona. Whilst searching for Tourist Info in George Square – dominated by a statue of Sir Walter Scott – surrounded by bright flower beds – I saw the Copthorne Hotel.

I entered, very sumptuous, Crystal chandeliers, a palace? Room, £110, breakfast extra! Something wanted ME to stay there!

"Treat yourself to some luxury!"

I beat a hasty exit, I even had a note on my file that I shouldn't stay there but the place did appear to be fit for a Queen. I put it down to a past life as Queen of Glasgow! I had such a welcome when landing at Glasgow Airport in 2004. I was first off the plane – as Queen's do!

I followed the directions for Tourist Info, which petered out before I got there. I walked on, found myself standing outside an impressive edifice, accosted an elderly couple. Did they know where Tourist Info was?

"It's probably closed by now" they'd answered.

My Heart sank, could they recommend somewhere.

"Try Browns Hotel".

They both had brown eyes. Something rose to my consciousness 'don't trust a man with brown eyes'. They insisted on guiding me to Tourist Info, they were so kind, but this had come to mind. I was in a dilemma. It was still open.

A charming girl manned the desk and I requested a B & B hotel with an evening meal. She tapped into her info screen. No luck. By now I was dowsing.

"What about the Rennie Mackintosh, it's a new hotel near the exhibition". Pendulum definitely felt that was good and that was where I went, feeling guilty about Browns, but thinking a new hotel might have better beds!

Happily I went to the Station, collected bags and boarded the Oban train. Where to sit? I *knew* the intended one as soon as I saw it, a two seater, no table, squashed between seats with tables, really dingy, and the window frame blocked the view!

I went further down the carriage, bustling with young foreign tourists. No, I had to have that seat and the man behind looked nice! Finally settled, I enjoyed looking down into the lochs and the mountains on either side. I noticed he kept popping up as well. I wondered if he'd been in the war. Finally I decided if I was meant to start a conversation I would!

I knew I needed a protector! Suddenly I'd said:

"You missed a good one there."

Then we slowly started chatting. Me leaning over the seat – I was squatting or kneeling in any case, it was too uncomfortable for my back to sit on, too low for the views.

Suddenly there was an announcement – the train was not going any further! We were to be bussed to Oban – the train divided at that point, half going to Fort William. There wasn't a second crew. In spite of us being the greater number, the distance to Fort William was greater.

It was like the war – on the platform the many nationalities chatting together. I was asked:

"Do you know what is going on". My reply had been:

"No but it's a nice evening, it's not raining, it's not too cold, we have much to be thankful for".

Two coaches eventually arrived and someone declaimed:

"Women and children first".

We all clambered aboard, it was a tight squash. The nice man and I sat together and we chatted all the way! His wife had tried dowsing!

I just survived – one point I thought I'd be sick – travel sick – I'd had a cup of soup on the train. We were only one hour late, 10.15. I grabbed a taxi to The Kelvin, which was right behind the station.

Entering the hotel I was followed by a young man I'd seen walking.

"Were you on the train?"

"Yes, I'm going on the Ocean Sailing Ship" or some such name.

I burst out laughing.

"I've just been chatting to the father of the girl who is running that ship".

We burst into peels of laughter. Believe it or not his name was Williams! Once more there was a protector for me!

I'd booked a room with private facilities and paying the bill before staying was new to me. It wasn't included. I said nothing, the difference would pay for the taxi. We then ascended a spiral staircase to the top of the building. A little room with a dormer window and NO facilities!

I dowsed if I was in the right room, Yes. No.14. For six months I'd lived in such a room before going to Australia in 1956. I was quite at home. I mentally gave it a good clean. The only eccentric thing was a cupboard door which didn't shut. That seemed par for the course after the bathroom door and the inner door of my room refusing to shut at the Kelvin Halls! Was it to do with those others refusing to open at Lincoln in '95!

The Healing

Gingerly I lay down and lay awake listening. Something was banging outside. At four A.M. it was time to get to grips with the anguish of not remembering my Father. Sunday morning, before breakfast at the Kelvin Halls, I'd climbed seven steps to snap the Copper pyramidal roof above the dining room.

Over breakfast, my new friend Pat had asked why I was going to Iona.

"It is to do with my Father."

I'd found myself wanting to cry. She'd held my hand, sensed that deep within me was a great pain, I called it anguish. I'd thought I'd dealt with it, obviously hadn't. Was that 'happening' due to that Copper Pyramid? Ever since I'd arrived I'd wanted to walk that particular path. It didn't go anywhere!

Room 14 at four A.M. I faced up to it all, sobbed my Heart out, sobbed again when Daddy said.

"It was your Mother's fault".

After his death from T.B. in 1943 she had never talked about him. I forgave them both, thanked them for allowing me to incarnate through them. Then I'd seen my dear friend, Ann Chapman, holding me in her loving arms and comforting me.

Thursday evening, I'd phoned Ann. Excitement suddenly gripped me, I'd wanted to share with her my excitement – she had understood. We have been friends from the early days of the Pre-School Playgroup meetings in Haywards Heath and at one time she'd helped me with running the M.Y. Club (Mothers and Young) at The Yews, Haywards Heath. The name M.Y. was my brainwave, I wanted not a Mother and Toddler Group, for that is exclusive and I knew from my personal experience when living in Havant, one can be extremely lonely when first becoming a Mum. For me the problem had been solved by the very good weekly group run by St Faiths.

The first group was with the help of the Cuckfield Playgroup in the Church Hall. I then had another brainwave, had an article in the Mid Sussex Times and we'd been overwhelmed by Mum's from Haywards Heath. Another club was obviously needed. One Mum knew about The Yews being available, said she'd run it, then couldn't, so I left the Cuckfield club and started the group at The Yews.

Before I could, I had to justify to Haywards Heath Social Services the reason for such a club, for The Yews in Boltro Rd 'belonged' to them. My justification, the Mental Health of Mothers. One young Mum Valerie Woods had been brought by a Social Worker, she was suffering from loneliness. She had a young baby Claire, husband out from early morning till late at night and the only person she had contact with was the milkman. The Club helped solve her problems. I ran it for over 13 years. On one occasion we had 56 mothers, some from afar as Forest Row, such was the need, but thirteen years on, clubs had sprouted everywhere. I left due to a spell of ill health but the club continued, but was then known as a Mother & Toddler!

Healing over, I'd slept. Trauma healed, I was free to go to the sacred Isle of Iona, a place of pilgrimage. At 7.20 the words came:

I AM WHAT I AM

THE WILLOW TREE

At long last the title for my book had been resolved, well I thought so in 1996! During the healing I'd thought of three willows. One in a park in Kent, the upright variety, one by the river at Stamford, weeping. That had sheltered me for a necessary pee! Then Frogmore, Windsor, a Sally Willow with 14 trunks!

Whilst the healing proceeded I'd seen a little frog-like creature. In thanksgiving I joined them in a triangle of love. In Celtic, I was in their land.

the Frog is the Lord of the Earth, the power of healing waters. (7) I was always buying cards depicting frogs, and for grandsons even a pair of three legged stools depicting frogs, one went in my case to New Zealand! I didn't after that.

Oban

I had a good breakfast, then exited The Kelvin. On the wall outside there was a Round Table plaque. That was very reassuring, my husband had been a Round Tabler. It couldn't be that eccentric if R.T. met there. I had been a member of Ladies Circle, the feminine counterpart, and that year was Chairman of Tangent, the ex Circlers club whose motto is 'Let Friendship Continue'.

I walked down the road, there was much building going on. I felt drawn to Tourist Info. I homed into a card depicting the Black Watch Tartan, and thought I'd better have a guide book. A book with the face of St. Columba caught my eye. If I was going to his island, I thought I'd better learn about him. I didn't like the piercing blue eyes. (8)

Then I headed for a large display of cards, but they were definitely a no no, but by the till, half hidden, were charity cards at only 20p. I bought six! That done, I waited patiently to cross a very busy road, then phoned my husband.

Dominating the skyline above the town is a huge circular folly which I wanted to see, I thought it would be peaceful up there, so I chose the shortest route, that was my folly, there were many steps!

The folly was full of arches. Monday morning was grass cutting morning with three smelly machines! Certainly a folly to have climbed it, there was no peace.

I descended, felt fruit was required but there was no greengrocer. The Supermarket was the answer it had a supply of delicious bagged English Victoria Plums, sporting a Union Jack! Then it was time for the ferry, so I returned to The Kelvin, collected my bags, another taxi, longer route – 20 p more!

Ferry Crossings

Mid-day, the large ferry departed for Mull. Stowing my bags, I'd said aloud: "Top Deck"!

It was echoed by a young man. The view – breath taking – real holiday brochure stuff – blue sky – blue water – blue green mountains – perfection.

The crossing completed, picking up my bags I tripped against a foot and looked up into face of he who'd echoed "top deck". I laughed.

"It's you again."

He laughed and then sat behind me on the coach for the winding thirty miles across the island to Fionnphort.

The chap in front of me, I'd sat behind on the Oban train! A very introverted character only wanting to read. I insisted on telling both of them they must be careful walking on Iona because of the peat bogs! Then I left them to their thoughts and me to mine, but I knew again they were my guardians.

I hadn't read 'Adonais (1) before leaving, I felt I couldn't. In 1818 there'd been no road, a rough journey, bad weather, awful food, Keats had gone down with a cold, forerunner of his T.B.

I thought about him, I felt I should remove from the road any T.B. which he might have left, for I reckoned he'd already got it and I also included anyone else's T.B. Nearing our destination, my Pendulum began swinging and did for several minutes as I mentally cleansed with orange light.

Then we'd arrived at Fionnphort and I'd purchased yet another ticket for the small ferry crossing of just half a mile.

Iona

I'd finally arrived on the magical isle thirty six miles from the Scottish mainland which Keats described in a letter to his brother Tom – 23, 26 July 1818.

'But I will first mention Icolmkill – I know not whether you have heard much about this Island, I never did before I came nigh it, It is rich in the most interesting Antiqu(I)ties. Who would expect to find the ruins of a fine Cathedral Church, of Cloister, Colleges, Mona(s)taries and Nunneries in so remote an Island? The Beginning of these things was in the sixth Century under the superstition of a would-be Bishop-saint who landed from Ireland and chose the spot from its Beauty- for at that time the now treeless place was covered with magnificent Woods. Columba in the Gaelic is Colm signifying Dove – Kill signifies Church and I is as good as Island- so I-colm-kill means the Island of Saint Columba's Church -Now this Saint Columba became the Dominic of the barbarian Christians of the north and was famed also far south – but more especially was reverenced by the Scots the Picts the Norwegians the Irish. In a course of years perhaps the Island was considered the most holy ground of the north, and the old kings of the aforementioned nations chose it for their burial place-'

The isle chosen by Columba on which to found a monastery. Iona became the centre for the Celtic Church which spread all the way to Northumbria.

Well I wasn't aware of all that either when I landed! A car appeared for the baggage but I was told to walk!

"Go through the ruins of the Nunnery".

Entering I felt I'd been there before!

Registration completed, I was led to my room, Room 14!

There was a wonderful view to Mull across deep blue water. Tea at four o'clock. Oh dear, I was gasping for a cuppa – no kettle so I asked if the bathroom water was drinkable. I looked for a key to lock the door. Couldn't find it, surely I hadn't lost it already. No, on that wonderful island everybody was taken on trust, no keys handed out – though they were available. I was given a glass of water, took it to the garden, lay down on a seat. Peace.

Rest over, I set off to explore the Abbey (St. Mary's Cathedral) according to hotel brochure. Returning for tea I'd been rebuffed! I'd thought another visitor was alone. She wasn't. However another lady was only too happy to chat, but first she had to finish counting tiny cowrie shells. She'd collected thirty three, I told her the significance – master number, associated with Jesus. Her name – Iona!

She recounted her morning adventure to Fingal's Cave. On reading it was opposite Iona I'd wondered if I could get there. Then I'd seen a superb photo whilst at Congress and thought:

"Well at least I now know what it looks like".

I knew the rocks were Basalt, I knew they stuck out and at Congress, I'd learnt there was an energy line going there.

Iona described the ascent holding on to a black pipe on a narrow ledge. I began to think. "Please Lord, spare me that one".

She added her husband would have been shocked to see her doing it; she had very bad eyesight, plus a bad back! A very courageous lady.

Keats wrote this to Tom in July 1818:-

'The finest thing is Fingal's Cave – it is entirely a hollowing out of Basalt Pillars.

Suppose now the Giants who rebelled against Jove had taken a whole Mass of black Columns and bound them together like bunches of matches – then with immense Axes had made a cavern in the body of these columns – of course the roof and floor must be composed of the broken ends of the Columns – such is Fingal's Cave except that the Sea has done the work of excavations and is continually dashing there – so that we walk along the sides of the cave on the pillars which are left as if for convenient Stairs – the roof is arched somewhat Gothic wise and the length of some of the entire side pillars if 50 feet. The length of the Cave is 120 feet and from its extremity the view into the sea through the large Arch at the entrance is very grand – the colour of the columns is a sort of black with a lurking gloom of purple ther(e)in – For solemnity and grandeur it far surpasses the finest Cathedral – at the extremity of the Cave there is a small perforation into another cave, at which the waters meeting and buffeting each other there is sometimes produced a report as of a cannon heard as far as Iona which must be 12 Miles – As we approached in the boat there was such a fine swell of the sea that the pillars appeared rising imm(ed)iately out of the Crystal – But it is impossible to describe it'

(9) John Keats Selected Letters

ON VISITING STAFFA
Not Aladdin magian
Ever such a work began;
Not the wizard of the Dee
Ever such a dream could see;
The spirit's hand, to wake ~~him up~~
Up he started in a trice.
'I am Lycidas' said he,
'Fam'd in funeral minstrelsy!'
This was architected thus
By the great Oceanus! –
Here his mighty water play
Hollow organs all the day;
Here by turns his dolphins all,
Finny palmers great and small,
Come to pay devotion due –
Each a mouth of pea(r)ls must strew,
~~Many a mortal comes to see~~

~~This Cathedral of the S~~

    Many a mortal of these days,
    Dares to pass our sacred ways,
    Dares to touch audaciously
    This Cathedral of the Sea!
    I have been the pontiff-priest
    Where the water never rest,
    Where a fledgy sea-bird choir
    Soars for ever; holy fire
    I have hid from mortal man;
    Proteus is my Sacristan.
    But the stupid eye of mortal
    Hath pass'd beyond the rocky portal;
    So for ever will I leave
    Such a taint, and soon unweave
    All the magic of the place.'
    'T is now free to stupid face,
    To cutters, and to Fashion boats,
    To cravats and to petticoats:-
    The great sea shall war it down
    For its fame shall not be flown
    At each farthing Quadrille dance.
    So saying, with a Spirit's glance
    He dived!

I'm sorry I am so indolent as to write such stuff as as this – it can't be helped'(9)

                p.133 John Keats Selected Letters, .

The above 'is almost an apocalypse, in which he conjured up the spirit of Lycidas whose body, Milton had supposed, might have been hurled 'beyong the stormy Hebrides.' The memory of Fingal's Cave went in its epic grandeur into 'Hyperion''. (p.245 1)

The Island guide recommended:

"Stick with the music, Fingal's Cave by Mendelssohn, it's much easier!" I love it. What a relief, and I never gave the trip another thought!

I'd seen the notice for the evening service for victims of violence and I felt one should also pray for the perpetrators. We agreed to go. Fortified, wearing Kit Mouat's thick Arran sweater, a very Scots lady indeed, my Pendulum took me for a walk.

Finding the Colour Ray

Carrying the map from the Gatekeeper Trust (2) I'd tried to distinguish landmarks but one clump of stones to my untrained eyes looked very much like another! I'd decided I needed a guide, one who knew the island and it's roads. Finally I climbed to a high point overlooking a valley. In the distance, the map informed that the shining sea and white sands, was the 'Atlantean Heart ' of Iona, the ' Bay at the back of the Ocean'.

In spite of the setting sun, for some don't recommend dowsing then, and also very windy, I dowsed what I was standing on. Was it a Ley Line or an energy line? 'No'. I'd felt I hadn't been brought to that vantage point for nothing, so I'd put the question:

'Would I know what it is that I'm searching for?' 'Yes'.

Finally I got it, I wasn't standing over anything! It was above my head, some twelve feet, the colour Indigo. I was dressed in the nearest thing to it. Dark navy blue Dash, the Arran topped with a woollen jacket, head wrapped up in an indigo/blue striped thick scarf, with a hole in the seam for the head; I'd looked every inch a nun! Imagine Mother Teresa – you won't be far off the mark!

I'd dowsed. The colour was flowing to the Abbey from the west. Then I knew my task on Iona. Find the other rays and if they flowed to or from the Abbey.

When I'd returned, dinner was being served. Tartan slippers on, I'd hurried in and enjoyed pork and apple in cider. Dinner over, in a corner I found a comfortable sofa .and heard someone talking about Agates. My cue, I called out something, they promptly came and joined me. Joy at the '95 York Congress had given me a little bag of mixed crystals, which I'd left on a bed, they had now done their stuff. I mentioned I dowsed. We were off.

They were also going to the service. We set off together. I sat down under the tower where the light was good. To my amazement Catherine rushed up.

"Sally, thank God I saw you, I can't take you to St. Columba's bay, my Asthma is too bad but come to coffee tomorrow morning".

"Thank you, I will".

That left the way clear for my true guide, who walked with a wonderful stick like a Bishops crook. I called her Betty Shepherdess, I loved her terminology, she was so full of knowledge and wisdom, who perceived what I was, what I needed.

After the Service hot drinks and talk . They'd asked me to dowse their problems, Iona joined us and it was late when we went to bed. I'd realigned the bed to see out the window, removed the electric blanket, slept fitfully, gazed across the darkened Sound. It was about 6.45 A.M. when finally God decided certain knowledge should be released through a dream.

I was having an argument.

"I want to see the Mother Superior".

"Go and see the Abbess".

"She is useless, I've been to her, she is useless, she MUST GO".

Then I'd slipped into another incarnation, for the next thing I knew was that I had had an abortion! I'd been raped! I'd aborted myself and caused dreadful damage!

Who did it?

"**MYSELF.** Myself, I couldn't possibly rape myself. "**MYSELF**".

After about the fourth **MYSELF** the penny dropped, **St. Columba**! No wonder I'd been compelled to buy the book, hadn't liked the eyes. I'd dealt with that, forgave him, healed my damaged self, then filled the bath with Ionian amber water. The sun was just glinting through the clouds, which before had obliterated the sky every time I'd looked.

I'd started singing gently and learnt:

"You are now whole".

I'd thought at the time it meant I'd finished with incarnation – I hadn't. I think it was St Etheldreda of Ely who was 'now whole'. I'd thanked my Lord and Master, pondered a second as to whether it was God Almighty. Asked:

"Are you my Lord and Master?"

A deep voice answered

"I AM" and then the word NOT tried to creep in. I'd decided if he was not, fingers would make an X **THEY DID NOT.** Then I'd realised the connection to Etheldreda. She'd refused to consummate her marriage to the Prince of the Fenland and later to the son of the King of York. That rape was the underlying cause. Finis! It was 10 September 1996 (10+9+1996 =44,) Master Number, the vibration of Golden Atlantis (3)

Next day I'd dowsed. I was the Abbess, I'd had to discover what had happened to her. She went to France. An Abbess again and was murdered. I'd sensed and felt terrible pain in an ankle and other parts of my body that evening. And what does 'Oh dear me, Oh dear me,' mean?

O Dio mio. I'd dowsed whether it was (Oh My God), no it wasn't, it was the euphemism for the English *'Oh damn me!'* (p.325 10) I would be damned, I'd lost my virginity!

Three years later in Horsham, a bit more of the jigsaw slotted in. I was with a small group of healers waiting for Barbara Stone, with her powerful Crystal Skull, she was late we were getting worried. We decided to send out energy, and I'd suddenly started saying "Oh dear, Oh dear, Oh Dearie Me".

I'd turned to leave the room, my friend Margaret Bull, a wonderful healer, said:

"Don't go, give us a song, Sall, you sing so beautifully".

Immediately I'd turned around, arms moving, singing, and occasionally an undertone of a lilting Irish melody. At the end, someone I'd never met, said:

"Do you want to know what I saw?"

"Yes".

"Ireland, a woman, probably a past life". I'd interrupted.

"I know, I know who."

I'd dowsed, a woman who'd been raped. I hadn't loved him but I'd loved him afterwards! Then she'd said.

"You were at the front, a lot of nuns behind you!"

"Oh my God, He'd raped a Nun." (Legs tingled in 2007 and 2009)

"What are you talking about?" said Margaret.

"St. Columba, he raped me in Ireland".

"Did he go to America?"

"No, he went to Iona, don't you remember the celebrations a couple of years ago?"

"No", none of them did.

I'd begun to wonder whether I'd lost my wits as well.

"I'm sure he's Columba, Columbus went to America."

"Well you'd better heal that time", said Margaret.

"I did on Iona".

Like everything, if one has experienced something or been somewhere, it tends to stay in the memory, if it means nothing to you, it goes again.

Back to Tuesday morning on Iona. Departing the bathroom I'd suddenly remembered a dream – me naked - people looking through the window! I'd hastily backed back, looked out carefully, extended an arm for a dressing gown – anyone walking past the window could have seen me!

Then I'd dressed carefully, putting other clothes into a royal blue knapsack.

Shorts, swimming costume, towel, waterproof square, cut from an old shower curtain, Omar Khayyám, plums, banana, later an orange from the breakfast basket. That was lunch. No waterproof – it wasn't going to rain!

We set off for the 9 A.M. service at the Abbey, Catherine wasn't there, so I couldn't ask if I could take Betty Shepherdess to coffee. We would meet at 10 A.M. which just gave me time to write six cards on a very nice desk in the room and stamp them. We set off, posted cards, found Catherine. There was much to learn. Whilst it was going on, energies flowed out of me to her. That completed, we were off.

Walking along, Betty Shepherdess identified the Heart and Throat Chakras of Iona, Angel and Signal Hills (2). She mentioned the artist John Duncan. He'd painted a famous picture, The White Horse, associated with Columba. Philistine that I was I hadn't heard of either. Suddenly we'd gone far enough together, she wished to return to her friend.

I was free! I could go to St. Columba's Bay, Root Chakra, alone. I'd known I needed to be. When I'd asked Catherine to be my guide, that had worried me.

Striding along I'd kept hearing in my head 'the mountains of Mourne', and kept adding 'where they go down to the sea'. I didn't know they were associated with Columba. I think that's where he raped me! Columba, highly born, related to Kings of Tara.(8) Was this an aspect within him which came to the fore on that occasion!

I'd kept to my instructions, go left; to my left a large burn, Loch Staonaig, for I'd spied what could be, possibly, a shorter, new path. I'd crossed a plateau, the Sacral Chakra, and then there was the bay!

Suddenly energies entered my fingers. I was at the outer edge of the Root Chakra, just as I'd experienced with Charles Holderness. Now I knew what that meant.

Reaching the sheltered rocks above the bay, it was hot, so clothes were discarded. Off came the Arran which then I tied round my bottom. Off came jacket, that went on top of my knapsack. It was a cloak! I was down to best striped Country Casuals T Shirt. Dressed thus, I descended to the valley and thence the beach. A lovely walk with beautiful huge brown grazing cattle, 'Daisy' beside the path.

Reaching the shingle a man appeared, he was leaving. I was having the bay to myself! I'd wanted Iona Marble – Betty Shepherdess said it had virtually all gone. I knew I could collect four stones and found a tiny green one and three Serpentine, typical of Iona – greeny striped with blue. They were Daddy, Mummy and Me! No Marble. I'd gone around some rocks, there was a rock pool, guarded by a huge one. Alone, I wasn't braving the sea, a rock pool was for me.

The Rock pool

Sun shining, stripped naked, holding gingerly to the huge rock, I took three steps into the pool and slid into icy water! I slowly adjusted, and felt an archetypal force rising, Amphitrite, Goddess of the Sea. Wife of Poseidon or Neptune, who'd rode on his Dolphin to woo her. Amphitrite means 'rubbing or wearing away on all sides (the shore) *(Gr.amphi-trio* for *tribo* (10). and Neptune then helps by breaking up the rocks with his trident! !

Lying there, legs kicking, I dressed myself in wonderful seaweeds. Lime, wine, brown, cream, playing as a little child – two and a half – and for a second I'd totally submerged, fully outstretched, looking at the sky, feeling I could stay for ever. Totally wonderful.

No I couldn't, sooner or later the tide would come in, sooner or later, others would arrive. Soon one did but not before I was clad; I heard his cough!

The cold immersion did wonders for my back. I gingerly placed a foot on the shingle and then onto my towel and donned bikini bottom but with my top dressed normally. Then I'd lunched and opened Omar Khayyám. I'd had just half an hour, one thirty I had to leave.

Omar Khayyám,

This was my Daddy's favourite book. I'd left his copy sitting on 'his' chair in the large bedroom. I'd told Ann. Suddenly I read verse 37:

'How Time is slipping underneath our Feet...'

So who's Omar?

'One of the most remarkable, as well as the most distinguished, of the poets of Persia, at the latter end of the twelfth century. He was altogether unprecedented in regard to the freedom of his religious opinions – or, rather, his boldness in denouncing hypocrisy and intolerance, and the enlightened views he took of the fanaticism and mistaken devotion of his countrymen.' (11)

He was also a mathematician and astronomer born in Naishpur on 18th May 1048. His 'Rubáíyát' or quatrains were adapted and translated by Edward FitzGerald in 1859 (12)

I looked at my watch – 1.30! Trousers, socks, trainers, everything on, I was off. St. Columba's Bay is reputed to be where he landed with twelve companions. No wonder I'd wanted to be alone. I returned up the valley – 'Daisy' still sitting by the path, I offered my hand, she stood up, I don't think she liked the smell of orange!

I said my farewells, at the point where I'd shed clothing, picked a tiny piece of heather, and climbed to the top where there was a small cairn. I'd added my little green stone to the top, it looked perfect, it hadn't felt right with the other three.

I returned via the other side of the burn, the path marked on the map; it was much quicker but I'd circumnavigated it, which felt important.

At the end of the path was a delightful sight. a pair of mating dragonflies! I watched for a long time, they even flew together which seemed symbolic of something!

I didn't return the way we'd come but descended a muddy track, making a detour to white sands pounded by Atlantic rollers. Approaching a white sand dune, I picked up a large oval stone. Surely I wasn't carrying that home! Next it was time for shorts and trainers tied onto knapsack. I played ball with the stone, caught it seven time, then hurled it away. It was as though I was unlocking a door.

Wonderful sand, I paddled along looking for stones, followed tracks of a dog, he'd known the way. (I'd left a book out for several weeks with a picture looking like footsteps in the sand. A Biology book (13), the picture represented 'Organization in Cells and Organisms'. The next course at the Abbey was 'Footsteps in the Sand'. It felt relevant. I spotted an oyster catcher, dowsed the rest were Dunlin. Then climbing from that wonder spot, I walked barefoot over the close cropped grass, the machair, to nearly where we'd entered.

Going along the road, I felt there was somebody behind me, I looked back, there was! Suddenly he was alongside – the nice chap from the ferry! I'd felt sooner or later on my walk we'd meet again. He came from Bath – that was important! The next day bussing across Mull, I'd tried to think of a rhyme – didn't succeed. 'There was a young man from Bath......?

We'd both had similar thoughts about day trippers. So easy to become superior! Then I'd thought.

"But I'm only a three day tripper!" – he'd thought the same. We'd parted. I decided to check out the last ferry, for after placing my stone on the cairn I'd been accosted by a young couple wanting to know.

Wednesday night I had nowhere to sleep for there was a National Rail Strike. My plans had been to return to Glasgow. Thursday night was fixed, Wednesday was free for wherever the Lord wished me to be! But there was no room on Iona.

Continuing my travail, I arrived at the Bishops House and discovered there was a Communion service at 6 P.M. in the Chapel of St. Columba. Just the job. I did so want to do that on Iona.

The Colours

I continued walking and seeing the Abbey from t'other side, remembered my **work**. I dowsed where colours entered. Yellow, blue, green, high above the chancel on the north wall. High above the altar, Amethyst. I walked on, up, and round to the front, passed the little chapel I'd entered on arrival.

I went to the obelisk, erected by the American Government in gratitude for the people of Iona rescuing and burying some sailors at the end of the last century. From there I could see the Abbey windows on the south side. I dowsed the remaining colours, Red, Indigo, Orange. With the exception of Amethyst, all were passing through the obelisk.

I walked on, came to the grave of John Smith, former leader of the Labour Party, who'd tragically died in 1995 at St. Bartholomew's Hospital. He'd wanted to save it, for it had been under the threat of closure.

I didn't know he was buried there, until telling people where I was going and then been asked:

"Are you going to see John Smith's grave?"

It hadn't been part of my itinerary. Suddenly I was face to face with it. An awful pain went into my belly! I could only assume he was the wrong way round, or if he wasn't, his gravestone was! All the stones, without exception had their names facing the Sound of Iona.

They were extremely difficult to read, for the small rectangular blocks were almost up to the boundary wall. There was his, not a small rectangle, but a huge grey oval with a carved pattern around, facing inwards. Presumably, so all who wished to pay their last respects could, without squeezing their bottoms on the wall!

I felt something was very wrong – dead flowers left by an admirer didn't help – so I mentally turned the memorial the other way.

Then I entered the Abbey, sitting where we had that morning. I tried to discover where the colours went. I looked at the Marble altar, carved with two plain panels. In front of these, on the second wide step, I sensed colours spiralling into the earth to a central point. The Amethyst ray divided, going into both. The colours exited out of the opposite hole and opposite windows. Amethyst went up high, out through the west window to Fingal's Cave.

That afternoon time moved very slowly but at last it was tea time! My friends were already there; I recounted my adventure, then Iona appeared and I said:

" I'm going to Church at 6 o'clock."

"Oh, that changes my plans, I'm coming to!" she'd replied and departed.

Betty S. said:

"I'm coming!"

Five minutes to go, Iona hadn't appeared. A poet had been carried away!

> 'You, O Lord are my Strength & Stay
> pay no attention to my crying,
> Your Golden thread is woven well
> Within the fabric and this dying.
>
> The other darker thread, the one
> cries out to you upon the Cross
> Your Golden thread is hard to see
> in this blank agony of loss.
>
> O present Help, come enter in
> and should I lose still further sight
> shine in and on this tread bare soul
> and flood the inner world with Light.
>
> Iona Bevan

A threesome again, we arrived with only a few seconds to spare and sat down in the front row of the tiny chapel. The Priest appeared in beautiful greeny blue robes, shimmering at times like the sea. He didn't appear to know the service but nevertheless took it beautifully. I felt spirituality, I hadn't in the Abbey, I left uplifted.

Such a wonderful day, I suggested the others might like to join me in a bottle of wine.

"I've got a bottle, share mine" Iona had said.

"Thank you". Then I'd thought.

"Why don't we all sit together for my last night."

I'd got my act together, I was leaving on the two thirty ferry to connect with the last bus across Mull, laying my head at The Kelvin once again.

I changed into the Black Watch trews and kept my guests waiting, then we all set off for the Healing Service, my third service that day! Betty S. laughed, she'd been to the Parish Church as well! I wondered if she was beating the bounds with her Bishops Crook.

The Healing Service

This was a simple and beautiful service under the tower. In the centre stood a wooden cross surrounded by night lights, two women, and a circle of kneelers. At the appropriate time those who felt in need of healing knelt there. Others waited around forming a large circle, hands upon each others shoulders. Each time the two women in the centre placed their hands on those kneeling, they said:

" Lord draw near" and then the outer circle said:

"Lord draw near, draw near, draw near and stay", which took a long time.

Service completed, I was motivated to touch the altar, for most of the time it was roped off, out of bounds. I seem to remember I've been motivated to do this before, the Lady Chapel in York Minster for one!

'The Bishop'

Back at the hotel there was a note on Reception bearing a name Iona knew. Sitting at the other end of the sitting room a gentleman played Patience. Iona thought the note was for him and that he was a Bishop, for she'd talked with him and his wife the previous evening.

"Do you think it's him?" she'd asked.

"Well why don't you go up and tell him", was my bright idea. She'd giggled.

"Do you think I can?" - and promptly did.

Then in the lovely lounge of the Columba, I channelled healing to the one we'd left behind and sensed she was someone very special.

Bedtime I placed a blanket under the sheet, having discovered the spare! That helped a bit with the back. Then I knew I must read 'Columba' (p.25. 8). The Milk cart's old White Horse, had foreknowledge of his death. Was that a message for me?

When I am driving in different localities, if I am being a conduit of healing, horses then appear, there are always two, one always brown.

Opposite was a poem I felt shed light on a certain matter! The Author's interpretation was that Columba was 'trying to renounce his desires and temptations!'

> I adore not the voice of birds,
> Nor the *sreod*, nor a destiny on the earthly world,
> Nor son, nor chance, nor woman;
> My drui is Christ the son of God. (8).

Skeins of Colour

Wednesday dawned, wet, misty. I needed grounding, so in my bath I added drops of Bergamot (14) and I thought about those colours, where they'd came from, where they went. Fingal's Cave was the destination for Amethyst.

Then I learnt the skeins emanated from the Tomb of the Holy Sepulchre, Jerusalem where I'd been in 1959. Granny Rose's ring had been this very year on Jude's little finger. I thought.

"If major rays are going through holy places, what is the colour going through the Kremlin Church?"

Remember my pink carnation went there after the York International Congress. (15). The answer:

"Purple".

I tried visualizing how they flowed; it wasn't easy. I needed a globe but eventually I worked out they flew out at Jerusalem, back in at Fingal's Cave.

Then through the earth back to Jerusalem, then out again to Wakaito, New Zealand, thus making a figure of eight, the laminiscate. On my return I told Christina my discovery, she wasn't surprised, she'd stood inside Fingal's Cave, sensed energies flowing there and hadn't wanted to leave!

That had taken some thought, I was nearly late for breakfast. No service that morning. I joined my friends and Betty S. on learning why I was late, remarked:

"You are always working very hard!"

She'd agreed to take me in the rain to the other end of the island. I told her friend what I'd seen during her healing, I'd remembered it in the bath! Wasn't I busy in that bath! I then asked if she would paint the colours I'd dowsed entering the Abbey. She'd agreed.

I then packed and said goodbye to Room 14.

Walk to the Crown Chakra

First port of call was The Pottery with Betty S. enquiring if John Duncan's picture of Columba's White Horse had arrived. It hadn't but I knew he was with me! He was an old horse who had, so the story goes, foretold the death of Columba, he'd pulled the milk cart, nothing glamorous, and Columba said his sad farewell to him. I'd known Black Beauty had taken me to Glasgow now I had a White Horse. (legs tingled at that as I typed in 2006!)

Then Betty S. showed me a large print of John Duncan's wonderful picture of St. Bride. Dressed in white, flowing long hair, being carried away over the sea by two angels. I'd been astonished, even more when she'd given me a postcard, which I later framed. I'd been very moved. My card is now faded and blue but in 2010 I caught up with the actual painting in the National Gallery of Scotland in Edinburgh. The power was indescribable.

I'd told Betty about my visit in 1994 to St. Bride's, Fleet Street, the Church of the Journalists. I went because it's crowning glory, the steeple, a four tier octagonal, 'is the original bride cake'! (16) I'd dowsed I should be there on the dot of 11 o'clock and I was and then I'd been shocked.

At the entrance I'd read the steeple was the inspiration **behind** the tiered wedding cake, not the other way, as I'd always imagined. A baker of fine cakes had lived and worked nearby, he it was who created the first tiered wedding cake from the vista he espied each day.

Benjamin Franklin knew that Church, did he take the design with him back to the U.S.A.? American 'Bride Cakes' are just as that steeple, not separated by pillars. (17)

Story over, we walked and talked of music, the Pentatonic scale, wondering if it was a five note scale based on a harp? None of my musical friends had ever heard of it!

Seeing rubbish tipped into a hole just north of the Crown Chakra, Dun I, distressed us. We walked on, then I looked back, aligned myself to the hill and sang a verse from that wonderful Hymn, which I always seemed to be singing.

'Sun and Moon bow down before him' (18)

This resulted in me learning I'd now be working on the Celestial level, whatever that was! Celestial had come through before leaving home; I'd thought of Celeste, Babar the Elephant's wife!

Retracing our steps, I'd suddenly known I had to leave Betty S, leave the path, walk on long wet grass. I was heading for The McLeod Centre, accommodation for those on courses or working at the Abbey. I walked up, then realised from the vantage point I could see where the Amethyst ray exited the Abbey. I walked down again. I was cold, hungry, wanting somewhere warm and found myself heading into the Abbey cloisters and thence the shop. Lovely music, warm, the vibes were good.

The Shop

I'd thought I wasn't buying anything on Iona but suddenly *knew* I was. I'd carefully looked, chose a couple of cards, then I realised I might need a basket! Then I'd come face to face with a Silver cross – St. Columba's pillow.

"Not another cross, £28 plus, oh no, haven't I got enough?" I mentally pleaded.

Thankfully, I remembered when faced with the same thing in 1987 in Canterbury Cathedral, I hadn't bought the Silver cross, but a cheaper pewter one, and with that in mind I'd seen at the end of the display, a shiny pewter cross. I searched further, beautiful Celtic Art letters caught my eye, I could have one for each grandchild. Beside them was a chair! I sat down, pulled out a plum, then a banana. An assistant came by and I made my requests:

" Please, do you have the missing letters?"

" No, it's the end of season."

So that was end of that plan.

"Could I have Columba's pillow in Pewter please?"

She'd wrapped it in a Tartan box. I paid and then set off down the road, passing the hotel, to what had once been The Manse, now a craft shop. Did they have the missing letters? No.

At other end was a little café recommended by Betty S. I'd have a hot drink.

The Café – Coffee & Cake!

A delicious array greeted my eyes but I chose the plainest, designed to be eaten with butter, and had requested:

"Please, a cup of black coffee."

"You can have a fill-up." came the reply.

Good Lord, two cups of proper coffee for I think 75p. – amazing.

Where was I to sit ? The café was pretty full , but one table had three spare seats.

I sat down, opposite was a man, I looked at his face, I recognised it!

"Were you at the Healing Service last night?" I enquired.

"No, I took the Service at the Bishops House," he'd replied.

"Oh yes, we came to it, sat in the front row, you took it so beautifully."

"Did I, I really don't know the Scottish service."

"Yes, we realized that!"

We were off, he asked if I would like another cup of coffee. I replied:

"Yes, I've got a free one!"

And I thought:

"Two cups of coffee, what am I heading for?"

I'd recently found if I drank coffee a healing might occur! (Legs tingled at that!)

He was a deeply troubled young man, told me of his burden. As he did, I realised St. Columba's Pillow, was for him. I looked at his face again, realised whom he had been and I placing my hand in the paper bag, said:

"I'm not a rich woman but I often find I have to buy things and give them away! This is for you".

"No, I can't"., he'd replied.

"Yes you can".

He'd taken it, opened it, his eyes had filled with tears. He had just been looking at that cross in the shop, which he hadn't liked. One reason, they sold Iona stones. He'd felt they should be given away. Nothing changes. Keats had also found Iona pebbles being sold. (1) And oh my legs tingled again as I typed this in 2006!

Before parting, I'd asked the Priest if he believed in reincarnation. He did. I said he'd been Columba. His face was the same shape as the picture on my book cover, the same piercing blue eyes. I did not tell him of the rape, but it was obvious why it had to be healed before our meeting. I'd asked him to pray for me.

I'd carried from Congress a large delicious scone, kept wondering when I eat it; it was then, the time had now come to brake bread. It was pretty crumbly, he didn't want any, but we ate a few crumbs.

I looked up as I'd left the old Manse, there was the bell above the Parish Church, my sign that everything was in order. Betty S. was waiting by the gate, I introduced them. They walked on up. I went into The Columba, said farewell to Betty's friend, collected her paintings, I wanted to change wet trousers and socks but my bags were gone. A quick warm wash , then we'd walked to the jetty, still NO bags. Where was the car?

The 'Bishop' was also looking for bags! The car then arrived and the bags placed at the head of the queue. Dear Betty decided she couldn't part with me yet and came on the ferry, complete with crook, which she'd offered me. I'd refused, I couldn't go off with that and said:

"Leave it to me."

"All right" .

Something then very strange happened. On her return to dry land, helping people with their bags onto the ferry, she'd hung it on a fence – it disappeared!

The Ferry Journey

Huddled on the ferry was a young woman in a yellow mac. She'd accosted the 'Bishop'. He'd looked surprised, we'd wondered why. I mislaid my ferry ticket, but in searching, found the name of the Oban hotel. I could now tell the 'Bishop's' wife where I was staying! Then the ticket appeared. I'd not placed it in my wallet, and I'd tried to be so careful.

Finally my dear friend had to leave, what a marvellous companion she'd been. She'd understood my need for protection, knew I was being well guarded. She'd felt safe leaving me in the vicinity of the 'Bishop'! Ooh how my legs tingled at that!

This is what Keats wrote to Tom, his brother, about Iona.

'I will first mention Icomkill - I know not whether you have heard much about this Island, I never did before I came nigh it. It is rich in the most interesting Antiqu(I)ties. Who would expect to find the ruins of a fine Cathedral Church, of Cloisters Colleges, Mona(s)taries and Nunneries in so remote an Island? The beginning of these things was in the sixth Century under the superstition of a would-be Bishop-saint who landed from Ireland and chose the spot from its Beauty – for at that time the now treeless place was covered with magnificent Woods. Columba in the Gaelic is Colm signifying Dove-Kill signifies Church and I is as good as Island-so I-colm-kill means the Island of Saint Columba's Church-Now this Saint Columba became the Dominic of the barbarian Christians of the north and was famed also far south-but more especially was reverenced by the Scots the Picts the Norwegians the Irish. In course of years perhaps the Island was considered the most holy ground of the north, and the old kings of the afore mentioned nations chose it for their burial place – We were shown a spot in the Churchyard where they say 61 kings are buried 48 Scotch from Fergus 2nd to Macbeth 8 Irish 4 Norwegian and 1 French – they lie in rows compact – Then we were shown other matters of later date but still very ancient many tombs of Highland Chieftains – their effigies in complete armour face upwards – black and moss covered – Abbots and Bishops of the island always of one of the chief Clans- There were plenty Macleans and Macdonnels, among these latter the famous Macdonel Lord of the Isles-There have been 300 Crosses in the Island but the Presbyterains destroyed all but two, one of which is a very fine one and completely covered with a shaggy coarse Moss-The old Schoolmaster an ignorant little man reckoned very clever, showed us these things-He is a Macklean and as much above 4 foot as he under 4 foot 3 inches-he stops at one glass of whiskey unless you press another and at the second unless you press a third. I am puzzled how to give you an Idea of Staffa. It can only be represented by a first rate drawing- One may compare the surface of the Island to a roof-this roof is supported by grand pillars of Basalt standing together as thick as honey combs. The finest thing is Fingal's Cave'. (8)

Mull

Back on terra firma , we'd waited, and waited for the bus. The woman, clad in the yellow mac, had kept repeating:

"Well if you cannot get her on to a bus, you must ring SALLY in Edinburgh, she will have to drive and come and get her."

She kept repeating "Sally". I was intrigued! Who was "Her?" A bedraggled woman in a palish pink raincoat who had to catch a flight to Minsk.

The 'Bishop' replied, alluding to the Rail Strike:

"Our problems are nothing compared with hers!"

How did the lady in yellow know who the tall thin man was? Through the Priest with whom I'd just had coffee! He'd recognised him, knew his name. He'd told me a party from Eastern Europe had arrived the day before, there had been a changeover of guests, those he'd made friends with gone, consequently he'd become lonely.

The coach arrived, we boarded. 'Bishop' and wife, then 'pink' lady, then me. I felt I had exchanged roles, I was now a guardian. I delved into my bag, produced an orange lidded pot holding raisins and almonds, proffered them backwards,then we'd settled to our thoughts.

Mull looked completely different. Silver, patched with lime green from the percolating sun, very restful, soothing, and good to see in a different light.

T'other side of Mull, it was much brighter, but alighting we were greeted by a cold wind. It was a large ferry, we struggled aboard and stowed our bags.

"You will come and join us" said 'Bishop's' wife to me.

"I'd love to, but first I'll change my wet socks" I'd replied.

Sitting on the cabin floor I'd found them, then my lace broke! I saw the 'Bishop' stride by. Feet clad once more I set off in the direction from whence he'd come. I'd just reached the upper deck – not top – when he'd returned.

"Can't see her anywhere" he'd announced.

I looked up into his face,

"I'm here" I said.

Together we set off to acquire welcome tea, we both chose coffee! I decided it might be nice to add a Danish Pastry to his biscuits, and collected a knife. Returning with our tray of goodies, there was no table. so it went on the deck and so did I. I was going to divide the Danish and my back wouldn't have appreciated leaning down. Division done, proffered, I'd then realised I had a huge mug of coffee, bigger than the 'Bishop's'. What was going on.

Eating, drinking, we'd chatted, and I'd found myself saying:

"I am a dowser".

To my astonishment I could hardly believe my ears. 'Bishop's' wife replied her good husband had been to one for his health! She didn't tell me he'd written about it in his first book 'A Year Lost and Found' (18) which I later read.

We were off.

I joined them on the seat, for pink coat wanted to show some photographs. I offered to move but no, I also had to see them. As she talked I realised it was about problems in Belarus; the unacknowledged fallout from Chernobyl.

I'd piped up.

"Do you know how in Ireland Belarus children were treated Homoeopathically?"

"No".

"They were treated with Granite, Marble and Limestone" (6) with the result they returned looking and behaving like normal children but the two who were not, returned as they'd come."

217

Lime Green

'Pink raincoat' inferred she'd been tested recently for radiation.

"They didn't know how I could have got it!"

I'd already placed a hand on her back, now taking her hand, I'd enquired

"What's your favourite colour?"

"LIME GREEN", and she pointed to a piece in her folder. My travel information folder was the same!

There and then I'd requested from unseen hands that LIME GREEN beyond the spectrum should take out the radiation. Years before I'd learnt from Janet Tintern, late Secretary of Fountain International, that Lime Green cleansed beyond the spectrum. Now I knew what! At Congress, the artist John Lawrie, speaking on Emotional Colour, had mentioned some people could see beyond the spectrum.

Then 'pink coat' gave me her card. Dr. Irina Grushevaya. President – International Association for Humanitarian Cooperation, so I'd given her my name sticker, printed with a rainbow background. She'd exclaimed:

"The Rainbow!".

"Yes".

It wasn't until finally home the full enormity of what God had set before me dawned. I had to laugh. It was only a general rail strike which allowed this meeting to happen. I also had knowledge how I could help, but that didn't come about. I never heard from Dr. Irina Grushevaya but the 'Bishop' did get her safely on a Glasgow coach.

Long Distance Healing

What would I have done? Used crystals to channel energies to those in need, using Homoeopathic 'poppy seed size' granules of Marble, for I had formulated a method that worked.

I had dowsed the under lying cause of a problem with the hands of the son of the Rev. Ellionna (Jane) Swann, in Canada, whom I'd known in England. No treatment he'd tried had healed them but within four days of this method they'd started healing.

He'd had to place a note under his pillow, in the form of a prayer, requesting the energies of the substances involved be sent during his hours of sleep, from a specified date till a specified date, all discovered through dowsing. I'd also written a similar note and placed it with the Homoeopathic substances on a large piece of Amethyst Crystal and that was all I did!

'Sense and Sensibility'

Breakfasting on Monday, I learnt 'Sense and Sensibility' was showing in Oban and before we'd parted Bishop's wife had said I should see it and then I'd headed for The Kelvin.

Two days walking on Iona had strengthened me sufficiently to carry my bags. This time my room was up Tartan clad stairs, complete with facilities, en suite, and a double bed!

Showered, dressed in a pretty rose skirt and matching stole, which I'd made two nights before leaving home, blouse with Jerusalem cuff-links, I'd entered the dining room with a miniature Vodka! A topped up 'In Flight' bottle from when I'd flown to Scotland for Duncan's wedding in 1988. I was making my own Bloody Mary!

Then I'd discovered anyone eating fish was entitled to a half of draught Guinness! Two huge fish pancakes arrived and I'd eaten as much as I could! Then I'd chosen the Scottish cheeseboard; a delicious array. Into handbag went one, thinking it might come in for lunch, but it became my breakfast! I was leaving on the first train, 8 A.M.. No cooked breakfast available. Next morning at 7 A.M. one roll outside the door plus cereal, which I didn't eat, had greeted me!

In a rush I'd set off for the cinema, not knowing it was such a walk, sense and sensibility had certainly left me! I should have had a pee, I should have worn a pad. I'll leave it to your imagination, all that coffee, then the booze, a rather damp me arrived at the cinema! One can't have everything! I did enjoy the film.

Next morning I'd quickly written a card to Elaine. Said with whom I should be travelling. The Very Revd Michael Mayne, Dean of Westminster Abbey, that was whom the 'Bishop' was!

A month before, Elaine had taken a notion to spend her birthday in two places in London, one being Westminster Abbey. That Sunday morning, as we'd entered they were praying for the sick, and I'd heard 'Sister Iona'. I'd felt then it was an omen.

Arriving at the train I'd found Michael Mayne and his loving wife Alison moving their chosen seats to where mine had been reserved! They'd wanted to know more about me! We had a lovely journey to Glasgow, and I'd mentioned the colour rays.

"What do you think goes through the Abbey?" he'd asked.

"I don't know", I'd replied.

Then he'd inquired

"Would you need to come when its empty to dowse them?"

"No, I could do it from home, I might even have a brochure".

We left it at that. He understood why I wore many rings, they were 'working' rings. Approaching Glasgow I'd removed them and Alison had given more instructions.

"Get a taxi, go straight to the Burrell exhibition, it's free, have lunch, it's very good there, come back on the bus. You must also go to the Rennie Mackintosh exhibition." and I'd replied:

"I'm staying at the Rennie Mackintosh Hotel!".

"Oh, that was next to ours, 'The Willow'. Oh, I thought, I *must be* in the right place.

"Do you like Pasta" said the Dean.

"Yes".

"Well after the exhibition go to................but YOU MUST BOOK". but somehow I didn't think I'd be in pasta mood that night.

When arising at 6.20, my stomach had felt slightly queasy. I'd taken drops of Rescue Remedy but a bit later I'd downed in water, a couple of drops of Green Peppermint, crème de Methe, for I wanted to be in control of events in Glasgow! I'd remembered the effect it had had on our journey from Southwell in '95, I'd felt very much in command.(8) At Queen Street Station, Glasgow we'd said goodbye. I'd been so touched they'd wished to travel with me.

Exhibitions

Having parked my luggage, I'd walked to a taxi emblazoned 'Ebony'. As we'd bumped along, the driver was very informative, even knowing where the Tunnel of Light was, just where I'd stood when meeting the brown eyed couple!

The Burrell, set in a large park some six miles outside Glasgow, had very nice loos! There was a poster for St. Mungo Museum of Religious Life and Art. I wished I could fit that in but that wish came true several years later when staying at 'The Willow'! Then I'd sought 'Information', re buses, but the trains ran roughly every 15 minutes, a much better bet.

Then I'd set off, the Dean being most emphatic I should see the stained glass windows, but I was badly in need of food. There was a delightful dining area, overlooking parkland, I ordered something exotic, stir fried red chicken.

"That will take 25 minutes."

"Well first I'll have some chicken pate".

It didn't come, I'd felt my stomach lining adhering, the chairs were not comfortable for my bad lumber region! Finally a lovely waitress enquired:

"Are you all right?"

"No". I'd replied

When delicious pate and superb salad finally arrived, not a lettuce leaf in sight or piece of flabby cucumber, there was no bread. I was too exhausted to seek it. The pate was very rich. Red Chicken arrived complete with brightly coloured veg; peppers red, green, yellow, mangetout, quite stunning. I'd never eaten anything like it. I ate the lot – blow the consequences!

I had no room for apple pie! The coffee was served in lovely deep coloured cups, green, blue, yellow, wine, edged with Gold, different coloured saucers and jugs, echoing the stained glass frieze above the windows.

Filled to brim, I wandered through the exhibition, knowing I had to see some Old Masters. I'd glanced at the plan, knew which gallery. When there, I'd looked over the side into the lower room. A very large tapestry of a White Horse greeted me! I'd descended again, had a good look at him, thanked him. He then led me to the stained glass exhibition from very special places, not like the restaurant Coats of Arms.

The glass ranged along two abutting walls. I'd homed into a French monk holding a reliquary of Mary Magdalene. I sat down, dowsed.

"Had that reliquary ever held HER bones?" NO. Then the Pendulum had swung 'Yes But'.

It had held bones but not hers. If the MONK believed they were hers, his thought processes could imbue 'them bones' with M.M. Energy. That sorted, I'd continued and nearly skipped the last exhibits, but the last piece caught my eye, all amber and opaque.

The Islip window from Westminster Abbey.

The week prior to my sixtieth birthday, a friend and I pilgrimaged to Ely. William Topliss-Green had joined us. After breakfast we'd gone into the garden and William had talked about his signet ring, the crest of the Islip family. My Auntie Smudge, his Mum, was a descendent. He'd rattled on about Oxford, at which point I knew my friend had to listen, she being an Oxford graduate.

I was astonished. Westminster Abbey is built from Islip stone . No wonder Abbot Islip, Abbot of Westminster Abbey, responsible for its completion, used it The chapel built to honour him, now honours the dead of the last war. The glass, is a pun on his name. He sits in a tree, under which on the left is an eye, the right, SLIP!

If you want to know about the village of Islip, read Robert Graves 'Good-Bye To All That'! (p.310 (19) His wife Nancy described exactly the home they required, which he'd then found! There are so many things in heaven and earth that we do not necessarily understand!

William had been very much in my mind, I'd meant to send a card, but ran out of energy. Now I had something to tell him but he didn't get the card, for waiting at home was a letter. He and Mim hoped to come and stay and I telephoned; far more exciting.

Excitement over, it was time to leave. I passed heads of Egyptian gods, statues of Mary Magdalene, other Saints, a party of young school children knew their names. At that point, my stomach began to make itself known. I chewed a couple of charcoal tablets! Over lunch I'd decided a train would be better for my digestion than a bumpy bus ride and probably quicker

It was a lovely walk through the park, advised by Alison, out to the depressing station. I wrote up my notes, talked to a young couple touring Scotland, then arrived at Central Station, from whence I would leave the next day. I sussed out the food shop, been told it was very good, bought a card, knew where to acquire lunch.

I set off for George Square, it was hot, a leaflet was thrust into my hand. House of Fraser promotion starting that night; I didn't think that was on my Agenda! I passed Tourist Info, who hadn't known where The Tunnel of Light was, even though the Queen had been there!

I was on my way to Glasgow's newest gallery, Gallery of Modern Art in the historic and elegant Royal Exchange, housed on four floors with different themes – Earth, Air, Fire, Water. Pretty grim some of them but in the basement was the Tunnel of Light. I hoped the Queen had as much fun as I did in the ever changing brilliant rainbow.

People were laughing, playing with tactile exhibits, some again rather grim, then I climbed a dappled staircase, due to the sun shining through stained glass windows, and finally at the top, reached a little uncompleted restaurant. I was thirsty but I didn't have a long cool drink but a pot of Earl Grey. I didn't know why. It was so hot I couldn't drink it, so requested ice cubes.

The carpet was orange, the walls lime green. I wondered if the elegant building required cleansing. I held my Pendulum and requested:

'Show me Yes' It did a 'No' swing, so I knew work was required so I spun in the cleansing colours of Lime Green and Orange, but that wasn't sufficient. A star was required, the energy of red Betelgeuse. I didn't know why but I felt it was right, which appeared confirmed as I exited by the red stained glass. This had taken some working out!

Next requirement was info regarding the Rennie Mackintosh exhibition, so I returned to Tourist Info. It was busy, I heard a couple of men, not British, talking about the exhibition, so I asked them and one said:

"I'll get you the leaflet".

It wasn't right, I put it back, and just as I was almost out the door the man rushed up with the right one. It was so strange and so kind, I felt they were German. The exhibition was open until eight o'clock.

I didn't retrace my steps to George Square but walked another way to Queen Street Station and entered from t' other side. I spied Boot's the Chemist, thought I'd pop in for a small packet of pads, I didn't want another accident. Years later when I stopped drinking coffee and tea, the problem ceased!

Five steps into Boots something shouted within me: "GET OUT, GET OUT".

I beat a hasty retreat, collected my bags and headed for the taxis. There stood EBONY! Don't know which of us was more shocked. We bumped together to the Rennie Mackintosh Hotel. I told him I'd been to the Tunnel of Light and remembered I hadn't tipped him! That rectified a little bit, he'd parted with:

"Until next time!"

The Hotel

Shocked to the core, I wearily climbed the steps. Same taxi twice in one day, what were the odds on that! Registering I told the Receptionist, then clutching bags climbed another spiral staircase, and walked along a landing to my room. ROOM 14!!!

A narrow room, boiling hot, dominated by superb long Tartan curtains, narrow due to the 'en suite'. Sun streamed in the windows and looking out I saw opposite 'Incorporated Dental Hospital'!

I collapsed on the bed, lying in deep shock, arms above my head went numb. What on earth was this all about. Three Room 14's, I hadn't the slightest idea. Fourteen had never come my way before.

Strength recovered, I had a shower. There were no instructions on its use nor was I too sure if the bath mat was freshly laundered. Suddenly I realised everything was blue. I'd left a peach soap container and soap on Iona.

"One always leaves something", the Dean had said.

I wonder why we do? Is it to leave a link of some sort? Still it was a good shower, then I crept out, there was no hook for dressing gown, no Courtesy Bowl, luckily I'd brought a shower cap from The Kelvin. A new hotel, it needed a bit of sorting.

I dressed in Dash – oh how I was looking forward to some different clothes. It was no good, I couldn't wear skirt or Tartan trews that night. Six o'clock on the dot I sallied forth, headed the wrong way, retraced my steps, went under a bridge cum arch to the buildings opposite. And then past the Art College – designed by the great man himself – then down the next street, passing graffito

– 'DASH' – that had a lovely spiral underneath! I was clothed a'right.

I turned into Sauchiehall Street, up to the McLellan Galleries and entered down a tunnel. I'd arrived at the biggest exhibition ever mounted by Glasgow Museums. Concession ticket in hand, I climbed another curved staircase to be faced with LIME GREEN. Shocked, I bought wrapping paper and two notebooks, one for Dr. Irina, and one for me.

Did I want the audio-guide, No, then thought, Yes but after trying, returned it. Me and cassette would not be in tune. Then I'd seen the beautiful white furniture, the famous long straight low backed chairs.

Suddenly I was face to face with the exhibit of the Willow Tea Rooms in Sauchiehall Street, Willow his favourite wood. His most complete total design achievement in collaboration with his wife. Based upon a Rossetti poem. On Elaine's birthday we'd walked past Dante Gabriel Rossetti's home.

Sonnets XXIV, XXV, XXVI, XXVII WILLOWWOOD

I

I sat with Love upon a woodside well,
leaning across the water, I and he;
Nor ever did he speak nor looked at me,
But touched his lute wherein was audible
The certain secret thing he had to tell:
Only our mirrored eyes met silently
In the low wave; and that sound came to be
The passionate voice I knew; and my tears fell.

And at their fall, his eyes beneath grew hers;
And with his foot and with his wing-feathers
He swept the spring that watered my Heart's drouth.
Then the dark ripples spread to waving hair,
And as I stooped, her own lips rising there
Bubbled with brimming kisses at my mouth.

II

And now Love sang: but his was such a song,
So meshed with half-remembrance hard to free,
As Souls disused in death's sterility
May sing when the new birthday tarries long.
And I was made aware of a dumb throng
That stood aloof, one form by every tree,
All mournful forms, for each was I or she,
The shades of those our days that had no tongue.

They looked on us, and knew us and were known;
While fast together, alive from the abyss,
Clung the soul-wrung implacable close kiss;
And pity of self through all made broken moan
Which said, 'For once, for once, for once alone!'
And still Love sang, and what he sang was this:-

III

'O Ye, all ye that Walk In Willow Wood',
That walk with hollow faces burning white;
What fathom-depth of soul-struck widowhood,
What long, what longer hours, one lifelong night,
Ere ye again, who so in vain have wooed
Your last hope lost, who so in vain invite
Your lips to that their unforgotten food,
Ere ye, ere ye again shall see the light!

Alas! The bitter banks in Willow wood,
With tear-spurge wan, with blood-wort burning red:
Alas! If ever such a pillow could
Steep deep the soul in sleep till she were dead, -
Better all life forget her than this thing,
That Willowwood should hold her wandering!'

IV

So sang he; and as meeting rose and rose
Together cling through the wind's wellaway,
Nor change at once, yet near the end of day
The leaves drop loosened where the Heart-stain glows, -
So when the song died did the kiss unclose;
And her face fell back drowned, and was as grey
As its grey eyes; and if it ever may
Meet mine again I know not if Love knows.

Only I know that I leaned low and drank
A long draught from the water where she sank,
Her breath and all her tears and all her soul:
And as I leaned, I know I felt Love's face
Pressed on my neck with moan of pity and grace
Till both our heads were in his aureole.

(20)

Sonnet III was his inspiration and the beautiful painting by his wife, *O Ye That Walk in Willow Wood* (20)

Sauchiehall Street

Sauchiehall Street means "alley of the willows", "Sauch" being Scots for "Willow" (20). There was I, Sally which means Willow, in a street representing my name; I was totally mind blown, what was God trying to do to me. I'd grown up in Hampstead Garden Suburb with a footpath along the edge of the garden – an alley to the next road. On marrying in 1957, I went to Cyprus as a young Army wife, our nickname had been, "The Willows".

I hardly took in the rest of that exhibition, I had no energy left for paintings, but I felt I should buy a book, a gift for my husband 'Part Seen, Part Imagined'. It was heavy, full of pictures (20) and the recipient had not been the slightest bit interested!

In ancient times the enchanted Willow was sacred to the moon Goddess and pertained to the sign Pisces. In Parkers' Astrology, Pisces head is crowned by two fishes, they mirror each other, as do our bodies, and above that is a white water lily, which no doubt could also be a lotus.(22 p125)

We reflect what we are, those who have the eyes to see may see things which others do not. A mirror reflects, it is up to us to make the reflection as good as possible. The Willow tree hangs over water, it is constantly reflected. In the picture Pisces is holding a long white ribbon attached to which is a moonstone. She could in fact be dowsing!

Fodder !

Hungry, I headed for the Pasta Palace but there was no room for me, it was full! Crestfallen, but I hadn't followed the instruction to book ahead! Now I had to look for myself. I walked uphill to the road behind, Bath Road. That felt right, for I'd met that young man from Bath! I continued down. There was no restaurant to be seen, I heard footsteps, turned around, asked a young woman if she knew anywhere.

"No, go to the Take Away, they will know".

I walked down towards Sauchiehall Street, stopped outside the Turkish Place, wondering whether I was to be fed on a cut price kebab. Something said:

"WE'LL TAKE YOU TO THE RIGHT PLACE" . There it was, right next door!

My Guardian Angel through my Higher Self had led me to 'The Jade Garden' - slogan: "The pleasure is yours and ours"! We have a lower and a higher self and those unseen Beings mingle and work with the latter.

Entering, climbing yet more stairs, I knew I was in the right place. Harmonious décor cosseted me which I hadn't felt entering the Pasta Palace. As I was guided to my table there was a lady sporting orange and lime green; I was certainly in the right place! It was busy but here I could relax, even the chair supported my back!

Chinese Scallops and Mushrooms sounded delicious and Apple Pie, even though I knew scallops would not be greeted with delight by my digestive system, and yes, I'd have a glass of white wine. Then I looked at the wine list, spotted aperitifs, top of the list, Pina Collada. I'd remembered my first in Times Square, New York, with my cousins. Coconut, I'd been homing into coconut for weeks. If I had that I wouldn't need apple pie pud, I thought, but it wasn't apple pie pud but apple pie bed that I was heading for!

Pina Collada

On arrival it was a delight to my eyes, parasolled, blue sword spearing slither of orange and a cherry and a LIME GREEN STRAW! didn't know the symbolism of a straw but I'd left a blue and white striped one under some plants! I'd wanted to remove it, I couldn't, but I'd had no trouble doing so on my return. The cocktail transported me into realms of delight, Seventh Heaven, so on went my rings to celebrate!

It was a very Yin/Yang Chinese Scallops and Mushrooms on rice, delicious but far too much, so I left with a doggy bag; I had tomorrow's lunch! Dinner completed, rings returned to bag, I crossed Sauchiehall Street, then up the opposite hill, and thus to my abode.

I wondered what to do, it was so hot. I switched on the telly, tried to get comfortable on the bed, began returning to reality.

The Dream

I didn't sleep. The quietest venue of my whole trip but my digestive system had finally given up, Glasgow received a lot of Hydrogen, and my back also decided to pack up. I lay on top of a pillow. Much happened. At one point my proboscis turned into a trunk, it waved from side to side, and it was intimated there were no relics of Mary Magdalene! It was so hot, yet not hot enough to do without a cover. My fourth duvet, I don't like them.

About 5 A.M. I'd dosed off, had a dream, shouted:

"You Bastard, You Bastard, now I'll never finish my book".

I felt a sword enter my throat and my voice ebb away. God couldn't surely have put me through all that for nothing, then I woke up. The relief, it was a dream, I was still alive and presumably for a purpose. I could still write my story.

I felt it was Siva, the destroyer and creator Hindu God, and that it was a sequence to a previous dream of dying I'd had in 1995, then I'd shouted:

"I'm dead, I'm dead".

My husband had woken me, said I wasn't! A couple of weeks before my travels, I'd thought about what book I might like for light reading. Suddenly, flinging my final bits into the little bag, I'd grabbed 'The Art of Dreaming' (23) thinking:

"Why that, it's not easy reading". I'd tried and then abandoned it and wondered if the book was for someone else..

Days passed, I hadn't even mentioned it. After the nightmare I knew! Then I'd slept until 6.30 and then my tummy needed Rescue Remedy, followed again by two drops of crème de Menthe in water. I would be in control for my journey. Neither would I have a cooked breakfast but water was required for the journey! I wasn't spending any more on bottled water. I'd shelled out 99p at Glasgow Queen Street Station! A real shock. At Euston, yes another brand, had been 30p cheaper. I'd kept the bottle and it was filled by the nice hotel waiter with delicious pure icy cold Glaswegian. The water comes via a Victorian aqueduct from Loch Katrine, and after it was installed when the next cholera epidemic raged, hardly any caught it in Glasgow.

Journey Home

I'd ordered a taxi for nine ten, even though the receptionist thought nine fifteen soon enough. I'd been emphatic, nine ten, knowing full well I would be dreadfully early. I'd taken photos, including the Dental Hospital, which when developed had Lime Green on the front!

Climbing up the stairs to get my bags, I'd been informed I'd climbed the spiral for the last time. Well I'd certainly climbed a lot of spiral staircases. Two hotels with twin ones which confirmed, for me, what I'd sensed about the rays flowing into the Abbey on Iona.

Bags in hand, I exited the hotel just as a superb taxi arrived with twelve safety features! Cabbie hearing I was London bound, said London taxis were good but Glaswegians were bone shakers, due to the roads. And it wasn't emblazoned Ebony. Ebony shares the symbolic meaning of Black. According to legend, the Throne of Pluto, God of the Underworld, is made of Ebony! That I felt was the message, I'd certainly visited the Underworld in my dream. (24)

Glasgow Central

I entered to the strains of 'Amazing Grace'. Perfect. I hadn't heard any Scottish music, let alone Bagpipes, the whole time I'd been away. Having loads of time, with no shopping required, I wondered what to do, so I'd gazed at the Indicator Board. The information was in Lime Green! Standing under the clock, I'd asked that any negativity left by me the previous Friday, be removed. Not wanting to stand for over half an hour, I hadn't known where to sit, then a woman in a white coat arose and there was a seat.

Before I knew it I was in conversation with the man sitting next to me and then his tall wife arrived, and stood towering over me. On learning they were from Melbourne, Australia, I'd said:

"Oh, I was there for the Olympic Games in 1956".

"So was I, at the Opening and Closing Ceremonies" said he.

"So was I" said I.

We looked at each other in astonishment, shook hands! Then we said why we had been in Glasgow and I was off.

There and then his wife wanted a dowsing demonstration - she was in the pharmaceutical industry - was really interested. She'd also been to the Gallery of Modern Art but only seen the Ground Floor Fire exhibition, which had left her upset by the grim aspects portrayed by some artists. I did feel that the

Tunnel of Light should have been 'highlighted' by the Museum. If I hadn't seen the photo of the Queen standing in it, I would never had known it was there, never gone and I'm sure the Aussie would have loved it.

I'd worn and used the big pear wood Pendulum all the week. That morning it retired, packed, it had been time for another. Years later I'd discovered what it emitted. Horizontal Negative Green found under domes! Very beneficial.

Fishing into my handbag's inner sanctum, out came a rose Quartz Pendulum caught on a bunch of safety pins! We tugged, and left a bit of chain on the station! It had journeyed to Glasgow hidden in my bra! Stripping off before dinner that first night I'd had a rusty line down my frontispiece! Sweat from the Glasgow heatwave had made the chain go rusty. Strange thing, the surname of the Secretary and Treasurer of the Dowsers being Rust! So that was the end of that chain. In due course I'd adorned it with a proper Silver one, no more rusty marks for me!

Dowsing demo over, I found my train to Kings Cross on the longer East Coast route, with many stops. I found my seat, B 01 complete with table but there were no other companions until Edinburgh. The seat faced the carriage wall. From the Magazine Rack the face of Joan Collins looked at me, we'd been at the same school, I a class below.

I enjoyed crossing Scotland and a lovely smiling lady joined me at Edinburgh. We'd chatted away, she'd worked for House of Fraser – I still had the leaflet from the day before! I'd wanted to throw it away but something had stopped me.

A few stations on, a South African couple took the remaining seats. Again I found myself giving a dowsing demonstration. This time I used Brigadier General Bell, carefully polished before leaving. I'd been wondering when he would be used. I'd placed him in the black velvet bag containing the crystals Joy had given me at York in 1995, left the crystal at home on a big bed.

I told various stories, how I acquired my latest Pendulum, they wanted to see it but it remained hidden, it wasn't appearing again that day.

Only when I'd written this story did I get the connection. It was in South

Africa in 1900 during the Boer War whilst in hospital he met a fellow officer who was a dowser. It was then that Colonel Bell had become interested in dowsing. A journey passes so quickly in the company of chattering and laughing good companions. Before I knew it, we'd arrived at Kings Cross!

I walked to Kings Cross Thameslink, (I don't think this now happens), remembering the route we had taken after our Ely pilgrimage in 1993, and I'd shown others the way. It was so badly sign posted. The train was on time but the seat completely finished my back.

Over supper with a bottle of white wine, I regaled my husband with the events of my holiday! By the end I was slightly tiddley! I looked up, there in the kitchen window was a tiny square of Lime Green!

Supper over, unpacked, eventually I'd gone to bed. The bliss of lying on my own well padded, well sprung bed cradling my back, cotton sheets and blankets to add or subtract – indescribable. I'd had an adventure but I was very happy being back home.

The Post

An invitation from Francis Holland School, Clarence Gate, to attend the opening of the new pool by Miss Joan Collins and the new wing blessed by the Bishop of London! After that journey with only her face to look at, no way was I missing that!

I went and had the pleasure of hearing the school hymn sung on the 118th anniversary.

"CHILDREN'S SONG"
Father in Heaven who lovest all,
O help Thy children when they call,
That they may build from age to age,
An undefiled heritage

Teach us to bear the yoke in youth
With steadfastness and careful truth,
That in our time Thy grace may give

The truth whereby the nations live.

Teach us to rule ourselves always,
Controlled and cleanly night and day;
That we may bring, if need arise,
No maimed or worthless sacrifice.

Teach us to look in all our ends,
On Thee for judge and not our friends.
That we with Thee may walk, uncowed
By fear or favour of the crowd.

Teach us by the strength that cannot seek
By deed or thought to hurt the weak,
That under Thee we may possess
Man's strength to comfort man's distress.

Teach us delight in simple things
And mirth that has no bitter springs,
Forgiveness free of evil done
And love to all men 'neath the sun.

From Puck of Pook's Hill by Rudyard Kipling.

I cannot under estimate the effect those words had on my upbringing. They imbued me with great emotion and still do.

I heard what the Actress said to the Bishop, or rather what she told the school, that Francis Holland had imbued her with the idea of becoming an actress! It was where she'd found she had a talent to write and that it had taught her 'discipline and hard work'. And then we had the pleasure of hearing the Bishop say he had listened to the Actress!

That night we went to dinner with Michael and Dorothy Darke, who'd bought my Mother's house after my marriage in 1957. We had all grown up near each other in Hampstead Garden Suburb.

Michael had written to The Times, my husband had seen the letter, contacted him, discovered they lived not far away. Michel's father, Harold Darke, had written the music to, 'In The Deep Mid Winter' my favourite Christmas carol when set to Darke in F.

My husband mentioned where I'd been. I found my programme, read out that the Chairman of the Governors was Madeline McLauchan. She was a great friend of the Darkes! Extraordinary. What a day for tying ends.

THREE ROOM FOURTEENS!!!

This was the revelation I discovered when reading 'Columba'.(8) I was back to the real reason for the Synod of Whitby, at which St. Wilfrid's rudeness and debating skills crushed Bishop Colman, the head of St. Columba's Church. The Synod had been called by the King of York, Etheldreda's father-in-law. He'd celebrated Easter when the Celtic Church, founded by Columba, prescribed it, **14th April**. His Roman Catholic wife however might be on her knees celebrating Palm Sunday! There was much unhappiness in that Royal Household, they couldn't eat their Easter Eggs together!

This was the real reason for that Synod! The King wanted to be in harmony with his wife and if it meant giving up being a follower of St. Columba and going over to be a follower of St. Peter, he would. St. Wilfrid was extremely rude – I'd seen the gentleman in a totally different light.

The **14th April** is the day the Jews celebrate the Feast of the Passover. It was the eve of the Passover when Jesus was crucified. It was St. John the Evangelist who instigated the tradition that his Church celebrated Easter on 14th April and this was the tradition followed by Columba and the Irish Church.

On that 14th April, Mary Magdalene must have been in torment. The man she loved lying dead in a tomb to which she could not go. Was that the reason I had to have three Room 14's, to bring home to people that that was the true date when Christ lay in the tomb of Joseph of Arimathea?

In 1997 I'd learnt more about Mary Magdalene and number 14 when reading the Bloodline of the Holy Grail, (p.114. 25).

'The first mention of Mary in the New Testament is actually the story of how she was raised from death as Jairus' daughter in AD17. Being 'raised' (symbolically, from eternal darkness) related to elevation of status within the 'Way' or, as we have seen, to release from spiritual death by excommunication. The term is still used in modern Freemasonry. However, since women were not excommunicated, Mary's event was plainly an initiatory raising.

First 'raisings' for boys were at the age of 12, and for girls at 14. (25)

So, if that was one of the things I had to learn and tell you, I have!

There was a theory then that the Crucifixion could not have taken place so quickly, the legalities would have taken longer but the legalities were already in place, one man was substituted for another in the face of a threatening crowd. Had I now discovered a reason why I was no longer moved at Easter Services, due to its fixing. Who did that initial fixing? The Roman Catholic Church of St. Peter.

I once had a picture of Mary Magdalene dressed in Lime Green on the cover of a note pad bought at the National Gallery by Mim Topliss-Green, painted by Rogier van de Weyden 1399 -1464.

Knapsacks!

It was strange, on leaving Iona when I met Alison Mayne, her back sported an ethnic knapsack, thick woven, red. A couple of weeks before, I'd found something similar in an outside shed. Relatively heavy, with handles, not a knapsack, I'd washed it really well, thinking I might take it to Iona. I hadn't but left it under the verandah. I'd decided to give it to St. Wilfrid's Church for their charity sales, for from my home I used to be able to see the spire in Haywards Heath.

On my return, I'd seen that bag in a totally different light, the bags had linked us together. I decided it was very good for carrying produce from the allotment! St. Wilfrid's were not having it, not after what I'd read. On my next journey it went with me, it matched my coat!

The Nightmare Message

When I returned I placed 'The Art of Dreaming' (23) upon Papa's Omar Khayyám, still upon his chair. Ten days later, vacuuming that bedroom, I homed into it and felt it contained a message, so I asked:

'What page?' The answer:' Page 212'.

I continued vacuuming. Going to bed I picked it up, it opened there! A quick glance rather shocked me. It would have to wait.

Next morning, working on the principle that all is prepared 'up there', with me bringing it and creating it down here' - via Sainsburys - I was in the midst of planning the next day's meal for twenty-five 'Tangents', but the message could wait no longer!

I had to get to grips and to discover the relevant bit, I dowsed page 212/213, for by then various subjects could all have been relevant!

Page 213 'Let's go back to the Church' - That was the message. Shocked, I couldn't go on saying I was a fringe member - I had to stand up and be counted regarding reincarnation. The Church, on the whole, does not believe in it. I felt if I had to seek advice, I had met a priest, a very wise man, whom I could talk to, Michael Mayne.

Still shocked, I'd gone shopping and nearly had an accident! But I never did seek his advice. However in August 2007, the week of the Patronal Festival of St. Bartholomew, I met separately two C of E priests, who when I'd mentioned I believed in reincarnation, hadn't throw up their hands in horror and strangely they were both connected to Churches dedicated to that Saint.

A month later I dowsed the colour going through Westminster Abbey, it was Lime Green! I wrote to Michael and he'd replied just before his very last service, that he'd chosen Lime Green for the one set of vestments he'd ordered for The Abbey!

Lime Green, that wonderful colour which cleanses beyond the spectrum.

1. Adonais, Life of Keats. Dorothy Hewlett, Hurst & Blackett, Ltd.
2. Gatekeeper Magazine
3. Cygnus Review, issue 8, 2009.www.cygnus-books.co.uk.
4. Tartan Book (Elaines)
5. Copyright Colour Publications 1988 Designed & Produced in Scotland
6. The Proving of Granite, Marble and Limestone, Nuala Eising, The Burren School of Homoeopathy, Caherawoneen, Kinvara, Co. Galway, Ireland, Tel: 091 -37382 7.
7. An Illustrated Encyclopaedia of Traditional Symbols, J.C. Cooper, Thames and Hudson ISBN 0-500-8
8. Columba, Ian Finlay, Chambers, ISBN 0-550-22542-027125-9
9. John Keats Selected Letters, Oxford University Press, ISBN 0-19-284053-3
10. Brewers Dictionary of Phrase & Fable
11. Rubáiyát of Omar Khayyám - I do not know the printers!
12. The Element Encyclopedia of Symbols, Udo Becker, Element ISBN 1-85230-560- 6
13. Biology, M.B.V. Roberts, Nelson, ISBN 0 17 448012 1
14. The Garden of Eden, Jill Bruce, Magdalena Press, ISBN 0-9523695-0-8
15. My Story, International Congress, York, 1993.
16. Phoenix of Fleet Street, Dewi Morgan, Charles Knight, ISBN 0 85314 196 7
17. Sun & Moon Hymn p.94

18. Year Lost & Found. Michael Mayne Darton, Longman and Todd Ltd.

19. Good-bye To All That, Robert Graves, Anchor Books, ISBN 0-385-09330-6

20. Part Seen, Part Imagined, Timothy Neat, Canongate Press, ISBN 0 86241 366 4

21. p.119, The House of Life, Rosetti, Oxford Standard Authors, Oxford University Press.

22. Parkers' Astrology, p.125 Julia and Derek Parker, DK, ISBN 0-86318-601-7.

23. The Art of Dreaming, Carlos Castaneda, Thorsons, ISBN 1855384722

24. The Element Encyclopedia of Symbols, Udo Becker, Element ISBN 1-85230-560- 6

25. Bloodline of the Holy Grail, Laurence Gardner, Element, ISBN 1-85230-870-2

14. Hawkwood 1996

Hawkwood College, Stroud, is an imposing early 19c Manor House, overlooking the Severn Vale, very beautiful. October 11th, my feet having hardly touched the ground, I went with Delia to 'Harmony With The Earth' with Dr. Patrick MacManaway.

Sunday morning was devoted to the Labyrinth. Coffee break there was nowhere to sit in the dining room. Everyone was either busily talking or immersed in their own thoughts, so I exited with my spoon ringing against the side of the mug, stirring non existent sugar, and entered the empty opposite room.

Above an imposing mantelpiece was a huge red and Gold embroidery of the Phoenix or Bennu Heron, beneath the Cosmic Egg of Creation . In the corner stood a large antique chest with one drawer not completely shut, full of old picture post cards, a polythene bag with more cards, and a brochure from The Museum of National Antiquities – Statens Historiska Museum – Stockholm 1953. (1)

Nosy Parker me opened it at Page 4, 'The Arrangement of the Collections'. I dowsed which period, Gothic Art. I'd looked at the Index, found the page but it was the previous page which had caught my eye.

The Bell Room with a photograph of bells! I couldn't believe it. What did it mean? I dowsed the writing, 'No' to everything. I looked at the photo again, then counted the bells. NINE. That was the clue.

We were just about to walk a seven path Labyrinth. The message was:

'in the future mankind should concentrate on a nine path'.

I returned to the dining-room, two people remained, one had piped up at the same time as me saying, "Chi Rho", regarding the start of a Greek Labyrinth. At that point I realized we were on the same wavelength! That's how I met Sandy McKenzie. The Chi Rho was the emblem of Emperor Constantine, painted on shields before the battle of Saxa Rubra in 312, which he won (2)

I told them what I'd discovered, so we went off to the garden. They were my guardians. I insisted we first sprinkled water from the nearby stream and then just as I entered the Labyrinth, I heard STOP. Spinning around, I saw Patrick and the class walking down towards us, like the tail of a comet. I was rooted to the spot, nothing would make me budge. They had all been meditating! We'd thought they'd walked it already!

He realized something had happened. I wasn't moving. He gracefully gave in, asked me to lead the group. I said a prayer, said it was our task now to find out how a nine path Labyrinth should be drawn and worked. The last time I'd spoken to that young man had been at Glasgow, his parting words being:

"I wonder what you will have discovered by the next time we meet!"

After I walked that Labyrinth, I stood under an ancient tree, then went in to the piano to work out the notes involved with the nine path, for before coffee we had been taught the notes pertaining to the seven path. I worked out eight notes, told them what they were on their return. I felt it had something to do with the Pentatonic scale.

I'd brought with me again the 'Pentatonic Songs' (3), hoping to discover the meaning of that scale, for Hawkwood was connected to Rudolf Steiner. I'd bought the songs at Rudolf Steiner Hall in London which, was it by chance, is right next door to my old school!

That was the message of the Bells. Nine Bells were rung for the funeral of a man, six for a woman, three for a child (2) Those who knew about such things would have got the message down the energy line. What energy lines we crossed or traversed to that destination in the Cotswolds I do not know but I was sure that somewhere we had passed a pub named the Nine Bells!

I'd also taken a five line 'Celtic Benediction', sent by Betty Shepherdess. I'd pondered what it was all about. I'd felt that these thoughts should be some of those meditated upon when walking the nine path Labyrinth.

Celtic Benediction

> Deep peace of the Running Wave to you
> Deep peace of the Flowing Air to you
> Deep peace of the Quiet earth to you
> Deep peace of the Shining Stars to you
> Deep peace of the Son of Peace to you

Before leaving Hawkwood I told Sandy about the Sussex Dowsers. Next thing I knew she was Chairman!

So that was what happened to me at Hawkwood. Unfortunately I don't know if any more work has been done on that particular Labyrinth, certainly not by me, for though it may seem strange, after the amazing things that happened to me at the '93 Congress, I'm not really into them!

Three Egyptian Pendulums

So far I haven't said much about Pendulums but this next story is about what happened when I came in contact with three Egyptian ones used for healing, but many more have now been made.

The course completed, late Sunday afternoon we'd driven to Gloucester to see Bogdam Joachim, proprietor of Emerald Innovations. Was it coincidence I'd worn an Emerald Green Jacket and Scarf?

He sold three Pendulums bearing Egyptian names, Osiris, Isis and Karnak. I'd wanted to see Osiris. On the phone he'd said that it transmitted an energy beyond the spectrum, Negative Green. A mite, *Fasciolopsis buskii,* (4) who some believe is a cause of Cancer, cannot flourish in that environment.

Osiris

Osiris amplifies Negative Green radiation. This radiation is strong and potentially harmful, so when not in use, the Pendulum must be enclosed with a Faraday Net, graph paper or Aluminium foil. I chose graph paper for I am allergic to that foil, I cannot touch it.

Osiris is so powerful that when used, it has to be earthed with white thread tied to a chair leg or door handle or table leg and only used by those with sufficient dowsing knowledge and skill. It can be used for teleradiesthesia, the early diagnosis and relief of Cancer, viral illness, vermin, agricultural pest control, and general research. In 2005 I'd used it to kill off T.B. Bacterium.

This was verified by Sandy, who had another form of Osiris. T.B. was listed amongst the many things Sandy's Osiris could be used for. Incidentally I didn't want to be near her Pendulum and neither did Delia. I don't think everyone is necessarily aware that for some sensitive people, these Pendulums may be dangerous, due to what they are emitting. One of the discoverers of Negative Green died through its over use, not realizing how dangerous it was.

I'd been quite scared but Bogdam felt I would be able to handle it! (5) We were short of time, very tired but we'd learnt and looked, for I couldn't touch them. When I decided to buy Osiris something within me had to be retuned before I could pick it up. There had to be a blessing.

Then I met – by chance? – a beautiful Polish woman who had once been his assistant, who said I would have to learn what else Negative Green could be used for.

Anyone who understands Radionics (and I don't) will know that Negative Green is the colour in the middle of the Radionics spectrum, where white meets black. This energy is found under the centre of the Pyramid. Experiments were made using a razor blade and a small Pyramid, and the blade lasted a year.

Lt. Col. Stevelinck wrote in "The Pendulum, (1952)"

'The fact that razor blades become sharpened when placed under a pyramidal shape is a physical phenomenon. When a blade is sharp it is because of the thinning of the steel edge. Under a microscope the steel molecules can be seen to be joined and oriented in one direction, that of the line of the blade. After tempering with oil, the secret is in orientating the blade in the direction of magnetic North; any other direction would produce bluntness.

After using a blade several times it becomes blunt and under the microscope small dents and unevenness are seen. To re-sharpen it must be reset, by returning the molecules to their correct positions.' (17)

After using Osiris, both healee and healer require cleansing and it is advised to use Isis which emits white light. I felt I didn't require Isis, I could manage the cleansing mentally. After using Osiris I quickly wrap it in graph paper, then mentally cleanse myself and the healee with white light. Next I wash my hands in cold water and mentally wash myself in Crystal clear water. Then I cleanse my healing room, open the window, shooshing out anything which should not be there and then shooshing in fresh energy.

I shoosh by first flinging my hands outward and then to draw in fresh energy, inward. I did the hand washing and window every time I did absent and present healing. It is important to do this, it rids me of anything which I might have taken on board whilst doing the healing. Miss Rene had told me she was very ill when first doing her work, she hadn't learnt to protect or cleanse herself.

Isis

'It is a Pendulum for beginners and advanced dowsers, has a high sensitivity and the capacity to cleanse itself by the constant emission of White Rays – its natural radiation. As a harmonizer and energizer it works through the whole colour spectrum. It can be used to test food, herbs, medication, medical diagnosis and treatment. To explore the Subtle Energy fields of objects, minerals, crystals and so on. There is also a single earring to be worn on the left ear by women, having the effect of strengthening the feminine vibrations, of recharging life energy .(5)

Delia bought Isis. Later, due to her skill at measurement, drawing, plus photography, Eric Ede made Isis in a chosen wood for me. I have had extraordinary swinging from it. It is not easy holding a four inch wooden Pendulum when it decides to not only swing in a vertical circle, like the London Eye, but then swing horizontally above one's hand, the momentum generated must be very great to keep it there.

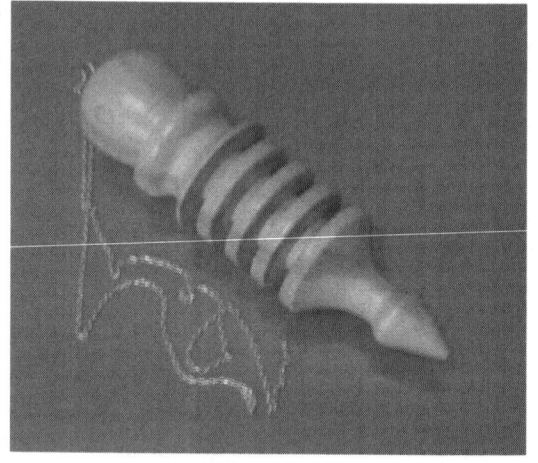

Enter Candida Albicans

In early December Delia brought an article regarding Candida, thinking we manifested many of the symptoms it is claimed to produce. I'd imagine most people do for they are multitudinous! This was not the first time I'd had something similar said but I had always felt I didn't have it. I thought further, maybe I didn't have Candida but maybe a growth of some other fungi in the wrong place.

I dowsed, I did. Where was it? The Stomach, Duodenum and Jejunum. What to do about it? Treat with Negative Green.

I started on Monday 9th December, continuing until the following Sunday. I held the Pendulum, already earthed by a white 'silk thread' to a door, by holding it in front of the Stomach, NOTHING HAPPENED, I held it in front of the Duodenum, ditto, I held it in front of the JEJUNUM, THE PENDULUM SWUNG! Why? I deduced that my mite, whatever you like to call it, Clostridium I later discovered, should be in the first two but not the last. I then dowsed what it fed on. Chocolate! Bananas!

Well I'd had my chocolate moments, then happily given it up, but bananas had been on the increase, from one to two small ones a day. I promptly gave them up, only to discover I then didn't want raisins. I had been consuming many. In my efforts to improve my digestive system I had given both up for long periods but never together, always to no avail.

Next thought. What was this mite doing to me? Answer: holding up the element Phosphorus in the Jejunum, affecting the magnetic system in those parts. That was a surprise. Three days after the treatment stopped, Wednesday preparing for the Tangent Christmas party in my house, I had a short break. Whilst sitting quietly, I'd seen little 'things' running back to the stomach and Duodenum!

To be in tune with Mother Earth's Magnetic Field then I needed to be in harmony with it for 8 Hertz was 'very good for us' (6). I'd learnt from Jack Temple that a Dowser functioned on it. So I'd dowsed the magnetic system within those three parts of my digestive system, discovered 0/10 on the Jejunum, 5/10 on the Duodenum and Stomach. After the healing all three came up to 10/10.

What did that refer to? Not to 8 Hertz. The magnetic field was working 10/10 but was it on the right Hertz? It was for the Jejunum and the

Duodenum but oh dear me the stomach was on 21 Hertz, in other words the wavelengths were occurring 21 times a second rather than 8. What did I do about it?

The problem had been caused by Geopathic Stress. Antidote: Very expensive Melissa Aromatherapy Oil which I'd bought in the summer. I added a few drops to a massaging oil and massaged my stomach twice a day for 6 days. Stopping bananas, chocolate and raisins helped the house keeping!

Dead Orgone Energy - DOE

Next step was DOE. I had read Barbara Ann Brennan's second book. Light Emerging. (6) I'd learnt that under New York State there was 40 yards of this negative energy which looked like a dark greyish-black goo. It accounted for much ill health. I'd wondered why she hadn't done anything about it!

I started doing something to remove that. To help, I invoked Gaia, the Earth Goddess. Next I started on the most ancient of places, the City of London. On New Year's Eve 1996 I used Osiris, which I repeated three times. In July, 2010 I visited again Stansted House and in their delightful Garden Centre I found the rose, 'City of London!'

Christmas '96 and Candida

Christmas 1996 was a learning time. A friend, phoned feeling deeply ill due to an infection of Thrush and all the different drugs she was on. My husband, some year's before, felt he had Candida, consequently we had a lot of books on the subject which I had never read. I delved into Candida, by Shirley S. Lorenzani, (7) and found it riveting!

I begun thinking on a much wider spectrum about those microbes which like living with us. As long as we are fit they stay in their appropriate homes. Once we become ill, maybe given antibiotics, they may well move on to where they are not required.

It was in New York State that Nystatin, the drug most commonly used for ridding the system of Candida, or Thrush infections, was developed and is named after it! (7). Some find it very effective, some go on an anti Candida diet to rid themselves of the menace, or there is the Homoeopathic Candida nosode, Candida Albicans (Monila Alb) (9). This timely reminder came from a new friend who entered my life the very afternoon I had written the above!

I'd thought about Candida, if there was a Pendulum which would knock out that bug from unwanted places. Answer: 'Yes', sold by Bogdam, but I couldn't find his information. Delia said:

"You aren't meant to, there is something else you have to learn".

I did, New Year's Eve! It was about the Egyptian God Ptah and a new Pendulum. That discovered, the information appeared. The file had slipped out of sight! I required Karnak.

An Opal Pendant

As my horizons widened that Christmas, I wondered, perusing MIMS, (10), the prescribing book for the British Medical Profession, if there was a new product on the market which might help me. I had an instinctive feeling I had to dowse and discover.

I looked at the booklet, put the question:

"Should I go to the Doctor?", "Yes".

I dowsed the relevant pages on Gastro intestinal problems, saying the drug names. I got "No" to everything. Then I looked at the article about the Triple therapy for Heliocobacter pylori treated with a cocktail of antibiotics, which had had much press earlier in the year.

To my astonishment, I found the Pendulum doing a YES BUT on H.pylori. Why? I required a drug but I'd got a "NO" to all the ones on offer in MIMS. How could I go to my Doctor and say I want *tri-potassium di-citrato bismuthate*, Bi_2O_3 but I don't want it under its name of De-Noltab! He would think I was bats! It's for gastric and duodenal ulcers. I thought again. What did I need it for? Healing the lining of the stomach, the epithelium, to allow a digestive enzyme to work.

If I didn't go to my Doctor, which Doctor had the Pendulum indicated I did go to? The one in the sky!

An Opal Pendulum would bring that chemical formula, energy frequency. Long ago I'd read it could increase the assimilation of protein (11). If we believe that all is already 'up there' one shouldn't be surprised at such revelations. The manufactured form would not have held the right vibrations for me, could certainly have had nasty side effects, for a third of patients do! (10)

Entities

What had stopped it and when? A previous illness 27 years ago, an entity entered! I healed that, sent it on its way after making sure I had enough protection. Protection comes in many forms: to cover oneself in yellow light is one. An entity maybe anything from a frog to a dead person, who enter a vulnerable person, quite often when undergoing an operation.

What to do? I ask them to leave, look up and go through the Tunnel of Light, telling them they will be met there by those of their kin who will then take them to where they truly belong, but there are also other methods.

My diet changed again, I had a great desire for Shropshire Blue Cheese and Stilton, which I ate for breakfast! I hadn't liked Blue Stilton for a long time. I'd homed into the Shropshire Blue just before Christmas. Those cheeses contain forms of penicillin mould!

When a change in a desire for food occurs, it is due to requirements in the Auric Field, the rebalancing of energies, a frequency change.(6)The Auric Field is a field of energy around us, unseen, but which can be dowsed and felt by healers, and I believe there are 22 levels, for that is the number I am able to dowse.

Briar Rose, Karnak, & Ptah!

Saturday 28 December I'd learnt:

"I AM THE LORD I AM"

The Divine Spark, sat in the centre of the 1000 petalled Lotus, in the Crown

Chakra.

In the bath on, January, 6th,1997, Epiphany, a special event occurred. I'd seen the core of my being! A candle sat in the midst of the Divine in the Crown Chakra. I decided as one grew in spirituality, he shone greater and greater.

First post Tuesday, 8 January, Karnak arrived, but I didn't open the packet until 1 o'clock, for I'd felt protection was required. This took a mental form of a large coat, a strange shaped hat, and long flat narrow shoes, which I'd wanted to make upturned at the points. I think I was thinking of the Chinese but I wasn't in China!

Karnak

Karnak is a copy of a sandstone Pendulum found in a sarcophagus in Karnak, in the Valley of the Kings, Egypt.

The Karnak Pendulum unscrews to hold a sample or witness. It transmits a little Negative Green, so should be kept in two pieces. I felt mine should hold a sample of Silver. I dowsed a piece of Silver wire, 1" long, folded in thirds, was required. If I kept it in two pieces I could lose the Silver, so I lined the little clear plastic bag it came in with graph paper and sealed it.

Polonium

I'd dowsed Karnak emitted the radioactive metallic element Polonium, discovered by Pierre and Marie Curie, named after her native Poland. No.84 in the Periodic Table, the element with the largest number of isotopes, 27. 5000 times as radioactive as Radium, found in Pitcheblend.(8) Bogdam Joachim's parents were Polish. It was always nice to find a connection!

It can be programmed to transmit anything. I dedicated the Pendulum for healing and only transmission. I dowsed there was a greater affinity between it and Polonium than the other energies it might transmit from the elements. I wondered why. Then I thought:

'Where is Karnak?

It is a village in modern Egypt on the east bank of the Nile that gave its name to the temple of Ammon, constructed by Seti I and Rameses I, around which the major part of the ancient city of Thebes was built. (8) I couldn't write more then about Karnac, I only had my enclopeadia available! I can now, I've been there, it is in the modern city of Luxor, it's huge and very impressive. Try visiting at lunch time, the crowds have then dispersed!.

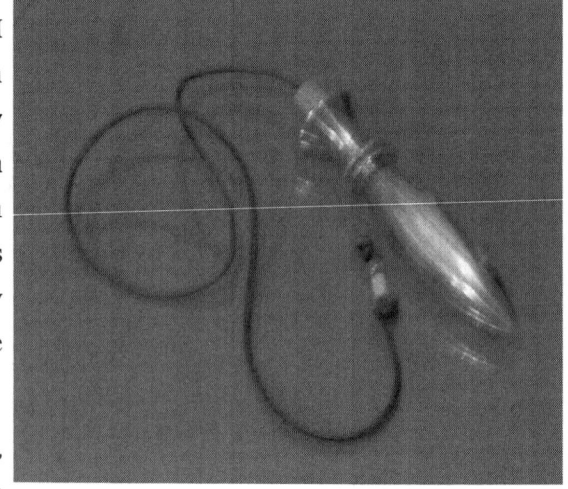

'In Egyptian mythology, Ammon is the king of the gods, the equivalent of Zeus or Jupiter.(12). The name is also spelt Amen/Amun, food for thought, I thought. I dowsed further. He, Ammon, controls the Karnak Pendulum through the energy of Polonium. Needless to say one should cleanse with white light after use.

Having discovered Karnak was in Egypt and Ammon, King of the Gods, the controller, I felt very drawn to pick up 'Egyptian Language', (12) bought half price in our village's antiquarian bookshop. I'd been thinking I should try and understand Hieroglyphics! I soon thought otherwise! The book would be returned, I'd get half my money back! That was not to be, my hand was stayed! What page did I then require? It opened at page 118, the Definite Article, with personal suffices.

I dowsed the translation, No. 3

Fie on thy coming after me to slay [me].

I'd got a Yes, to *coming after me!* Why? Did I need more protection, "No", was something after me, "No". Then I got it. It referred to the next Pendulum I should have, egg shaped, two eggs, one upon the other, hollow, made of Copper. Filled with sand. I'm afraid it still isn't made!

I thought about it's name, thought of Set and Rameses, Horus, none of those, I fetched 'Ancient Egyptian Religion', turned to page 44, it was PTAH, the great creator god. (13)

Ptah:

I read the translation of a text in praise of the creative power of Ptah, which covered even the creator-god Atum himself or Ammon or Amen if you prefer.

'The gods who took form from Ptah...Ptah the great, being the tongue and Heart of Ra... The form as tongue and the form as Heart are as the image of Atum; the great and mighty is Ptah who vivifies... Thoth took form by it, Horus took form by it, by Ptah. It came to pass that Heart and tongue have power over all limbs ...' (13)

Well, I think you should have got the message, I need not quote further! We have returned to one of the beginnings in the belief of man. The Bible was written after the Egyptian Ancient Religion, parts being based on their beliefs. (14)

Next morning I thought what was Ptah for. To restore the life force of humanity to 10/10, or if you prefer, 100% by taking away the side effects or the lowering effects of vaccines and inoculations. They now save life but do not necessarily strengthen the human body in the long term.

By dowsing one may discover that each generation who are vaccinated, their life force has decreased, in other words they do not have the resilience against other illnesses, which those before, if they survived their childhood, did.

Earlier that week I knew Saturday 11 January would be a very special day. 11 + 1 + 1997 = 38 = 11, first Master Number, eleven went up to Heaven. On waking I prayed to the Earth Mother, asking if there was anything else I could do.

"No, it's all going according to plan".

Opening my eyes I homed into the wild rose on the wall paper. Turning onto my stomach I thought about it's symbolism.

Winter time, the wild rose has no protection, bar it's thorns. I thought I should use it as a symbol of protection and I sort of put myself in the centre of the bare rose, thinking of the Crown of Thorns of Jesus, and the 'thorn in my side', the Hydrogen problem, the burps.

Still on my stomach, I had the most wonderful visualization. Amber flooded my Third Eye, but disappeared quickly. Black took its place. I felt amber had been blocked. What was blocking it?

I heard gleeful laughter, demons, they were in the core of my being! The core star is one and a half inches above the navel. It is the central core '.the level of our inner source or the localized divinity within us. It is from this inner source that all creativity from within arises' and is related to our divine essence. (6 p.14 and 29). In Barbara's book there are wonderful pictures depicting it.

I asked them to leave but they didn't want to, they went on laughing. I decided to turn my thorns inward, catch and hang them outside, just like sheep's wool caught on wire and briar's. That done, I enquired where they had come from.

Mars! I sent them there with all my love, then a great GRUNT escaped. Then I'd known the time had come to use Karnak but before I did Ammon had a surprise in store. I received a most wonderful healing from the Egyptian King of the Gods. (8)

Still on my tummy, I sensed an energy, as though someone was holding a swinging Pendulum, which spiralled slowly down my spine, then up the left side of my body, then down the right, finally ending a little way from the base at the base Chakra. Something within felt I needed the healing power of that Pendulum before it could be used for anyone else. But what was the healing for?

I didn't work that out until 15 January 2001. It was four years since I'd written Briar Rose. The previous week I started rereading the story and decided to check my diaries. I dowsed using the nearest thing to hand, an egg shaped tea infuser! The healing had been for my mental level, which links the

Higher Mind to the Lower Mind. It had been upset when I nearly broken off my engagement! Was that chance?

I could have written on Saturday or Sunday but I didn't. At the time I'd never thought what my healing had been for. In fact I had completely forgotten about it and was very thankful that for once I had written up the diaries.

Ammon was healing the Antakarana, the bridge between the upper and lower Triads (15 p.56) And where was Karnak whilst I was discovering this. In my pocket, I'd had to keep him there all over the weekend, or under the pillow! No wonder he came but I never imagined it was going to be used in such a way.

Before I had my bath I looked in the mirror, I WAS BETTER and then in the bath, the words which came were "I AM AT PEACE". When I saw Delia she immediately said:

"You look different, your energy has changed!"

We hadn't met since before Christmas.

Before getting up that Saturday, I phoned a very sick Ann, told her what had happened. We decided I would channel absent healing to her after breakfast using Karnak. I oriented a chair, imagining her sitting there, I stood still, I couldn't use the Pendulum, something was happening in the room, something not experienced before. It was very, very quiet, I felt it was Ammon.

Saturday became a really busy day, I used Karnak on Delia. I suddenly found I was swinging the Pendulum as far out in her Auric Field as I could stretch. We wondered why. She'd lacked Polonium on the 13th level.

By Sunday I'd given the matter much thought. Delia had popped in again. We worked out that we all have the elements up to Tin, No 50, on the Periodic Table. We physically need all of those from food, after that we are not all requiring the rest. We only need those which are connected to our diseases. They are missing and missing on various levels from the Auric Field and they have to be healed.

When I'd first seen Karnak, I was frightened, it looked like a miniature Brass torpedo. I didn't want it near me. Not surprising now knowing what it is emitting. But Ammon or rather Amen/Ra had not yet finished with me.

The previous Sunday I 'd started reading 'Ley Lines' (16) bought just before Christmas from a 'cut-price' Horsham shop specializing in 'bookends'. £4.99, published 1999, bang up to date. On 18th January 2001, lying in the bath, the chosen reading was page 51:-

'Sir Norman Lockyer – astronomer, scientist, and founder and editor of the distinguished scientific Journal *Nature* – began investigating the temples of ancient Egypt to test a hypothesis that they were deliberately constructed to point towards the rising and setting of the heavenly bodies at particular times of the year.

He found, for example, THAT THE TEMPLE OF AMEN/RA AT KARNAK HAS ITS MAIN AXIS DIRECTED TO SUNSET AT THE SUMMER SOLSTICE' (My caps). Amen/Ra had an axial passageway 500 yards long giving an accurate alignment. ' He tried to do the same thing at Stonehenge but due to the ruinous condition, he failed.'

I was gob-smacked.

Over the years I'd discovered that very often special events occurred in my life on a birthday of a member of my family. The eighteenth was such a one, Madeleine's birthday.

Dressing was difficult, nothing recently worn. Shades of purple were required. It wasn't until I'd typed the following, done immediately, that I'd realized the cover was purple! I felt there was something I had to discover. I did.

Karnak, wrapped up, lay on the unmade bed. I couldn't move it. Using Isis, facing south-east, the time around eleven forty-four, I dowsed. 'Is Polonium relevant'. 'Yes'. Finally I discovered that at sunset on the Summer Solstice every year Polonium enters Planet Earth at every place where ancients placed their stones on an alignment for the setting sun .

Polonium has the largest number of isotopes, 27, (that's a special number), and is 5,000 times as radioactive as Radium, liberating large amounts of heat. (8) It would be very interesting if somebody with the necessary equipment could detect any change in the radioactivity at this time of the year at Karnak.

I wanted to get this story finished. I dowsed:

'Was there more for me to learn? "Yes". That evening I read 'Pendulums' and 'Negative Green', by Bruce Copen (17) and seen the exact description I'd written of the protection required when Karnak arrived. I'd gone to bed very late, didn't sleep well, had the most awful burps. I hadn't suffered like that for months. I'd started thinking.

What was it about the indigestion that mucked up my sleeping – I realized it was to do with Hertz – something I had eaten or drunk that day had been on the wrong frequency. I suddenly realized I'd had a mug of delicious Almond Tea, that was the only thing different. At 5 A.M. KARNAK popped into my consciousness. The wrapped Pendulum was under the pillow. What had that got to do with it. TEA contains Polonium. The amount of radioactivity was sufficient to disturb my Hertz wavelength. So what to do about it.

Ipecacuanha (Ipecac-root) came to mind; I'd never used that. Chief action is on the ramifications of the pneumongastric nerve. I didn't know what that was. After much searching through medical books I discovered it was the VAGUS nerve, the motor nerve, the soft palate, pharynx and larynx, and the sensory nerve of the Heart, lungs and gut.(18) It goes down round the oesophagus, into the stomach and is very important!

Homoeopathic 'Ipecacuanha producing spasmodic irritation in chest and stomach. Indicated after indigestible food, raisin, cakes etc.'(19) Well some may think I'm a nutty old fruit cake but I can't digest it!

None at the local chemist.

I thought about the protection I'd used on the arrival of Karnak. I realized it didn't appear Egyptian. It suddenly dawned that it was *very Chinese*. Was it Mandarin? My head shook 'No' very violently. My head acts as a Pendulum. Up and down is 'Yes', side to side, is 'No'.

I then thought about a previous Chinese incarnation, was it me or my wife, for once I'd discovered I'd been an Emperor and met my Empress. 'No'. Then I'd thought about MY FATHER. I'd threatened to dowse his photo with Karnak, at which my body reacted strongly. It had been him!

Francium

Long ago I'd dowsed where the elements entered and when. Friday, I dowsed with the Tea Infuser if there was an element which should be available to negate Polonium. 'Yes'. Francium, homing in on Lime Green to the left breast Chakra. Francium had been blocked for nineteen and half years due to poisons on a plant from a garden centre. I dowsed it out; I held a Pendulum and let it swing to remove the poisons. It took fifteen minutes. I felt pain in my left temple and a buzzing in my left ear.

Francium is another radioactive element, No. 87. a multiple of three (3 x 29,), add two and nine, (2 + 9 = 11) you get eleven, which is where I think this story started. Where dowsing is concerned, verification is absolutely necessary. I think I had it; the tea infuser as the Pendulum, number eleven, and china tea not to mention the guise of my father and the purple of the book and clothes.

Briar Rose

Now back to 1997. Sunday morning there was no lying abed. I was reading a lesson at the eight o'clock service and sat in my usual Sunday place. I unhooked the kneeler which I'd used for months for the Friday service, it bore the Briar Rose. How I laughed to myself. Oh my Grandma Rose, oh my Royal Fusilier badge.

'The rose (and lily) in the Occident occupy the position of the Lotus in the Orient In Christianity the White Rose is innocence, purity, the thorns of the rose are the sins of the Fall and the red rose, (as per the one I knelt upon), grew from the drops of Christ's blood on Calvary but Greeks and Romans believed it came from the blood of Adonis.(22)

But there is more to the Briar Rose than that. It symbolizes (23 p.150.) the hidden feminine waiting to be united with her counterpart, lost, after Christianity became male oriented. In European Folk Tales, the story of Briar Rose is the same as Sleeping Beauty. She pricks her finger on a poisoned spindle and a great Briar Rose grows up around her until a hundred years or maybe one thousand have passed, and the handsome prince slashes his way through the hedge to find and marry her.

'The image of the impetuous prince slashing his way through the thicket of thorn bushes in an attempt to find his lost princess, his "other half", is particularly significant for our modern world. The wounded male brandishing

This brooch belonged to my mother.

his sword is not only hurt and frustrated, he is also dangerous.

The sooner he is united with his own lost, scorned, and repudiated feminine side, the better!" (22)

When we realize that everything is universal, everything carries symbolism, that the archetypal forces are to be found within us, healing can occur. Through this healing I found PEACE.

I now back track to 1989, a sweltering day, 24 July. That day I found my Father, for I cannot remember him or much of my childhood.

I'd gone to London for my first check-up after my Laser treatment. I travelled on four buses, six trains and two taxis. The heat seemed to unite people, we'd smiled at each other, as we'd suffered and mopped our brows. A young girl shared her fan, an Indian made sure I'd gone in the right direction, help was given everywhere.

The Buying of a Tiddlywink!

After the check-up when I'd spilt the beans about what Jack Temple had discovered, I'd gone to the British Museum, then Hatton Garden. I was hunting crystals. My destination R. Holt & Co at 98, recommended by Magda Palmer in The Healing Power of Crystals. (20) They had a wonderful array of gem and semi precious stones but not plain Quartz Crystal. Exiting I'd had a headache. This can happen if one is not used to being in their presence. It was due to me not closing down my Chakras to a suitable level. What I should have done was to stand outside for a few seconds before entering, and ask the Chakras to close to an appropriate level.

I had to hunt again and my destination was Fulham. They directed me to the nearest tube, Faringdon Street. I trotted down Greville Street, not then beautiful; quite seedy. I'd suddenly stopped. On the pavement was a board – 'SILVER AND GOLD BOUGHT'.

'Gilt Edged Jewellery'

Now I'd seen signs like that before but never been tempted to enter but this time I was! I dived in! At home there was a useless piece of Silver, I enquired what I could get for it. Not much, £3.00 per ounce. Then I pointed at my watch. That had given up the ghost the previous week, I enquired:.

"Please do you do batteries?"

"Yes, it will take fifteen minutes."

The shop was tiny, with two tiny counters but it was beautifully cool, it would give me respite and rest. I did have one or two reservations, one being the cost, no room to move, and no room to sit! The only chair was occupied by an elderly man, speaking a foreign tongue, to him behind the counter.

At the other counter a man was examining a tray of rings. I glanced at them, they were not expensive. I then looked down and discovered that under my glass fronted counter there were shelves also displaying rings. I looked closer. The rings were set with green stones. At the end of one row there was a strange looking one, it had a green round disc, like a Tiddlywink, with two Silver leaves at the bottom. which in fact were white Gold.

As I looked, I heard the words:

"Buy it, Buy it."

When my watch was done and dusted, four quid, two more than last time – I had a little conversation:

"Please, how much is that ring and what is the stone?"

Answer:

"£100, JADE".

Next question:

"Please, is the ring old?"

"Yes".

"How old?

"Ten years"

."I don't call that old" said I.

Then the elderly man had chipped in.

"How old is old?"

By this time the tiny shop was completely full; a man by the door said he thought it was older, either nineteen thirties or forties and then he'd put the stone in his mouth and I think, bit it! That done, he confirmed it was Jade.

Well I had not gone to London to spend £100 on a ring, I had gone to buy a few crystals for healing. Rational thinking woman took over and had thoughts of how many stones and crystals she could buy with £100. However, as jewellers do, I had been persuaded to try it on, so did on my right little finger.

For over thirty years I'd worn my grandmother's Gold engagement ring but I'd removed it on becoming a dowser. I'd dowsed Gold was not good for me. Please don't think Granny Rose had tiny fingers, I had had the ring made smaller. I didn't think a Tiddlywink would be practical there but again this voice kept saying.

"Buy It, Buy It".

The jeweller said he would put the ring aside for a day.

Outside, perched on a handy bollard, I read Magda's views on Jade. (20) It contained Silicon, Oxygen, Magnesium and Calcium. I realised holistically that would be very good for me but I also learnt that though tough, if knocked, it could break. Well that's no good, I thought, I'll chip the disc in no time. Most impractical.

I proceeded on my way, three trains and one taxi, because I'd got on the wrong train. Finally I arrived at the other firm listed in my book, Gregory, Bottley and Lloyd (G.B. & L) in Fulham, not an area I knew. The taxi driver seemed surprised I wished to go there. It was a rather unprepossessing door. I peered at the name-board, there was Burke's Peerage, that was reassuring. Then at that moment the door opened, someone popped out and I popped in. I dashed down the stairs and entered a dark Aladdin's cave, filled with dark chests of drawers, totally different to Holts. The countless drawers of hidden bits of treasure which I didn't have time to explore.

G.B. & L were established in 1850 and it didn't look as though it had changed since then! It had, their original premises looked vast, they'd only been in Fulham since 1982. However G.B.L. have now decamped to the coast, so don't go trekking to Fulham. (21)

I realised I could spend a fortune if once my eyes ever looked within and later as the years passed I did acquire some wonderful treasures but that hot day I'd bought what I'd set out for! Four crystals.

Then I walked around the corner to West Brompton Station and started my journey home, including sitting in the Guards Van! I thought of my younger days travelling First Class with my Mother. After my Father died she'd had a well paid job. I had a little chuckle to myself - back to front as usual.

On meeting my husband I regaled him with the days events, including the fact that I'd seen a ring.

No comment.

Next day Celia Flexman, plus grand-daughter Lucy, came to lunch. I told her about the ring. After lunch Celia asked if I had Jasmine tea. I found an old packet and started getting the cups, pink, Victoriana Rose, Paragon.

In 1981 I'd been given two after demonstrating 'Icings for Christmas' to raise money for the proposed St. Catherines Hospice in Crawley. My inspiration had been Katie Stewart's NSPCC cookery demonstration in Clair Hall, Haywards Heath. As I'd watched, I'd known I could demonstrate, not cookery, but cake decorating. Then I'd gone to a meeting about the proposed Hospice and the funds required. I left Clair Hall with the idea of giving a cake icing demonstration and thus it came about. Three hundred came in the morning, two hundred more in the afternoon. This could not have taken place without a wonderful committee under the leadership of Jean Clifton.

There were cakes to buy, decorations to buy and a raffle, total raised £1500. The cups had been a 'thank you' from them, because they said, no matter whatever I was doing when anyone dropped in, I would always give them a cuppa in a beautiful bone china cup! Now I wasn't alone on the stage, I'd had a gas cooker and an assistant, a student of mine, trained in Home Economics, Jane de Pinna.

Now back to the pink cups. Pink was definitely WRONG. I heard again the voice:

"Get the green ones."

Immediately I'd known which ones, but going to a different cupboard I'd questioned whether green meant *Royal*Paragon '*Water Lilly*'. Definitely not. I had guessed correctly. I had just two of these hand painted Paragon, all the rest broken. They were very special to my Mother. Completely circular, stylized green flowers around the rim, very nineteen-thirty.

Now my Mother was in hospital just before her marriage and my Father bought all the furniture. To her horror she'd discovered most of it was green. Maybe the tea service was a wedding gift by someone in the know, for I'd got the feeling writing this, he hadn't bought it but I'd originally thought he had!

Next morning I got up at six-thirty to make a cake. I'm afraid Thomas The Tank Engine didn't fit in very well with the events which were unfolding. I decided I would take no more orders for children's' cakes. I'd never really enjoyed doing them. Cake in oven, I put my muesli together, topped by round slices of half a large kiwi – green again, the colour of Jade.

I was commanded to:

"Take it upstairs and sit on the bed in the little healing room"

THEN THE THOUGHT CAME.

'I wonder if Jade has got anything to do with my Father?'.

I fetched Magda's book. (20)

At the beginning there is a large section about the Zodiac, which I'd never read 'Not interested in all that stuff' had been my reaction on purchase. Just to prove how ignorant I was, I looked for February 6 at the beginning, 'Sign by

Sign and Stone by Stone', then realised it was not like a calender, at which it opened at p.90, 'Second Half Aquarius; Talisman JADE!'

On learning that the Chinese Emperor Wen Di in the second century A.D. had thirty Jade discs, more than twelve inches in diameter, placed above and below him in his tomb, I'd felt there must be more to my Tiddlywink than met the eye. It clinched it. If the Emperor felt the need for Giant Tiddlywinks in his tomb, who was I to question the reason for a tiddley one! The ring might look as though it was from a Christmas Cracker but obviously not. I phoned Celia – she advised:

"You should buy the ring, Sally."

I phoned the jewellers, requested the ring be kept until my next London trip. It was strange, they didn't appear to want my address, telephone number or a deposit!

I switched on Radio 3, Borodin's Polovtsian Dances issued forth, the bit which had the famous song 'Oh my beloved'. That nearly finished me off, but there was no time for tears, there was a wedding cake to do but I felt extraordinarily happy.

The post arrived, with one of those things which if you send them back you might win thousands of pounds! Usually they go straight in the bin, but this one didn't. I'd fallen about laughing because a few days earlier I'd been told I would receive some money. Well I had, a penny! However I did read it, I did do it, and I did post it back and I put the penny or to be correct, 1p, in a safe place!

I have a money-box stemming from my childhood bearing the inscription:

'Take care of the pennies and the pounds will take care of themselves'!

Well I had just to 'wait and see'!

It was early to bed, I woke again about 3 A.M. needing to release gas. I burped and burped away but that done, I didn't pop back to sleep. I felt I must be awake for a reason. I thought about something my husband had said a couple of nights before. He was worried I might end up a complete nut-case. I couldn't blame him so I decided to meditate on the problem in the morning. The answer was:

"BE TRUE TO YOURSELF, DO YOUR OWN THING, BE YOURSELF

LEARN FROM OTHER PEOPLE, READ BOOKS BUT FIND YOUR OWN WAY"!

I'd then been told that all the advice I would ever need I would find contained in my bookcase, in the notebook my Father had filled with quotations. It had suddenly clicked. It was my Father who was talking and guiding me.

I was overjoyed and overwhelmed but I had that wedding cake to complete. No time to wade through Father's quotations. They would have to wait until after lunch. Then I'd gone into my bedroom for a hymn book for 'Abide with Me' was going through my head. There was the Notebook, I removed it, it fell open at a page I had never read.

The quotation was already marked with two lines:

'Thy friend has a friend, and thy friend's friend, a friend – be discreet!'

The Talmud

Other events had also happened that week. It meant that for the time being I had to keep my mouth shut! Something, I did find rather difficult!

In my efforts to heal my memories, to remember my Father, I'd been to his school, Dulwich College, but they couldn't help. Then St. George's, Hanover Square, where I'd been a bridesmaid. In May 1989 I'd walked all around Lord's Cricket Ground on the One day test against Australia. Lords is in my blood. Aged three, I'd made my mark upon the hallowed ground performing head over heals with frilly pants on show! Not quite like the beautiful streaker who suddenly interrupted play that day!

My Father had played Real Tennis, I'd longed to go inside and see the court but I'd been too shy to ask. I'd been turned inside-out seeing men with their orange and yellow striped MCC ties, no matter what age, and I still am!

Match over, we'd walked to Baker Street, past Abbey Lodge where my

Father's sister, Eve Fettes had lived. I think my talent for cake decorating must have come from her. She'd made exquisite clothes for me but also had dressed a doll as a bride, complete with silk underwear. Just imagine how I'd loved my Princess Elizabeth!

Next we'd passed my old school. It had been a walk down memory lane. It wouldn't have occurred if my husband hadn't suddenly been given those tickets.

But where did I find my Father? In my small bedroom, sitting cross legged upon a bed cover the colours of an MCC tie, the room where my Mother had spent the last weeks of her life, the room in which I discovered I could dowse.

That bedroom had been our eldest son's, and when I'd learnt about harmful earth radiations, I'd wondered how he had survived his childhood there. Now I knew. He'd been protected by his Grandfather. At that point the floodgates had burst.

I was typing this story and eating my breakfast at the same time. Abandoning both, I'd sobbed my Heart out on my husband's chest, who'd wondered what on earth had happened. Five minutes before I'd appeared perfectly normal delivering a bowel of porridge to his bedside, then had appeared this deeply sobbing woman, who when asked what on earth was the matter, could only reply that she had found her Father, long since dead!

I expect, poor man, he'd wondered whether I should be taken to St. Francis Hospital, then the local hospital for 'nut-cases' but now flats!

Allegro Taylor, the author of 'I Fly Out with Bright Feathers' (22) discovered at the end of her search for the truth about healing, that her Father had been her Guide. Like me, she'd thought she had lost him. It was also Allegro who'd given me the idea of a ring. I'd looked in Brighton for Amethyst, meant to be good for healers, but for several months Jade had been coming into my head. I'd thought of book ends, no doubt they'd have cost a fortune – then I'd discovered I could put the books upon the windowsill!

This wasn't the first time I'd been in a shop for one thing and exited with something else! Well I hadn't bought the ring there and then but I could have searched forever. However it was certainly the first time I'd heard "Buy It, Buy It". The voice had never been so clear.

When I have instructions I usually obey, but this time I'd refused, due no doubt to money being involved. It's easy following instructions which cause little inconvenience, like sitting on a bed or thinking about the colour blue, but spending precious lolly is another matter. I suppose my LINEAR, brain took control. Deep down inside I'd certainly known I should buy that ring but it was so strange I'd wanted to know why. I'd failed to trust my intuition, the right brain.

Poor Daddy, what a difficult, backward, slow learning child, did you beget. One who perpetually does things the wrong way round and doesn't know when her leg is being pulled!

"I thank you for revealing yourself, my search is ended, I am at Peace. For my guidance you have left me something quite priceless, countless words of wisdom garnered from time immemorial. You had time to find and write them down, no doubt when you were isolated, in hospital with T.B."

One morning when everything had finally fallen into place, I'd awoken with the tune and words of Puccini's beautiful aria from Gianni Schicchi running through my head.

'Oh My Beloved Father'

('O mio babbino caro)'.

I still when hearing it want to cry. I know that singing played a great part in his life, that he had a wonderful voice and now my voice is used as a channel of sound in healing.

Finding the Lolly!

I'd gone to Brighton with my Mother's diamond ring, a three stone affair. She never had an engagement ring, it meant nothing to me, so I'd sold it. Back to London I went, first to Hatton Garden, named after one of Queen Elizabeth's courtiers. Into R. Holt & Co. I went, and exited with a lapis lazuli necklace.

Lapis Lazuli

One must be very careful with this Crystal, it is extremely powerful and if used on the Third Eye or Crown Chakra can have an effect on the brain. It certainly did things to mine, consequently it can have the effect of hallucinating drugs. It shouldn't, according to Magda, be worn for long periods, but I wore my necklace of small stones for a year, not removing it, and then I never wore it again. It had done its work, it had shielded me during the process of my spiritual development.

Then I'd bought the Tiddlywink.

I had a friend who was particularly interested in that ring, so a few months later I returned to the little shop. The atmosphere was quite different. I'd been greeted by :

"Hallo Lady",

A little woman sat behind the counter by the door. I showed her the ring. She said it had been designed by a Russian who was coming later that day, and would I like to leave the ring. I didn't, but later that day I returned and discovered that the only other Jade Tiddlywinks designed by Nassib & Co were possessed by the Shah of Persia!

So money did come, through a ring whose middle stone was of poor quality! (22)

1. The Museum of National Antiquities, Stockholm 1953.
2. Brewers Dictionary of Phrase and Fable 3.Pentatonic Songs, Elisabeth Lebret,
3. The Waldorf School Association of Ontario 1985.
4. The Cure For All Cancers, Hulda Regehr Clark, ProMotion Publishing (1993) 10387
5. Emerald Innovations, 16, Orchard Road, Longlevens, Gloucester, GL2 0HX.

6. Light Emerging, Barbara Ann Brennan, Batam New Age Books, ISBN 0-553-35456-6

7. Candida, Shirley S. Lorenzani, Ph.D. A Keats Original Health Book, ISBN 0-87983-375-0

8. The Hutchinson Encyclopedia, 1995 Edition, Helicon, ISBN 1-85986-018-4

9. Ainsworths, 40-44 High Street, Caterham, Surrey, CR3 5UB 10.MIMS,

10. Monthly Index of Medical Specialities, May 1996.

11. The Healing Crystal, Geoffrey Keyte, Blandford Press, ISBN 0-7137-2099-9

12. Egyptian Language, Sir E.A. Wallis Budge, RKP, ISBN 0 7100 1129 6 Needs Friars Road, Suite 231, San Deigo, California, 92120, USA.

13. Ancient Egyptian Religion, Stephen Quirke, British Museum Press, ISBN 0-7141-0966-5

14. Light from the Ancient Past, Finegan, Princetown University Press.

15. New Age Healing, p.56 Brenda Johnston,

16. Ley Lines, Danny Sullivan, Piatkus, ISBN 0-7499-2017-3

17. The Pendulum.. Negative Green Academic Publications, Bruce Copen Laboratories Ltd. Lindfield Enterprise Park, Lindfield, West Sussex RH16 2LX.

18. An Introduction to the Symptoms and Signs of Surgical Disease, Norman Browse, Arnold, ISBN 0 7131 4303 7

19. Boericke's Materia Medica, Jain Publishers New Delhi

20. The Healing Power of Crystals, Magda Palmer, Rider, ISBN 0-7126-1778

21. brianlloyd@bottley.co.uk www.bottley.co.uk Gregory, Bottley, Lloyd, Tel: 01304 372500 or 07729167195

22. I Fly Out with Bright Feathers, Fontana Original, ISBN 000-637224-4

15. Cirencester Again – October 1997

Stepping Stones across the Landscape

First comes Dentistry!

I didn't go directly to Cirencester, I spent a night with John and Pru Cuninghame, near Tewkesbury, then I'd tried to follow him to Cirencester but lost him on the way!There isn't much for me to say about that Congress; all my notes disappeared, but the first person I did meet was a Dentist, Bob Brewer who lived in Colchester but is no longer on Planet Earth.

He didn't agree with Amalgam fillings, due to the damage of escaping methyl Mercury and thought we should all have them out. Not the view of my dentist, but I did know people for whom it was the right treatment.

However for me, I wasn't putting myself through all that trauma, I am grateful to my dentist and his skills and advice. so what did I do about the escaping Methyl Mercury?

On 17th December, I found a NHS Dental Care chart, I dowsed the relevant teeth and mentally placed circles of Chrome, shiny Silver Chrome, around the teeth with Amalgam. The Pendulum had swung for each tooth, and for some much circling was required. I knew when the work was completed, the Pendulum stopped swinging. Some Amalgam fillings didn't require the treatment, they were very old ones.

This little bit of enlightenment came after we'd suffered a burglary; a most ghastly shock, a ghastly nightmare to receive at midnight after celebrating a son's birthday. The front door refused to open, it had been locked from inside. Intruders had taken the Silver. It took my husband a long time to recover. He'd felt guilty because he'd put it out, and then not away, even after I'd reported burglars were about. I'd received some warning, though I didn't realise it until afterwards. Two days before, I'd moved a piece, it was hidden, it didn't go and I'd bought 'Cheering Tea' in Brighton.

I also worked on the problem of WHY Mercury is so very dangerous. A large healing took place on 27th January at the home of June Holloway, another amazing healer, we were eight in all and I'd read the story. It was a very esoteric healing and where I'd found all the info, now in 2010 I cannot remember or find!

The Story

'Mercury ' stole Silver from Io, Jupiter's 3rd largest moon, for Astarte to try and Silver the 'black side' of the moon! I reckoned Astarte is the 'black side' of Diana. Silver was once known as Diana and they are both moon goddesses. Mercury is also known as Quicksilver. 'He is the patron of travellers, and also rogues, vagabonds and thieves! Hence the name of the god is used to denote both a messenger and a thief'.(1)

> Delay leads impotent and snail-pac'd beggary
> Then fiery expedition be my wing,
> Jove's Mercury, and herald for a king.
> Shakespeare: Richard 111, 1v, 3(1)

This Sunrise of Wonder

Now to the Conference dinner. I met Sue Brown, whom I'd first met in 1995 at the York Congress. On a beautiful Saturday afternoon we'd sat together in the back row at something or other and I'd wondered why I was there; I'd been bored stiff!

Sue is an archaeological dowser. In very cold weather she and her friend Anthea Bezant dowsed the north side of Waden Hill, Avebury in the presence of a group from Bristol University's Geophysics Department. Their equipment packed up but Sue then dowsed some of the circular barrows. The orientation of the buried was not east - west, therefore it was pre Christian. Her findings were later verified by one of the Geophysicists, they were Bronze Age.

Here she was again, and she'd wanted to know what I had been up to! I'd told her about Iona. Next morning she'd appeared, book in hand, 'This Sunrise of Wonder' (2).

"Is this the man you have been talking about?"

"Yes" I'd replied.

The author was the Dean of Westminster Abbey! Delia was with me, said she'd get it, and she'd finally produced it on the 21st February!

Next day, Thinking Day in the Girl Guides, 'This Sunrise of Wonder' came with me into the bath. I'd learnt, when three, his Father, a priest, had committed suicide. No wonder he'd asked if I had healed my trauma at the loss of my Father.

That afternoon listening to my husband's recording of Mozart's Magic Flute, I'd said how I used to play a record on my Father's gramophone, a most wonderful aria sung by a bass. Emotion had welled. My husband couldn't understand why I couldn't recall my childhood. I said, I'd read that when children suffered a trauma, they may block it out.

I then decided it was time I should try and do something about it. I contacted Julia Collett, who'd previously been to me for help. She'd been trained by Dr. Roger Woolger, Ph.D. in past life therapy. My visit was a revelation. I learnt that when a parent dies, part of a child may go off with them, but when asked this question, I'd vehemently replied:

"No, I went to the Kingdom of Aluminium". As we know, Aluminium may be a contributory cause of Alzheimer's, loss of memory.

Now back to Sue Brown. We went to the Chapel. The whole place swarmed with flies, millions, it was thoroughly horrifying. I dowsed the colour that should have been there was deep pink but it was wrong, it was green! I sang, the colour changed, and we mentally cleaned the whole place out!

A fortnight before, Jude and I went on an emergency visit to Paul d'Auria. He could hardly move, he'd requested healing and Jude had enrolled my help.

Paul was an amazing man, a television commercials designer/director, who'd astonished the medical profession with how he'd combated his rare Cancer, Thymoma, an 'extremely rare tumour arising from the Thymus gland in the chest. He far, far, outlived the prognosis of a few months to live, which he partly believed was due to the wonderful healing he'd received from many therapists including Jude. The Wandsworth Cancer Centre has now been renamed the Paul d'Auria Centre but is becoming known as 'Paul's Centre!'

On the way Jude had asked if I would like to go to Walsingham again.

"Sally, I'm going to rent the Methodist Church, would you like to join me, I

Paul d'Auria and his wife Caroline: 'I always try to keep one step ahead of the doctors'   Daily Mail, Tuesday, December 3, 1996.

shall be working during the day, you can do what you like?"

I declined, explaining:

"No, I can't I'm going to Cirencester."

Then I'd given it more thought, decided a drive right across England might be just the thing to do!

The Congress over, I spent Sunday night with Christopher and Veronica Strong and apparently we'd talked about the Blue Light!

Her parting gift had been her book, 'Stepping Stones into the Unknown' 'An

Inspirational Guide to Your Intuitions and Sixth Sense.(3) inscribed with:

'To Sally,

Thanks for the most delightful evening.

Veronica.'

I could also say the same thing! A very insightful book detailing why children may have problems due to food, how she'd discovered through a dowser what caused her migraines and how moving beds helped the whole family. I would recommend it.

Monday morning, 6 October I left Christopher and Veronica for my epic journey. Before leaving home, I'd wondered what music to play for company. Then the day before departure a tape had arrived.

At the wedding of my cousin's son, Richard, I'd met the composer Ian Hughes. He'd been in need of help. He'd received it under the stars! I was well oiled. Now he wanted to come down to Sussex for more, but I'd known he should meet Jude, they had much in common with their T.V. Work, so right across England, from Evesham to Warwick, Warwick to Daventry, Great Brington, Peterborough, Wisbech, Kings Lynn, Fakenham, East Barsham, Houghton St. Giles the sounds blasted out, in particular The Celtic Warrior!

I stopped off at The Blue Boar, Watford Gap, for Chicken and Broccoli at

£4.99, and paid my respects to the late Princess Diana at the gates to Althorpe. Finally I'd arrived at Jude's abode, first having lost my way in the numerous lanes. I was exhausted but Jude had found a good watering hole some miles away at Wells-next-the-Sea! It was a memorable meal. A bit of shot snapped off a crowned tooth!

Little Walsingham

Abbey Ruins and Walsingham Shrine

Walsingham is one of the great holy places in England, where pilgrims have come to worship for nearly a thousand years. It all began in 1061, when Lady Richeldis de Faverches had a vision of the Virgin Mary, who told her to build a Holy House like that in Nazareth. This shrine was duly built and became famous for miracles. There were already two holy wells at Walsingham, and these became famous for their healing water, especially for headaches and stomach problems.

Later they degenerated into wishing wells; the wisher knelt on a stone between them and dipped a hand into each well while making a silent wish, and finally took a sip of water from each well.

In 1931 it was decided to build a new shrine, and while the site was being excavated an ancient well was discovered. It was found to link directly to the two wells in the Abbey ruins and so was incorporated into the new shrine. Today over a hundred thousand pilgrims visit Walsingham annually. The holy well is in the Anglican Shrine in the village; the original two wells can be visited in the Abbey grounds where they are close to a Norman archway.' (4)

Tuesday, Ian came to Walsingham and I sang to him! Being a Channel of Healing to musicians, I found quite daunting. They also found it a challenge, wondering what notes I was singing! All I can say is that the healing helped Ian when in Walsingham.

I then took them to the Swallows' Restaurant for a little bite. Three soups, three crumbles, £10.20. The service was slow, but that gave us plenty of time to talk.

Ian tragically died in his forties, his was the music for Poldark, Howards Way, Children of the New Forest and the wonderful award winning music for the Mousehole Cat. He was also the first conductor of the Cornish Sinfonia. I miss him greatly, attending his concerts had brought another dimension into my life.

After Walsingham I'd driven down the Norfolk coast, through bird watching country. I stopped off at Clay for a pub lunch and heard the tinkling of the yachts. It was a time of remembrance, I'd taken young birders there. Finally I'd reached dear William and Mim Topliss Green at Roughton.

William fell in love with me when I was three and he was ten and it was his father who'd stepped into the breach and given me away on my wedding day, my 'Uncle Bill Topliss Green'. The man who had been given the job, had been suddenly whisked away to report on a football match elsewhere in the world! He had known me from before the time I was born, he was Alan Hoby of the Sunday Express and my father had been his mentor. I loved staying at Roughton, a world away from my life down south.

Friday I went to Norwich Cathedral and was transfixed by the ceiling boss of the Green Man.

After a very psychic experience with that gentleman I'd met Antoinette Watts for lunch.

Antoinette had grown up in Cuckfield, her parents, the Sharpe's, lived in

Copyhold Lane. Her Aunts, Veronica and Madeleine Mayo lived at Mytton Cottage They were three talented sisters, potters, musicians, writers, and her mother also ran the Marionette Theatre at Christmas. We'd met at a pantomime in the Church in 1991, she'd wanted to know about dowsing, so suddenly after Christmas there she was on the doorstep announcing she'd been here before and I'd made her wedding cake!

Lunch over, I'd gone to Thetford, paid my respects to Thomas Paine, the pamphleteer, the author of 'The Rights of Man', and 'Age of Reason'. He'd played an active part in the American and French Revolutions, but was considered a traitor in Britain. The wonderful gilded statue was given by the Thomas Paine Foundation of America in 1964 and I snapped it!

He is believed to have been born in Thetford. My friend, Hazel Burgess for years researched everything to do with Tom and gained her Doctorate at The School of Studies in Religion at the University of Sydney. This year, 2010, her ground breaking research has finally been published . 'Thomas Paine, A Collection of Unknown Writings'.(5) There is a new statue in Lewes and if you like beer, there is a Tom Paine strong, but slightly sweeter than bitter light ale, brewed by the Lewes brewery of Harvey's,

That done, I'd made my way to Bury St. Edmonds, had a lovely night in The Priory Hotel, which seemed the right place for someone who'd once been a nun!

The Wessex Cancer Help Centre now Cancerwise

Saturday I was at home! I went off again on Sunday! Destination, the beautiful Goodwood House, for the annual Wessex Cancer Help Centre's (WCHC) Conference to hear Leslie Kenton speak and a very good speaker was she. The Centre now has a new name, Cancerwise (6) I'd taken a new friend, Kathryn Wallace, now the Rev. Kathryn Wallace Holmes, a wonderful Interfaith Minister. At the conference a lady fell, I was again a C of H! I'd felt shattered eating my lunch.

I had first contacted the WCHC in 1988, seeking advice for my pre Cancer of the cervix. Later I'd wanted information regarding Aluminium. Julian Kenyon advised me to see their Chairman, David Holmes, F.S.A.E., F.R.S.A., M.R.S.H., M.I.H.E., Painter, Sculptor & Lecturer.

I duly went to his home, Wentworth House, Emsworth, situated almost on the foreshore, and was really shocked when he'd asked me to dowse, not only the house but his health because then I had so little knowledge of the subject. I'd felt very bad at taking him a cake wrapped in Aluminium foil.

Aluminium

This is a toxic element and is classed as a heavy metal because it may accumulate in the body it is a neuro-toxin and can cause brain deterioration as well as depletion of phosphate and bone minerals. It can produce changes in brain structure similar to those seen in Alzheimer's disease.

Sources include cooking vessels, antacids, some baking powders and food additives, tea bags, dried milk, instant coffee, table salt and many anti-perspirants as well as cereals and vegetables. Soya milk contains more than cows milk. Excessive levels in the body can be detected by hair mineral analysis'.

(Nutritional Health Bible. Linda Lazarideds.)

At this time I'd dowsed Jack Temple's list of Homoeopathic extraction tablets, putting the question:

"Is there something here that could help with the problem, extract the Aluminium?"

"Yes"

I'd dowsed the list, found something, phoned Jack and told him, which resulted in him saying:

"You are a very accurate dowser!"

When I'd been prescribed Gaviscon in 1987 for my digestive problem, it did the trick for a couple of days and then I'd begun feeling really ill. I'd returned the bottle to the chemist. In those days it contained Aluminium. However Homoeopathic Alumina is the remedy if one has suffered many teeth abscess. I had had many and had always treated them with Belladona which worked well, but after this knowledge, when the next came along, I'd used Alumina 6.

Well David had filled me in with the harm which Aluminium may cause and the WSCC sent me reams of extracts on the subject.

I was deeply moved when he'd given me a print of his wonderful painting of Chichester Cathedral, he'd seen the emotion in my face. My mother loved the

Cathedral, lived a stone's throw away. We met again in the Army & Navy store with Jude, she seeking advice on starting a Healing Centre He sadly died on March 22nd 1998.

Conference over, we visited Diane Shillingford. I'd first met Diane on Sunday, 8th June 1997 on the way down from being on the summit of the mini Silbury Hill at Lewes. I'd read in Church, and before the Sussex Dowsers started dowsing, I'd felt we should ask those unseen for permission! What I said I cannot remember. From the mount the points of midsummer and midwinter sunrise and sunset are marked on the horizon by prehistoric mounds. I wasn't interested in the dowsing, so I'd begun walking down and there on a bend was Diane, who'd said:

"I could have done that!"

My thought had then been,

"Why hadn't she!"

We'd started chatting, she'd asked where I came from, I'd said Cuckfield and her next question had been?

"Do you know Judy Porter?!"

"Yes" I'd replied.

"Oh, I have a friend staying in her cottage at the moment!"

Then I mentioned the next field trip to Glastonbury and the early start which was involved. Diane had immediately said I could stay with her in Chichester and that was the start of our friendship in this life. Now this Sunday she thought I was the Salvation Army! It was my rain hat! My husband had insisted I had this after loosing my Barbour's hood on that epic journey to Wales. I'd bought one, he'd then seen this at the pony shop, (Penfolds Saddlery), insisted I exchanged it. And thus I have a hat trimmed with Black Watch Tartan, which is still admired and I feel gives me protection!

By the time it was all over I had driven over 800 miles and I was more than shattered when I got back that Sunday evening! For some 800 miles would be nothing, but for me it was!

1. Brewers Dictionary of Phrase & Fable, Cassell

2. This Sunrise of Wonder, Michael Mayne, Fount, ISBN 0-00-627870-1

3. Stepping Stones into the Unknown, Veronika Strong, ISBN 0-9530944-0-5 Stepping Stones, PO Box 108, Evesham, WE11 8ZL Tel: 01386 833 899   email: christopher.ssitu@btopenworld.com

4. Atlas of Magical Britain, Janet and Colin Bord, Bracken, ISBN 1-85891-094-3

5. Thomas Paine, A Collection of Unknown Writings. Hazel Burgess. Palgrove Macmillan, ISBN 978-0-230-23971-5

6. Cancerwise, Tavern House, City Business Centre, Basin Road, Chichester, West Sussex. 01243 778516 enquiries@cancerwise.org.uk www.cancerwise.org.uk

16. Ascension Day '98

Remember May, 1998, the weather was hot, it was especially hot on Ascension Day. Delia and I were in the Brecon Beacons, staying at what once had been the Infirmary of the Workhouse, opposite Crickhowell.

Ty Croeso Hotel, House of Welcome, is perched upon the side of a steep hill, approached by a very narrow steep lane, which immediately descends, so that when faced with a sharp right hand turn over a small bridge spanning a canal, the bonnet of my car looked heavenward. I'd almost stalled when we'd arrived two days earlier for a three night 'welcome break'. It was a very friendly place. Our first surprise, Mine Hostess had grown up in Balcombe, the next village up the road from Cuckfield, daughter of Dr. Wynn Jones. Departing to explore on Wednesday my eye caught a notice. Boat trips were to be had on the canal from Brecon. I'd always wanted to go on a canal boat, but in the end we didn't have time.

Thursday we'd explored the Black Mountains, arrived back early so decided on a walk along the tree lined tow path, it looked cool and inviting on that sweltering day. Just as we'd crossed the tiny bridge a canal boat had sailed under.

"Oh, I would like to have a ride on that" I'd said

"Well you'll have to run after it" said Delia.

I did.

"Hey, please could we hitch a lift" I'd called.

"No, problem", came the reply.

The boat was steered to the bank, a tiny gangplank placed, Delia from the rear saying;

"I'm not sure about this",

"I'll go first" I'd called, and over I went.

Three men in a boat, that's what they were, all unattached but five standing on the tiny deck at the stern end was too many for the helmsman, so he who had been fore'ard was told to go back again! He turned to me, saying:

"Would you like to see below",

"Yes Please", I'd replied.

Down the narrow companionway I descended, and the interior of this long vessel was all spick and span. We then went up the other companionway, there was a deck chair, I decided to sit but not before we had started to chat.

"Where do you come from"? says I,

"Waltham Abbey", says he,

"Oh, my Granny lived at Epping," says I

"That's just up the road". Says he.

I then said where I came from.

Looking at me very hard, he'd announced:

"I was evacuated there for two years in the war, I lived down Brook Street, my Grandfather is buried in the Churchyard, his name was Hayden. I went to the School, I was 10, I'm now 65". His best friend had been Raymond Smith. He was Ronald Le Carpentier and he said he would love to hear from anyone who remembered him, not to mention who remembered his grandparents. He lived with his daughter who ran a pub, The Sultan Public House, Seward Stone Road, Waltham Abbey, Essex. I promised to send him a card of Cuckfield. I did.

So my wish had been granted on Ascension Day, a day that always means a lot to me. I'd known I had to be in that hotel on that day for a couple of months. It was the icing on the cake but I'd felt it was also a thank you for the work we were doing whilst there.

When I visit such a place I may dowse whether it needs healing and cleansing, for stones hold memories. Wednesday evening we'd read the history of the Infirmary, built after the Workhouse. Staying there reminded me of our own Workhouse, which later became Cuckfield Hospital, built a distance from Cuckfield Town, but the walk to get there was nothing compared with what the destitute had to contend with to get to The Dardy.

Once there they had a magnificent view over Crickhowell and that was about all. So we'd both tried to heal that time, and my ride on the canal boat had been my reward. Three bridges later we'd parted company but not before Ronald Le Carpentier gave us both a good kiss on both cheeks!

On my return I decided to write this story in Holy Trinity Church magazine, which resulted in a Happy Ending!

At 6.30 P.M. on Saturday 2nd August there was a knock at the front door and there stood Ronald Le Carpentier and his wife. Someone had sent his best friend, Raymond Smith, a copy of my story and Raymond had contacted him. They had spent the afternoon together, then he had looked for his grandfather's grave, failed to find it. We all had a cup of tea and then returned to the Churchyard and searched and searched.

Finally, after I quite thought the gravestone had disappeared, he'd spotted on a flat 'book' stone, the end two letters of Hayden, next to a grave of someone buried in 1969, not where you would expect to find the grave of his grandfather, who had died in 1945. He was so happy to have found the grave, especially as previously other members of his family, even after searching through the Parish Records, had failed to do so. His wife was determined to find the house where my grandmother, Rose Hubbard, had lived on Epping Common, Syringa Cottage! Whether she did or not I do not know. God does move in mysterious ways. This was the third time I'd met people connected to Cuckfield.

17. Ripon 1998
The Icing on the Cake

In 1998, the B.S.D. 's Congress was at another new venue, The University College of RIPON & YORK St. JOHN. I'd never been to Ripon. If going that far I dearly wanted to include Hexham, but that wasn't to be.

How to get there? Originally Delia was going to drive, we were going to have a week's holiday but later she'd known her back wasn't strong enough – I knew my husband wouldn't be happy at the thought of me driving that far in my Y Reg, even if I had been to Wales and Newmarket that year.

September neared, how were we going there? I picked up the address sheet of the Earth Energies Group, homed into Anne, the one who'd jumped into my car when going to Avebury in '94, whom I'd only seen once since then.

Yes, she was going with Kate Fortlage, Chairman of Surrey Dowsers. It was Kate who'd said Old Meg was a 'horrid old girl,' at the 1997 Cirencester Congress(2) Kate was taking her 'people carrier', it had seats to spare, so that got sorted .

Anne thought she knew where we could stay on Thursday night, but having tried three venues she'd given up, not even carrying out her thought of phoning to see if we could stay at the College! She was a very, very busy woman, but she hadn't told us she'd given up! She'd merely put the thought out 'someone else could find it'. On Tuesday Delia had phoned at 2.30 P.M., panic in her voice, I was in the middle of a much needed rest.

"Anne hasn't booked us in anywhere".

For several weeks I had had the address of the couple Jude and I had met in Hunmanby (1) My story of after the 1995 Congress. I'd wondered whether to contact Liz, I'd dowsed. 'No'. Now I dowsed again, the answer was 'YES'. Sometime before I'd moved the scrap of paper from beside my kitchen table but that Tuesday afternoon I couldn't remember where I'd put it. I'd searched twice through my envelope of old addresses, then I'd found it, I'd placed it under the little calendar to do with Jude's Calendar Club, a money raising venture for The Triangle Healing Centre. I'd phoned and left a message on the Answer-phone.

Next morning she'd phoned. She did know of a b & b in Helmsley, and would find out if they had space for four. Four minutes later she'd confirmed they had, it was 9.30 and I had to confirm by 9.45. I had to make sure Anne had not found anything, for I didn't know she'd just given up on the job. I prayed someone would answer the phone and I wouldn't be greeted by yet another Answer-phone. My prayer was answered, she hadn't booked anywhere, so I'd immediately confirmed the booking. What a relief to know we had a roof over our heads, £16.50 b & b, Anne had got to thinking of £50.00 for the night at which I'd baulked. How times have changed!

Not only did I have to sort all that out, I'd had 8 telephone calls after Delia's. I was off to New Zealand a fortnight later for a month, I had much to think about!

I was wearing a little Tiger's Eye pendant, made at Holy Trinity Primary School, by the son I was going to visit. I'd even put it on a large piece of Tiger's Eye, finally I'd looked up why.

'It is helpful for individuals seeking clarity and for those who must deal intelligently with the scattered details which must be brought together into some pattern'.(3)

Well it certainly worked!

Kate collected me from East Croydon Station, I'd gone again on Thames Link and this time allowed plenty of time, I didn't want a repeat of my start for Glasgow when I'd nearly missed the train. We'd then set off to collect Delia and Anne and finally started off north at 11 A.M. We'd lunched at the Blue Boar, it made me remember my stop the year before on my epic drive from Cirencester to Walsingham. My lunch this time was much lighter and suited my digestive system. We'd then sat back in our very comfortable seats. We used our minds on some very heavy rain clouds for by using the mind it is possible to shift clouds. We just caught the edge of the storm.

At Selby, passing the Abbey, it looked so beautiful, we decided to stop. It was cuppa time but that proved rather elusive at 5 o'clock! We spent longer in the Abbey than anticipated. There was a very interesting document. The Stars and Stripes of the U.S.A. stemmed from two families in that area. Reading that, I knew I had work to do. We thought of President Clinton and his family, he was in the midst of his mess!

Then we'd driven down wonderful windy lanes, me saying:

"Of course the animals made these originally".

That apparently was wrong, for during the Congress we learnt those windy lanes are above deep windy subterranean water courses. I don't think my remark was wrong, the land hadn't sunk, the animals homed into them and so made the tracks, which are now our roads.

We finally arrived. Over the bridge down into the beautiful market town of Helmsley. We'd supped in a very good Italian restaurant, they had various pasta dishes but I had smoked salmon and avocado, for in those days I could digest them, but I can't now! I was sharing with Delia and didn't want to give her a noisy night, I didn't, I'd slept, she didn't, due to the traffic! She lived in London, wasn't used to noise. I was.

Supper over, we'd walked to the Sayers, got a bit lost, but it was all for a purpose. It was wonderful meeting up after three years. When I got home, I discovered on the kitchen wall the post card Liz had sent after that meeting. The beautiful brickwork of The Old Rectory no longer stood out, the colours now tints of Aqua.

Looking at it, reminded me of the walk I'd taken beside the sparkling little river, after ordering my supper for I'd discovered I'd lost a very special Pendulum. I couldn't sit there wondering where I'd left it. It was quite safe, sitting on my seat in the 'people carrier'. It was there for a purpose.

Next morning before breakfast, Delia and I had a brisk walk, we were impressed with the vibrancy of the cottage gardens. They'd looked a lot healthier than down south. After breakfast we'd set off for the market; Liz had said there was a man selling Crystal jewellery from whom she had a marvellous Labradorite pendant.

The name rang bells, I knew I had some, but where was it? It wasn't till I got home I realised, I'd given it to Jack Temple. Then I had a message, he had to move it, I'd phoned. At Congress I'd seen him selling his book 'The Healer' (With a foreword by Sarah Ferguson, Duchess of York.) (4) but I never saw it, so I didn't buy it. So when I phoned I asked if I could have a copy. On the cover was:

"Going to Jack Temple was a life-enhancing experience. He

cured me, my sister, my mother and my children of

all our ailments. He is a genius miracle worker".

Jerry Hall

Advice on Labradorite

'When in trouble wear Labradorite. Carry a slice or chunk of the stone in your pocket, place it above the car dashboard, by the kitchen sink, or behind your head whilst sleeping – in fact anywhere you choose. But be sure to let the light catch its iridescent colours which rival a tropical butterfly's wings.......

The composition of Labradorite includes tiny plates of Iron. These are helpful in straightening the spine and bringing the vertebrae in line with the magnetic north and south poles on Earth, an effect known as polarization. When the stone is used for healing purposes, salt should be taken with food. This gem is now just starting to be recognized. It is the stone of today and the future.' (5)

But I've shot ahead.

At this point I managed to lose everyone and decided to continue my walk up the road, where the river ran. Delia had turned right. I never saw her again. I went round that market four times, I crossed in and out the stalls, looked down between them, never spied her or the Crystal man.

Instead of going to Hexham, I'd agreed to walk to Rievaulx Abbey, 3 miles down part of the Cumbrian Way. Delia and I were going together. Ann and Kate were driving, they'd be there in a hour.

Eventually I decided to set off and met a young couple, who'd spent the night in luxury at the Black Swan, somewhere Jenny Peacock of the Cuckfield Wives had recommended. She then had phoned at 8.30 A.M. on Wednesday with the news it had changed! Her husband had just stayed at £100 per night. I told them I'd lost my friend and charged on. She eventually caught up with them, they told her. But the funny thing was I thought Delia was ahead of me and she thought I was behind her. Eventually when she did appear at Rievaulx, her greeting was:

"You're a bloody awful dowser".

"I agree".

Then she'd added she'd thought I was behind her. My reply:

"So are you".

We had a good laugh. I hadn't dowsed, I had prayed, and as I strode along I'd come to the conclusion it was a walk to be done alone. She'd also come to that conclusion. I'd dressed in white, white trainers, it was muddy, I could have worn little waterproof boots, the sort stable girls wear. I'd worn them the day before but no, they wouldn't have been right. Cistercians wore white!

Rievaulx was founded in 1132 on the instigation of St. Bernard of Clairvaux. It became the most important Cistercian Abbey in Britain.(6) As I walked along, I'd started singing Frére Jacque dormez-vous, but lest you think they were all peaceful monks who'd founded that Abbey, oh no. St. Bernard had had an Army at his disposal for the local landowner wanted his lands increased, so he was only too happy to have him come along and had given him the site.

Our bedroom had overlooked his erstwhile castle and I couldn't help wondering at the time why it seemed so important to take a photo from our window. This began to make sense after I'd read the guide book.

Rievaulx is now under the auspices of English Heritage, so there are loos, money to pay and guide books. Hanging from my right hand was a picture of

St. Wilfrid's Church, Haywards Heath, printed upon a blue cloth bag, containing a smart 'doggy bag,' – half Kate's pasta dish; I'd felt we couldn't leave it, why I didn't know, thinking it might be an offering somewhere or even feed me. I didn't realise why until our return. The weight of the pasta turned the bag into a Pendulum!

As we walked about, the bag began swinging back and forth, guiding us in the right direction. Every now and again it started circling, then I knew I was over an energy point needing attention.

The S.E. end of the awe inspiring Abbey Church was encased in an edifice of scaffolding, which I'd spied from the road, it was upsetting the energy lines flowing through that magnificent structure. We'd just felt English Heritage knew not what they were doing. What did we do? We mentally removed it!

Going to somewhere like that can be a very powerful experience for people who are sensitive, especially to past lives. Delia and I by the end of our exploration felt truly ill, needing Rescue Remedy. Once we'd been part of that Cistercian Abbey, we had been badly treated, we had been ill, we had sinned, a sin much debated at the moment within the Anglican Communion!

As I'd healed the Infirmary, healing and cleansing the stones, I'd homed into the Black Death. I had the most horrible experience trying to walk up a staircase. That was after I'd entered the dining room, when I'd had a lovely welcome. I'd obviously been an Abbess or something, for I was going to be given the very best wine, the next thing I knew I was feeling absolutely dreadful!

I am mentioning this in case other people suffer likewise but may not know the reason. We may perceive on different levels what is appropriate for us to know. Anne had found it a lovely place, but on our trip to Fountains Abbey the next day, she had found it the reverse but I had had a very nice time. I'd spoken to their 'Doctor' who'd told me of the illnesses suffered there. WORMS appeared to be the worst, he'd started with Pleurisy, mentioning Pulmonaria, Measles, Black Death but WORMS was his bête noire but he'd added there'd been plenty of other things as well. So I drew the conclusion that Delia and I had had many lives at Rievaulx but I certainly hadn't at Fountains Abbey.

The Staff at Rievaulx said we'd get a good lunch at. 'The Hare', a couple of miles up the road. We just hoped it would still be open, for it had gone 2 o'clock. It was, they should have closed but they hadn't and we were rewarded with a superb lunch. I downed a much needed pint of Guinness sitting outside in the sunshine.

Then I'd wanted a pud and entered the pub to order. A family in the bay window was eating a wonderful one. I knew I needn't look any further. It came upon a dark green glass plate, sprinkled with icing sugar, a gorgeous hot dark sponge pudding with toffee sauce, decorated with strawberry, blackberry and raspberry, too much for me, so Delia and Anne happily helped me out!

Suddenly down the steps came one handsome man after another wearing long socks with 'boy scout' tabs.

"What are you doing" called I.

"Fishing" came the reply.

Then a rather stocky chap, with a large cigar, came to the table, and homed into Kate; they were on a Shoot. She also shot. The chaps I'd noticed sitting outside, I'd thought might be gamekeepers, all trooped into a Landrover and set off. As I'd walked to Rievaulx I'd heard much jollity, and wondered where it came from, I think it could have been that lot!

Then we set off for Ripon and at 4 P.M. arrived at the College, but we didn't enter for three of us missed the entrance and so we had a drive around Ripon! However, Delia, sitting on the left had seen it but had 'known' we first had to do the drive! If it hadn't been for Golden yellow 'Degree Ceremony' notices stuck around the place, I'm not sure we would have ever found it again!

Kate, Delia and I had single rooms on the third floor. Anne, having booked late, was out in the sticks with no bathroom but she'd had the best room the night before. Delia and I had certainly felt like 'maids', for the others had been behind the house in a delightful quiet cottage.

It was wonderful seeing old friends, making new ones, catching up on people's names. The dowsers are an amazing mix with so much knowledge. I didn't sleep well, I burped away, but with cotton sheets and blankets on the bed, I was perfectly cosy, whilst those who were used to duvets, were cold.

Next morning, I discovered we did have bathrooms, lots of hot water, that someone had a terrible cough and an elderly lady was very cold. I became a C of H, and set about trying to warm her up, me in my new thin cotton striped navy blue and white dressing gown! I'd made it on Monday and Tuesday for the Congress, based on Delia's, the material bought in a car boot sale!

I didn't want to attend the first lecture, water dowsing was not my scene, but I'd known I had to. Sitting there, definitely emitting negative thoughts, I suddenly realised I had work to do.

I homed into the water, which the lecturer had been dowsing or at least the direction his fancy equipment kept pointing at. I pulled up my windcheater baring my breast, covered by a *Jumper* T. shirt decorated with motives to do with the sea.

Three weeks before in Horsham I'd dived into *Jumpers*, bought it and promptly worn it. Now I dowsed the motives, scallop shell, seahorses, fish, a spiral shell, crab. It was the crab and I had to place it where the water was. I didn't know why but I'm sure anyone who knows about Cancer (in the Zodiac) will. That done I could leave. I crept out, Delia later saying she thought I'd been rude to do so.

Next to the Lecture Hall were two chapels, once they had been one. I entered the Peace Chapel, which was connected to Iona and made by the Students in 1995. Columba was definitely there. In the large chapel singing was going on, which I found rather distracting. I stayed for a little while, then walked out into the sunshine and met a young woman in a dark green anorak. We chatted, she was on the Ripon Diocese Lay Readers Course and was very interested in Dowsing.

The night before at the Presidents reception there had been several 'dog collars' heading for the bar, thus I'd learnt they had been nothing to do with us.

Next I wandered round the campus, St. Wilfrid swinging back and forth. I found the bell outside the Peace Chapel, so I said something to the B.S.D.'s founder. Only on my return did I realise I had left my heavy Brass Pendulum, named after him, sitting on the sideboard.

I had to stop every now and again when the bag indicated, let it do its own thing. I picked up I was over a Burial Ground, so I dealt with that, then found myself walking past our block. I knew it was ours for I'd spied the flower bed beneath the window, it was the only one, then I'd seen what we were sleeping above – The Health Centre! No wonder I'd had a dreadful night.

I set about clearing out all the negative energies from that place and of course the buried Souls. Some of them had been there to try and get help for their illnesses! I felt I was doing a 'Joy' for she wasn't at the Congress. It was the sort of thing she would have discovered.

The next two presentations were up my street and then it was Fountains Abbey where my bag again performed, finding Chakra points and other things. I didn't want to do what the rest did, that's when I'd gone off to the Infirmary and 'spoke' to the Doctor but I came back at the end and did the last exercise.

I'd bought a new Mager Rosette, invented by the French dowser Henri Mager. The disk has eight segments, white, purple, blue, green, yellow, red, grey, black. Water dowsers, apart from others, find it very useful to determine the quality of water. If dowsing with a Pendulum, the colour wanted is held between the finger and thumb, the Pendulum in the other hand. If rods are being used, it is held between the finger and palm alongside the rod. Different colours relate to different metals, red equates to Iron. In healing, it can determine the colour a person may require. The Rosette is sold by the B.S.D.

Twenty years before Beulah and Philip Garcin, the B.S.D.'s tutors at Lincoln, had been dowsing at Fountains Abbey with the Clive Beadon. He was working on the theory why the High Priests in Solomon's Temple had gems on their breastplates. He'd discovered that these stones, if placed on the site of the High Altar, would alter the colour of the energy lines flowing through a sacred structure like Fountains Abbey

Dowsing at Fountains Abbey

They would alter the energy field, in fact obliterate what was flowing. Beulah placed a stone on the altar. We'd then dowsed with the Mager Rosette the colour then emanating from the ground. It completely obliterated the other colours, it was purple and I got it right.

They interpreted this to mean that when Priests processed down the aisle the colours would flow with them and out on the lines, which then spread into the countryside to heal.

That learnt, we'd returned to Ripon, 'met the the Council', after which I'd known I could buy three books. One I had ordered months before but I'd forgotten its name and so had Deirdre! I homed into it, dowsed, got a 'NO,' then I'd checked my dowsing. Where I stood the energy changed because a tree had once stood there and those who'd chopped it down hadn't sought it's permission, so there and then I asked it to forgive them. I was so relieved on getting home to discovered it was the right book!

Much energy flowed at dinner, it had the previous night as well for I'd had two glasses of red wine, one donated by Allen Heiss from the States for he wasn't drinking. Sunday I had nothing. I was wearing a pair of Amethyst earrings. Allen had used that stone to stop his drinking four years before. It was his special rods which had inspired me to have mine made after the 1996 Congress. I'd forgotten to bring those as well but that didn't stop him giving me another lesson with his.

Whether it was the Amethyst ear-rings or not which stopped me drinking wine I do not know but I did know before dinner that I didn't want anything to drink including water. No way did I wish to drink it in that dining-room that night or Sunday lunch.

We had a free evening and I found myself listening to a group who were thinking of setting up a training based on the CIA enabling one to discover what one wanted from the Universe. I didn't think I required that. 'Distant viewing' I think it was called. It can be very useful but for me it would be a form of spying or prying.

I then found my friend David Beale, the giver of my wonderful Pendulum at the York Congress; he was in need of healing again. It doesn't matter where you do these things. A large room with a bar and smoky atmosphere doesn't hinder. He'd sat back and lapped it up. He had a friend beside him whom I will call 'Olive Oil'.

'Olive Oil' had had a large melanoma just above his eye. He'd asked if I hadn't noticed it at previous Congresses. Well last year it was getting so bad he'd thought he'd better do something about it.

He'd massaged into it, Virgin Cold Pressed Olive Oil, three times a day and held a bottle of Aniseed. Within three weeks it had gone. He was experimenting for curing ailments, all sorts of spices and plants. An amazing, lovely man. I knew he could help Delia!

At that point she'd arrived with her companion. David needed his bed. I'd wondered what to do. I stood up, burped a bit, decided to sit beside the lady who'd had the awful cough, so pulled up a chair and enquired:

"Why, what caused it?"

"A big Solar Flare last Wednesday, it affected Television and Radios."

I couldn't believe it. That was the answer to why on Wednesday our T.V. had decided to become black and white! So there I was channelling healing again. In the back ground, ten feet away, a group of women danced, they were not dowsers! It was like a cabaret act.

The healing completed, we'd chatted, my burps came up, and in return for her healing she said she would treat me She was Editor of the Radionics Society Magazine, a very hard working woman. That night she mentally radioniced me and her list the next morning was as long as my arm! I had things I had no knowledge of which had all been dealt with and I'd slept very, very well.

Before bed, I made a mental decision. If I should attend a Communion Service at the Cathedral, I would awake at 6.40, have a hot bath, then go. Long before I'd decided to skip the first lecture. I didn't want to know about dowsing for oil, I'd heard the speaker before. I might miss breakfast so I asked Delia to try and save me some.

Wilfrid on left arm, not hanging down, I felt guided to walk across the campus and out the second entrance, then down the road and turn right, then past a hall with a little bear on the door, a playgroup or something, attached to Holy Trinity Church at the cross roads. That made me feel good remembering Cuckfield's Holy Trinity. I wondered if I had to go there, but no, I turned left, walked on, turned right, then left again, I was going past the hospital I felt there was a reason for that!

At the end I recognised the road. We'd driven down it the day before and when I looked back there was a sign – Cathedral. I walked along, it was such a beautiful cold crisp morning and the pavements all washed and clean from the night's rain. I crossed another road, then I spied a little elderly lady coming from a side turning.' Yes', I thought, 'she looks the sort who'd go to Communion, she'll guide me there.'

She disappeared up a narrow steep alley, I followed. Nearing the top I got the words

"Ever been had".

The lady had disappeared into the paper shop! I looked up the street, there in front across the wide road, was the entrance! I walked up, went in and of course she followed, paper under her arm.

St. Wilfrid

Built in AD672, this was Wilfrid's first Church, dedicated to St. Peter. Now the Cathedral is dedicated to both.(7)

St. Wilfrid, still over arm, I followed the lady and came to the choir stalls. The service was to be held in front of the High Altar. Beside the entrance were the most wonderful spiralling gleaming Silver sculptures, bit like huge Christmas Tree decorations, symbolising the descent of the Holy Spirit.

Two people stood there, a lady handing out Ripon Cathedral 'The Eucharist, Traditional Language' booklets and an elderly man. I'd told him it was my first visit, and he'd said,

"YOU MUST SEE THE WOODEN SCULPTURES OF THE STATIONS OF THE CROSS". Oh, I'd thought, I've been commanded once again to do something and had better do it after the Service, never mind breakfast, for breakfast was from 8 till 8.30.

The front cover of the booklet had a beautiful picture of three holy people dressed in blue, *The Rublev Trinity,* (they looked female), the back, a copy of the stained glass window dedicated to Wilfrid. Oh I did want a copy of that and at the end of the service I was able to buy it from the nice lady. Then I'd set off for the Stations of the Cross.

They were wonderful, huge, made by a carpenter, I think, who'd either had an accident or had been ill, and this had been his therapy. Unfortunately all the leaflets had gone. It was on loan. One could touch them, the figures were inlaid in the wood, clenched fists, some large, some small, but No 4 reduced me to tears.

'Mary, mother of Jesus, putting her hand on his as he carried

his burden of the stake'.

Only the arms, proper arms made of wood, the hands made of something very special, were attached to the large piece of wood, nothing inlaid on this one. I just knew it wasn't his mother, it had been his wife, Mary Magdalene, 3 months pregnant, that was the chord which seemed to touch me, now why do I write that? I had read 'Bloodline of the Holy Grail, The Hidden Lineage of Jesus Revealed' (8). It made a lot of sense to me.

Then I'd stopped at No.12, I'd thought it was the last, I'd turned and there high up before me was the window of St. Wilfrid. He seemed to call me a lot of things, daughter, lover, mother! I was quite bewildered. I'd turned again and then saw two more Stations of the Cross. It was the last one, No 15 which also stirred me deeply, an oval with rays flowing outward from it, carved in the main piece of wood.

I knew I wanted photos of No.15 and No. 4 and those who were guiding me agreed. No 15 done, I'd headed back towards No.4. Almost opposite was a lady on a ladder, who was touching up her wonderful floral arrangement, before a pillar, husband dutifully holding black plastic bin liner. We started talking, I showed my St. Wilfrid bag.

"You know this Cathedral is dedicated to him". she'd enquired.

"Yes". I'd replied.

"Can you see the black tiles under the transept, that's the outline of his High Altar, underneath is the crypt of his original Church. You should see it. It's locked now because of the Services, could you come back later at 2 P.M.".

"No, I'm leaving, I cannot go then, we will have left", I'd replied

"You see the sacristan ....(a tall slim young man in red cassock), ask him if he can quickly unlock it for you now. He might just let you go down before the service starts at 9.30!" He did, saying:

"Bear with me one second".

People were already sitting in the nave for the next service.

The next thing I knew he was giving a slight nod and pointing me down some narrow steps right beside a large pillar.

I tried to make myself invisible and hurriedly crept down a narrow low passage, which ended beside a tiny cell with five niches holding lights, only four were working. Originally they'd held caskets of sacred relics, (bones and other objects associated with saints) which Wilfrid had brought from Rome, for use in the dedication of his new Churches. Ripon was considered by his contemporaries the finest building west of the Alps! (9)

It was the most wonderful experience. The power was incredible, I was again moved to tears. Again the saint talked to me. I couldn't but feel that those two had deeply loved each other and my legs tingled editing this in 2010. Another even smaller cell led to a narrow staircase, which exited in the choir. I'd returned, knelt, prayed, SANG, hoping it was not being heard by those waiting for the service.

The night before leaving home I'd looked very hard at the tea-towel of Hexham Abbey stuck on the back door, a birthday present from a friend. I'd looked particularly hard at the flight of stairs and said:

"I'm coming to see you!"

Well I got the stairs but a different lot! When I'd written this part of the story I knew it was time to cover the tea-towel with the one I'd bought at Rievaulx.

There had been no need to go to Hexham, this was where I had to come.

'That crypt is believed to be the oldest complete Saxon crypt in England. It reminds us of the tomb of Jesus and proclaims His life with us today.' (9)

On reading that after my return a great surge of energy had flowed through my legs. Where did that idea come from? I had to wait until Christmas for a friend's present, 'The English Cathedrals' published 1950, (10) full of architectural photographs. I'd wondered, whether she was expecting me to study the history of our Cathedrals, the intention of the book.? I wasn't doing that. Then I applied my brains, looked up Hexham, looked up Ely, these were the gems for me.

' ...built around A.D.670...its central chamber and wandering passages are strangely reminiscent of the grottoes beneath the Church of the Nativity at

Bethlehem; the same arrangements are found at Wilfrid's other surviving crypt beneath Hexham Abbey. It is a strange coincidence that the shipwrecked Gaulish bishop, Arculf, should at this very time have been relating his travels in the Holy Land, and setting down plans for the sanctuaries in Iona, whence the narrative was *SENT TO* YORK (my italics) as a gift to the Northumbrian King Aldfrith.' (10) That was. Etheldreda's father in law! No surprise to me after that. Wilfrid would no doubt have seen them.

As flower arranger and husband talked, they'd mentioned the Dean would love to dig up the place to find the rest of Wilfrid's Church and his remains, but they could be elsewhere. I said the Dowsers would be able to find the outline without any trouble. However, whilst waiting to go down, I quickly dowsed if his bones were there, they weren't!

Marvelling how once again I'd been led step by step, moment by moment, I left. As I'd entered the crypt, I'd wondered whether my friend had been there the previous year.

On my return I checked, she hadn't, she'd been concerned with the obelisk in the centre of the Market Square, little knowing she was carrying one. It was her birthday present and birthday was whilst she was away! I didn't know Ripon had an obelisk, neither did she, but she had descended to the crypt at Hexham..

When I looked up at the obelisk I was amazed at the symbols atop, there was a whole collection. The one at the bottom hooked me, I didn't know why. It turned out to be the symbol of psi from the Greek alphabet, used in Physics,Y. which came to light during the riveting final lecture.

Above, the blue sky held half of the waning moon. I photographed the lot. I felt it was a pretty powerful spot. Then I had asked directions back to the College. I went past the Roman Catholic Church dedicated to St. Wilfrid. It had at one end an extremely interesting little Pyramid roof but I felt no need to venture in, so walked on to the College, entered the Peace Chapel and thanked St. Columba and wondered how to get my breakfast!

I stood outside the lecture hall, trying to look through the opaque and clear striped glass door, it was impossible. I wondered whether to enter and look for Delia but she suddenly appeared. She'd dowsed a little earlier to see if she could leave, 'No', but a bit later known she could, and like me the previous day, she had wanted to escape.

In her bedroom wrapped beautifully in peach napkins, were two pieces of lifeless toast, little packets of strawberry jam and Flora. I told her of my happenings, how wonderful it had been, which was lovely to share with an understanding good friend.

Then I'd required strong tea with lots of brown sugar to restore my energies. Perfect timing, it was coffee break. Then we knew a recently bereaved man needed healing, he'd had a go at healing my back when I'd got to Glasgow. We returned to the Peace Chapel and there, with all the chitter chatter of a coffee break going on outside, I sang a Requiem.

Another man, none of us knew, entered just before I started and said on completion, the sounds were still reverberating around those walls. All four of us were nearly in tears, it had been so beautiful and the dear man for whom it was sung, knew it was for him and his wife and my legs tingled reading that in 2010.

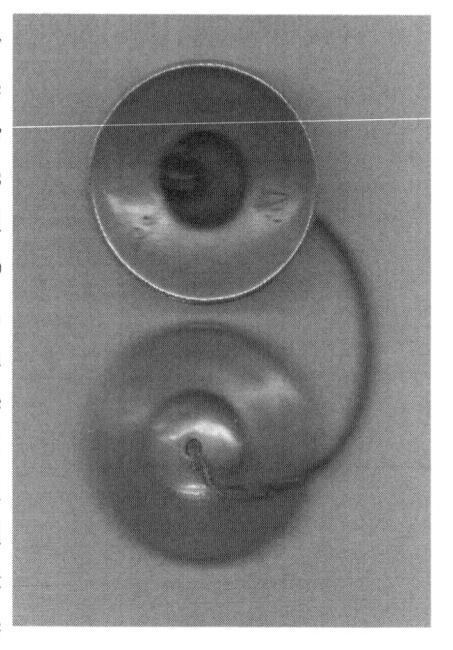

If you have ever heard *tingshaws or Tibetan bowls or bells*, that was the sound at the end. I'd brought *tingshaws* with me, only acquired the previous week. They'd been in the window of Jill Larkin's shop, Seventh Heaven, a shop selling crystals and other unusual stuff, in Cuckfield, a little shop set back from the others, which used to have a passage from the car park, now sadly sealed off. The bells were antique, bought from Tibetan monks in Glastonbury. I'd known they were probably for me, but first I'd had to earn the money and the money had come from the one time owner of Colonel Bell's home! Gavina Guest.

Quickly packing before lunch, I discovered the sheet had a pale green mark. St. Wilfrid had done a leak! The Pasta dish had turned on it's side! Never eaten, never a gift to the Gods, it had served its purpose! Its final resting place, the waste paper basket! Then after tucking into a good lunch we'd set off. I was home just before 10 o'clock and that is the tale of what happened at Ripon, my seventh Congress of Dowsers.

Midnight, I felt the time was right to open a letter from New Zealand. A bed was being offered by an Aukland dowser who'd been at Glasgow. I had first intended visiting N.Z. in 1956 but fate had intervened, a marriage proposal! I never got there, I'd returned from Australia.

I was going now to see two little grandchildren, Emma, four months and Tom, not quite three, in their home overlooking Lyttelton Harbour. Lyttleton is where the first English settlers landed and they had to walk over the Port Hills to the city they founded at Christchurch. Now there is a tunnel! !

So why did I need a bed in Aukland? Well the family were going away. I hadn't wanted to stay on in South Island and fly home from Christchurch, with none of them to wave me goodbye, so I'd decided to explore the wonderful North Island – in the end I didn't.

I saw part of the wet and windy city of Wellington at the southern tip. My hosts had woken me with the news there had been an almighty storm during the night – bridges were down – no travel on road or rail was possible. They'd fixed me up with a flight and at 9.30 A.M. I'd flown out from Wellington and up to Aukland and it was from Aukland that I flew home.

Dowsers are to be found all over the world. Dowsing has been used down the centuries. The ancient Chinese were some of the first. We'd learnt at the final lecture that physicists are discovering what dowsers have always discovered, their ideas are having to change, but ours aren't!

New Zealand Dowsers!

On my return from N.Z I wrote to the Editors of the B.S.D. Journal.

'Dear Editors,

I wondered whether you would be interested to include a small report on my meeting with the President and Vice President of the New Zealand Dowsers in October 1998.

It came about through asking Deirdre for their Secretary's address. On my return from the Ripon Congress, Judith Rubie had replied, an answer to prayer, for I had written requesting guidance on my stay in Aukland, but my letter wasn't written to her! She kindly offered to meet me and let me stay with her at Whangaparaoa, 45K outside Aukland. Judith had attended the Glasgow Congress. I wondered whether I would recognise her.

My second night we went out to dinner with the President, Janice Tait, and Vice President, Albino Gola. Everyone was very relieved when we all decided to dowse what food we ate. I learnt much particularly in regard to microwaves and how they were responsible for the cough that was sweeping New Zealand. I had it, so did Rubie, we had both been staying with people who were using them. I brought back a very powerful object, invented by Albino and Rubie, all done by dowsing. The Spider Web Coil, emitting eastern radiation. They had never written about it but I had needed to sit in front of it for 35 minutes. Something had really zapped me whilst in New Zealand. I simply knew I had to buy one. I have since used it to help others and discovered, on a very esoteric level, what it does.

At the end of the meal our waiter wanted information about dowsing and healing, for people at the next table had overheard our conversation. Thus the word is spread.

It is wonderful to belong to an organisation which is world wide and I felt very privileged and humble that they wished to meet me. There are just over 80 members in their association, how lucky we are to have so many in Great Britain.

1. My story re Hunmanby and York 1995
2. My Cirencester story 1994
3. Love is in the Earth, Melody, ISBN 0-9628190-3-4
4. The Healer, Jack Temple, Element, ISBN 1-86204-312-4
5. The Healing Power of Crystals, Magda Palmer, Rider, ISBN 0-7126-1778-7
6. Rievaulx Abbey, English Heritage, ISBN 1 85074 465 3
7. Ripon Cathedral Leaflet
8. Bloodline of the Holy Grail. Laurence Gardner, Element, ISBN 1-85230-870-2
9. Ripon Cathedral Guide
10. The English Cathedrals, Herbert Felton and John Harvey, Batsford

18. White Horses and Crop Circles

July 1999, the B.S.D Earth Energies Group held a 'flexible' three day meeting site dowsing Avebury, White Horses and crop circles, both of which decorate the Wiltshire landscape in great profusion. People could come and go whenever they chose and I knew I had to go, for I had a great desire to walk and look at those horses.

In the pub that night, at a long wooden table, twelve had supped together. Suddenly I'd remembered my mission, and thumping the table had said:

"Hey guys, do any of you know anything about mobile phone masts?"

"Yes, we have one in Glastonbury " Sig Lonegren had replied.

They told me of the problems it had caused; a murder, a bank robbery, a feeling that something was wrong, illness. Someone was monitoring it. I was given his phone number and duly phoned him. I learnt a Liberal Democrat MP was researching them.

Some weeks later, a Monday morning, I'd plucked up my courage and phoned the Houses of Parliament. I managed to speak to the relevant person and thus a big file on all the research till then on the harmful aspects of the masts came into my being. As soon as I'd put the phone down, Jude rang, said her husband's relation, Margaret Campion, was also very worried about, so I'd promptly ordered another file for her. Now Margaret had clout, she was on the PCC (Parochial Church Council) and she would be living very close to it!

Now why did I want to know? Some months before, late one Sunday evening, wanting to go to bed, I'd felt I had to read the Church Magazine and so discovered the proposal to put on or up the tower, a mast. Climbing wearily up the stairs, I'd called out to my husband the news and to my surprise, what he said was not something I'm going to print!

Next day I'd phoned a friend who's husband was also on the PCC, hoping he could do something about it but when she'd phoned a few days later, she'd said it was me who could to do something about it! Oh!

Having learnt of the murder, the bank robbery and the feeling that something was wrong, I'd reported all to the Vicar. The PCC then deliberated again, it was even stevens! To his great credit, (in my eyes) the Vicar made the final decision. It was nay, so we didn't have the mast. In some quarters however, I wasn't flavour of the month for years, for due to this decision, the finances of the Church were deprived of several thousands a year.

It was interesting, the Press got involved, questioned passers bye, some felt their prayers wouldn't be answered, if there was a mast in the tower.

I also had the Church dowsed by a dowser from Brighton, so that we had a record of the colours flowing through and if the mast had been erected, he was going to re-dowse to see if the colours had changed.

So my friend was quite right, I was able to do something about it. I'm pretty sure she'd dowsed that!

Well the next couple of days we did walk up hill and down dale looking at the White Horses and even a Crop Circle had appeared on the Sunday morning, after we had viewed the area from the hill above on Friday night and someone had said:

"There should be a Crop Circle there".

When it had appeared I knew it would not be wise for me to walk in, so I'd climbed the hill again and viewed it from there. Crop Circles may be made by man, may come as a result of thought by man, but they also come from God Knows Where and that can be determined scientifically, the enzymes have changed in the stalks.

Sunday afternoon we'd met at a village hosting a Crop Circle conference. In a very hot marquee one stall immediately hooked me ; I'd seen a T-shirt bearing a *WHITE HORSE* and known immediately that was the real reason I had gone to see the White Horses. I had to have it .

It wasn't my size. My cheque book was at home and cards no use, and I didn't have enough cash, so what was I to do; could I order and pay later?

Then the artist Anka had appeared. The horse was from a pack of Shamanic Wisdom cards entitled, 'A pathway into the Millennium' created from an ancient original pack painted on buffalo skin. They had once belonged to a Shaman. I had the privilege of holding them, for they were very fragile and it was wonderful meeting Anka, but Shamans, Wisdom Cards, I wasn't too sure about that. However I did want to know what the horse symbolised. On hearing the words I had been truly shocked, for once Jesus had called me to be his Old Grey Mare!

HORSE

'Allow horse to carry your needs on his back, bringing out your personal power and Warrior energy. He brings compassion, healing, strength, leadership and gentleness. He is the energy of a free spirit, which comes to lead us into the future with those qualities and brings peace into the land. He is also a communicator between us and the spirit world carrying messages in our dreams.'(1)

I wanted those words, they seemed so pertinent to me but the only way I could have them was by buying the cards. I didn't want to do that. I had a strong feeling that I didn't want to buy the cards in that marquee. then Anka had said:

"Why don't I send them with the T-shirt?"

"Will you trust me" I'd replied.

"Yes".

So I'd waited, and waited, and finally when the time was right, Friday 2nd September, the cards and T. shirt arrived.

I still wasn't too sure about the cards but I'd opened them that night and they went with me to my bedroom. There I'd looked and read them very carefully. I seemed to need 'The Hand'. I carried it, felt energy and finally placed it under my pillow.

This card was a *Key* card, used to see our present pathway.

The 'symbol brings forth a blessing and a healing upon a part of your life. It is a means for an understanding and communication with others and the divine. It represents our spirituality, and is most importantly an imprint of the self and brings forth self-discovery, and self-healing. Finding our place, making our mark. Giving but also needing to receive. Conductor of spiritual energy.'(1)

That was what I had under my pillow. At ten past one I'd got up to have a pee and in the loo received the message:

"*You should worship the hand which feeds you*".

What on earth did that mean. Did I have to worship him who gave me my housekeeping! No, I didn't think that was the message - I went back to sleep but not before having stuck with micropore a green Opal in my tummy button. I just hoped it wouldn't get crushed or broken. It was there for a couple of hours, then it too went under the pillow. The Opal had been a present from my family in New Zealand.

I didn't wonder at the time why I did that, but now editing this, I thought I should find out why, so turned to Melody for enlightenment

Green Opal

Amongst other things 'it can cleanse the body internally to promote rejuvenation....The energy instils a knowledge that one is always in control of, and may command the outcome of, ones life.' (2) So now you know what a green Opal might do for you, but of course it is also connected to the green Heart Chakra.

I remembered again next morning the message and puzzled again, then exiting the loo, it had clicked. I have found over the years, the loo is the place to receive messages, especially when treating someone else. In I'd pop, have a pee, violà, be told what I first had to discover! Many healers get messages in that smallest room!

It was *Saturday, EARTH MOTHER DAY,* that was who needed to be worshipped. In the bath. I thought about prayer. The prayer I said before falling asleep.

'Dear Lord and Father of Mankind, forgive my foolish ways, re-clothe me in my rightful mind, in deeper reverence praise'.

It had to be amended.

Dear Lord and Father, *Dear Lady and Mother,* of mankind, please forgive my foolish ways, re-clothe me in my rightful mind in deeper reverence praise'.

That was Step One.

Step Two was reading again the prayer which Jesus taught should be said in conjunction with 'The Lords Prayer, found in The Gospel of Peace of Jesus Christ.(3)

"Our Mother which art upon earth, hallowed be thy name.
Thy kingdom come, and thy will be done in us, as it is in thee.
As thou sendest every day thy angels, send them to us also.
Forgive us our sins, as we atone all our sins against thee.
And lead us not into sickness, but deliver us from all evil,
for thine is the earth, the body, and the health. Amen"

Afterwards Jesus spoke to them and ended with:

"I give the peace of your Earthly Mother to your body, and the peace of your

Heavenly Father to your spirit. And let the peace of both reign among the Sons of Men".(2)

I sat very quietly on the end of a bed after reading that – I was deeply moved – then I'd learnt:

'The Kingdom of God is Mine'.

1. Shamanic Wisdom Cards, A Pathway into the Millennium, Anka ™1998, 01225 703291 or 01249 814129
2. Love is in the Earth, Melody, ISBN 0-9628190-3-4
3. The Gospel of Peace of Jesus Christ, by the disciple John, The C.W. Daniel Company Ltd., ISBN 0 85207 103 5

19. Kosmed

The Times on 26th October 1999 had an article re a new Russian treatment machine, The Kosmed, which my husband had left out for me to read. The next day, Elaine said:

"Have you read about the Kosmed?"

I hadn't and it was nearly midnight when I'd suddenly thought I'd better.

'What the Russian researchers discovered was that they could trigger self-healing by stimulating the C-fibres of the neural network. The C-fibres, which make up 70 per cent of the network are responsible for general cell maintenance and are used by the body to deliver its own pharmaceutical messages in the form of proteins call neuropeptides' (1)

Having digested that, I'd wondered if the same could be achieved with a Pendulum, so had mentally asked if so. The answer had immediately shot back:
'Yes'.

I'd continued my questions:-

"What shape, what size, what metal?",

I then departed to the kitchen and as I did so,

'Wiggle, Wiggle, Wiggle,' came into my mind.

Then I'd got the measurements and drawn them on the paper. It was 12.22 A.M. on 28 October 1999, the Feast Day of St. Simon and St. Jude, and the latter is Patron Saint of Lost Causes.

That night Jude had a party celebrating the third anniversary of The Triangle Healing Centre. Almost at the door the last four suddenly started talking about the Kosmed and I'd said what I'd discovered.

"We'll have to find a foundry," someone remarked.

It was Elaine's husband, looking for something in Yellow Pages some months later, who'd spotted' White Eagle Foundry' in Cuckfield Road, Hurstpierpoint.

Off we'd toddled and the rest had fallen into place.

After learning of our requirement, the owner had said:

"You'll need a 'pattern', they cost a lot to make". I'd replied:

"I think I could make it out of icing!"

He looked astonished, and I'd explained:

"It's a very hard icing, I don't think it will melt or break as you press the sand around to make the mould." It didn't.

Recipe: GELATINE PASTE (Pastilage)

    50 ml/3 dessert spoons. cold water

    5 ml Gelatine

    250 grams/½ lb.. sifted icing sugar

Method: Place water and gelatine in a small bowl over a saucepan of water. Bring to the boil and allow to simmer until mixture is really hot and decreased, stirring occasionally. Throw half away, then add a tablespoon at a time of icing sugar, stirring with a wooden spoon, until really thick, then tip out onto remaining sugar and continue to knead well until it does not feel sticky. Pop quickly into a plastic bag, to stop it drying.

This is extremely hard, has to be used quickly, so placing it over something warm, a boiler, hot water bottle, etc., or down a bra, will keep it usable for longer.

This mixture can be added to fondant icing to make modelling paste for flowers etc. Mix half and half.

Fondant Icing

This is enough to cover one 6/7" fruit cake or up to a 4 egg sponge.

500g/1 lb. Icing Sugar, or maybe more if eggs are slightly larger

60g/ 2 oz. egg white. (medium egg)

60 g/2 oz. Glucose Syrup,

Squeeze Lemon.

<u>Method</u>: If possible use a mixer, it's far easier, or roomy bowl, cleansed with boiling water to remove any grease. It also helps with the mixing to have the bowl warm.

Place syrup in jar in saucepan containing cold water, bring to the boil and simmer until syrup is runny. (Don't forget to loosen lid.) There is no need to sift the icing sugar unless it is lumpy.

Put sugar, egg white, lemon juice and then glucose into bowl or mixer. If bowl, stir with wooden spoon, (not one used for curry!) - metal can discolour icing. When mixed, turn out onto a board or table, liberally dusted with icing sugar and then kneed with hands until smooth and pliable. Place in plastic bag for several hours if possible. It gets rid of any air bubbles. I wear Marigold gloves, kept specially for icing, for the kneading. Of course you can buy ready mixed icing but home-made is far nicer!

Dust table/board thickly with sifted icing sugar and roll icing out to required shape. Glaze cake with egg white and then lift icing with hands and place carefully over cake. Smooth, using plenty of sugar and finish off with cornflour if necessary. Prick out any cushions of air with a fine needle or hat pin.

Store remaining fondant in poly bag in fridge or freeze but never store cakes covered with Fondant in Tupperware or plastic, unless freezing. This is the opposite to cakes covered with royal icing.

So that's how you make fondant icing.

Christmas came, I was making Christmas icing decorations, and with the left overs made the 'patterns'!

On Tuesday 14 March I'd suddenly taken it into my head to take the 'patterns'! And what had they chosen to smelt that day - Aluminium! I couldn't believe it. I'd watched fascinated as a huge ladle filled with the gleaming silver stuff had been carried very gently to fill a large pile of small moulds.

On collecting six Wiggle, Wiggle, Wiggle, the bill stated they were BRASS

SNAKES. Elaine had already observed,

"You have drawn the Caduceus"!

I hadn't, I'd drawn half, but Wiggle, Wiggle, Wiggle, did represent the aspect of healing which the Caduceus represents. The intertwining snakes used in Egyptian temples of healing, handed down to Aesculapius, the Greek and Roman God of Medicine, which a serpent may possess. (2) (After his death, Zeus placed him among the stars as the constellation Ophiuchus, the Serpent Holder.)

Then I'd discovered each 'Snake' wanted a Gold chain and a nice velvet pouch to live in!

This is what we are, our bodies are like the sand encasing the 'pattern' or mould of our Heart. When we pray, raise our vibration, it is like pouring precious metals into the mould. We need to do it as often as possible, keep renewing, then pouring wherever it is needed on or in Planet Earth or the Universe.

In September, I'd gone to the Ripon Congress of Dowsers and Wiggle, Wiggle, Wiggle, went too. Friday night, I'd cast my eyes over the book stall. They'd alighted upon 'The Cosmic Serpent' (3) and the cover bore a snake!

I wasn't too sure I wanted that. Then someone needing help appeared, and for some reason only known to her, she nicknamed me 'Daisy'! I'd replaced the book and we went off. The next night I'd shown Wiggle, Wiggle, Wiggle, to a very eminent man, Professor Peter Stuart, who said:

"It's the Cosmic Serpent"!

Sunday I looked for the book; it had gone!

I couldn't remember it's name, so I'd phoned the B.S.D. They did and I'd said:

"I'll pick it up at the next London lecture".

Then husband had put his foot down and I must say he didn't often do that!

"You are not going to London on 31st October".

Why not? The trains were in chaos. However Delia was going to the lecture, said she'd collect it but I had to wait until her next Sussex visit, 9th December, but it was perfect timing.

I was reading in the bath 'The Woman with the Alabaster Jar'. Margaret Starbird's riveting book about Mary Magdalene (4) but that was abandoned for the Cosmic Serpent. If I needed verification that that was the correct choice, I had it for I'd watched the first two programmes about the Conquistadors. (I'd known I had to watch them.) Delia had also brought a Neal's Yard leaflet entitled 'Spirit of the Amazon'. I'd even watched the exact location in the Amazonian Rain Forest the previous Friday.

The Shamans, under the influence of their hallucinogens, more often than not saw snakes. Jeremy Narby, an Anthropologist, who'd gone to study the locals way of life, had seen snakes when he'd tried it. He hadn't believed what the Shamans told him. Ten years on, he'd concluded that what they saw and described, was exactly the description of DNA by Crick and Watson. I'd liked the way he wrote,his personal adventure story, as the 'Praise' on the back cover stated :-

The Cosmic Serpent is a personal adventure, a fascinating study of anthropology and ethnopharmacology, and a revolutionary look at how intelligence and consciousness may come into being. In a first-person narrative of scientific discovery that opens new perspectives on biology, anthropology, and the limits of rationalism, Jeremy Narby reveals how startlingly different the world around us appears when we open our minds to it.'

Some days later I'd reached page 57. A picture of the human brain, There in the very centre was WIGGLE, WIGGLE, WIGGLE!

A picture taken from an article: "Brain and mind in Desana shamanism" by Gerardo Reichel-Dolmatoff depicted an anaconda.

'The Desdana believed the fissure occupied by the reptile was a depression that was formed in the beginning of time (of mythical and embryological time) by the Cosmic anaconda'.(3)

Jilly Wootton's birthday present had been a Wiggle, Wiggle, Wiggle, and according to Jude, using it that night what Jilly had seen was 'mind blowing' but Jude had not enlightened me further. Sunday morning, I'd taken 'The Cosmic Serpent', to Jilly for her enlightenment.

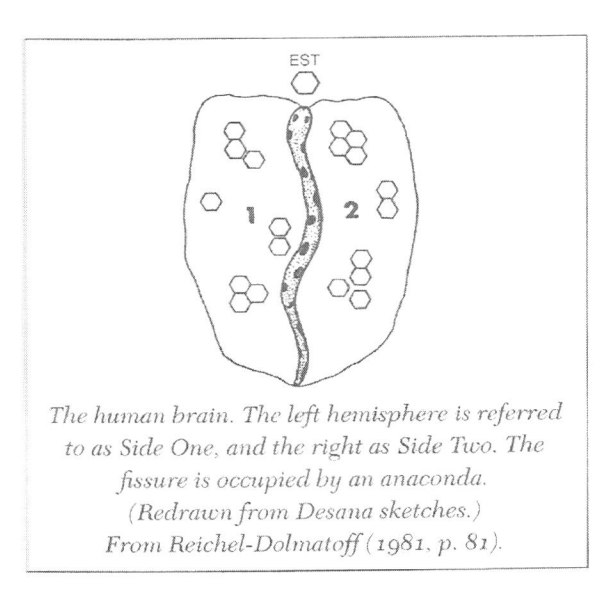

The human brain. The left hemisphere is referred to as Side One, and the right as Side Two. The fissure is occupied by an anaconda. (Redrawn from Desana sketches.) From Reichel-Dolmatoff (1981, p. 81).

On 19th December I'd learnt that Wiggle, Wiggle, Wiggle, linked into the Cosmic Serpent surrounding the planet, which is the same as DNA:

'The earth is surrounded by a layer of DNA-based life that made the atmosphere breathable and created the ozone layer, which protects our genetic matter against ultraviolet and mutagenic rays'. I'd been astonished, humbled, that the means had been given me to help humanity.

In July Elaine's birthday present had also been a Wiggle, Wiggle, Wiggle, but I was going to have to wait till November for my birthday present, but I couldn't wait, Wiggle, Wiggle, Wiggle, was required before then!

The night of the feast day of Mary Magdalen, 22nd July, I used it on my foot for Psoriasis, which I'd had for several months. Foot wiggled, almost jumped, all over the place as Wiggle, Wiggle, Wiggle worked but first I'd had to pray to the right deities before it would. I'd never, when using a Pendulum before for healing, had such a reaction like it. I then discovered every time it was used it would not become active until the right prayer had been said.

Now in the spring of 2010 I couldn't give you a picture of W.W.W. for he'd done a bunk. I couldn't find him anywhere but then I did! He'd fallen behind the wine rack in the hall!

October 18th, 2002, patronal feast day of St. Luke, Patron Saint of Healers , I'd read this beautiful poem.

Eternity

> He who binds to himself a joy
> Does the wingèd life destroy
> But he who kisses the joy as it flies
> Lives in eternity's sun rise. *William Blake (5)*

St. Luke's Day 2003. standing in the kitchen at 7.30 A.M. I'd seen the most wonderful sunrise. I'd looked at the sun, it entered my Third Eye, mesmerised, I read the poem again.

In November I took to Dr. Julian Kenyon at his Dove Clinic for Integrated Medicine in Twyford the remaining two W.W.W. He already had a Kosmed. Russian doctors were working with him on "TELOS *Technologies*." Jude and I had met them on 14th November at a special seminar on Telos Structured Water. They allowed me to watch what they were doing, which was heating water and when it became steam they did their magic and transformed it somehow for healing purposes. I'd known they should have the last one. However they said all their work was now done on computers and dowsing no longer used but I'd insisted they had it, but whether they ever used it I do not know.

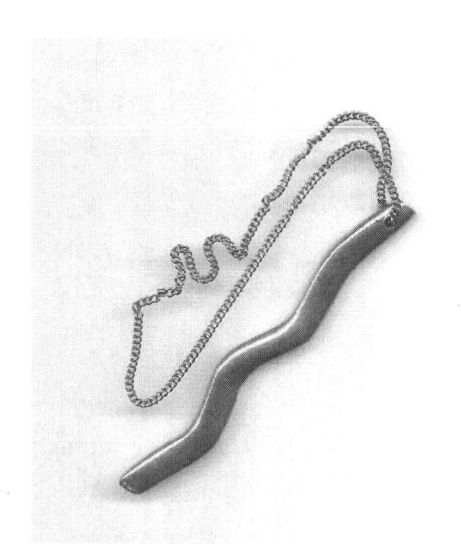

So that is the tale of Wiggle, Wiggle, Wiggle.

1. The Times, 26th October 1999

2. Brewers Dictionary of Phrase & Fable, Cassell

3. The Cosmic Serpent, DNA and the Origins of Knowledge, Jeremy Narby, Tarcher/Putnam, ISBN 0-87477-964-

4. The Woman with the Alabaster Jar, Bear & Company Publishing, ISBN 1-879181-03-7

5. Poem for the Day, Edited by Nicholas Albery, Sinclair Stevenson, ISBN 1-85619-499-X

20. Ripon 2000

Etheldreda of Ely and Wilfrid of Ripon

The B.S.D. Congress in 2000 was again at the College of Ripon and St. John. Saturday night after dinner I was asked if I believed in reincarnation.

"Do you believe it or not? Why is it that dowsers never mention it" I said a few things.

"Well you obviously do".

"Yes, but if someone had said that to me fifteen years ago I would have said:

"No" but life and my thoughts changed after I became a dowser".

Breakfast, Sunday morning, I was sitting next- but- one to a complete stranger, a well known American dowser, Barbara Prisbie, who had joined a team of Editors for the Journal. Suddenly she'd leant towards me, saying :

"Would you write something for the next Journal, you look as though you're bursting to say something and please could I have a photo".

I'd been taken aback, thought for a few seconds and then said:

"Could it be about reincarnation?"

A pause for thought,

"I don't see why not".

" I could write a story about Ripon and St. Wilfrid."

Christians may not believe in reincarnation due to its lack of mention in the New Testament but once it had been. In AD 553 those attending the Ecumenical Church Council in Constantinople agreed that all reference to reincarnation and karma was expunged for the Byzantine Emperor Justinian's wife, Theodora, wished it! (1) However a little bit escaped:- Matthew 17 v.10-13

'The disciples put a question to him. Why then do our teachers say that Elijah must come first? He replied Yes Elijah will come and set everything right. But I tell you that Elijah has already come, and they failed to recognize him, and worked their will upon him; in the same way the Son of Man is to suffer at their hands'.

Then the disciples understood that he meant John the Baptist.

This was foretold in Malachi 4. v 5. 'I will send you the prophet Elijah before the great and terrible day of the Lord comes' (2).

So to illustrate my belief, here is the love story of two saints. but it never appeared in the Journal. Why I do not know, all I do is that I first typed it, and then was requested to put it on disc, which was never returned.

I know I've been all sorts of people, good and bad, plus a butterfly, a fish, a goat and learnt whom my parents were. I've learnt history, visited places, none of which would have happened if those lives had not come to light.

Dowsing was my means of verification. When being a channel of healing between friends, we were always having to forgive each other for the hurts and harms we had caused in previous lives; something to remember if you work in the field of healing. Now the story of two saints.

Etheldreda of Ely and Wilfrid of Ripon

In 1992 a bundle of tourist attraction leaflets plopped through the letterbox of a friend. She dowsed if any were relevant. One was. Ely and a pilgrimage was required so in 1993 we went and William Topliss-Green had joined us.

Dowsing occasionally she'd tried to find out when but got no answer. Finally it fell to me, whilst sitting quietly in August 1993. It would be 17th November, the week before my 60th birthday.

If God deems something should happen, which is very important, it will. For six weeks, on and off, we'd looked after two little grandchildren, Becky and Hayley, for their other Granny, Hazel had become very ill. Us pilgrims were on tenterhooks, I knew I would not go if I was still needed.

Hazel sadly didn't recover, her funeral was the day before our departure. Five days earlier I'd told my husband. To my surprise he hadn't made his usual negative remarks, but said :

"That's a very special Cathedral, it has a special tower".

I was astonished, he seemed pleased we were going. We'd set off, we knew whom we represented, knew we had work to do. We were both channels of healing.

Crisp November weather greeted us, we explored, waited till dusk. On entering the darkened west end, into my consciousness had come:-

"They are blind, they do not know what they are doing!"

Why? An altar had been placed underneath the octagonal tower. We'd felt the tower acted like a chimney to the surrounding fenland, drawing up negative energy. The altar blocked it.

We went to St. Dunstan's chapel and prayed. We'd lifted the altar and suspended it on the tip of the new moon! After I had lifted it down again my companion had made holes in it like 'Gouda cheese', and thus allowed energy to flow through.

Then we'd gone to an exquisite Evensong. I'd learnt that the 8 A.M. Communion Service would be in the Chapel of St. Etheldreda. I'd known I had to go.

A lovely cold, crisp, morning had greeted me. The narrow streets, empty. I'd been early.

The Cathedral was suffused with pink light, streaming through the great east window; under which was the chapel of St. Etheldreda. It was such a contrast from the darkness and glowing candles and brass of the previous night. I'd felt so privileged to be in that place all by myself.

Later with William we'd both returned to the Cathedral, for there was work to be done. You may remember he was mentioned in the Glasgow story about the Islip window.

My job had been to place a twelve sided dodecahedron up the octagonal tower. A dodecahedron is a regular solid, having twelve equal pentagonal bases. A pentagon holds heat, so it is a very powerful symbol. As we'd exited, I'd noticed the great brass bell, the connection I always recognize as being from Colonel Bell.

Then we'd said goodbye to William and set off for St. Etheldreda's Roman Catholic Church. It had a relic – her left hand – found in Sussex in 1810. I knelt before it, I found myself cutting off my left hand, placing it in the shrine. When all was over and I'd restitched my hand back on, I stood up. My hand had become pretty warm.

What my friend sensed whilst all this was going on, I do not know. She'd simply said:

"What does it feel like to have a Church named after you?"

I didn't know, I still couldn't believe. Behind the altar was a stained glass window with three saints – Wilfrid, Mary, Etheldreda. I was deeply shocked. The colour of my clothes were the same as hers. Indigo. As I'd walked down the aisle I could have wept. Then we had lunch and I had a delicious rabbit stew.

Returning on the London bound train, I truly felt I was in the care of the man who'd loved me, Wilfrid.

On our return, my husband had said:

"When I was in the Art Transitus – Lower Sixth Form – at U.C.S. I drew the Octagon to scale, it was very difficult".

I couldn't believe it. As I'd looked at that magnificent structure, I'd felt he'd played a part in its building. Next morning he'd produced the next shock. I was standing in the hall when he'd suddenly appeared brandishing an axe in my face. I'd screamed.

"Keep away, what do you think you're doing?"

"I've cleaned, polished and re-fixed it, the head was loose. I did it whilst you were away!"

That night I read that Owen, Etheldreda's chief retainer, emulated her when she fled to a Nunnery. (See below). He became a monk and had presented himself at a monastery:

'in poor clothes, carrying an axe and a bill hook, to show he aspired to nothing higher than to be a woodcutter for the brethren. (3)

Shocked, I certainly had no doubt as to who he was in that life, and besides he'd kept correcting my pronunciation of her name! I'd done the washing, as I took it outside to put on the line, my husband had called:

"Go and see what I have done for the arch."

I did but I didn't retrace my steps. I continued to walk all round our oblong garden. I'd known what I was doing. I was in a cloister. At one point I picked the frailest, palest, fragrant Penelope rose which I held to my breast.

Finally when I'd circumnavigated my cloister, I'd stopped and turned towards the sun. With deep emotion I'd tried to sing some of the verses of the School Hymn. The tears had rolled. Tears contain the pure elements, the elements of God.(4)

>"Father in Heaven who lovest all,
> Oh hear they children when they call,
> that they may build from age to age,
> an undefiled heritage.
>
> Teach us to bear the yoke in youth,
> with steadfastness and careful Truth,
> that in our time They grace may give,
> The truth whereby the Nations live."
>
> Songs of Praise 488, Rudyard Kipling

Where did we go that afternoon? To the woodcutters for the arch. My 60th Birthday present. When one is 60 one passes through the arch, it is the end of an era, one returns to zero.

I'd gone out in a daze, I homed into staves whilst sitting there. I wondered if

I'd ever been tethered to one. Yes, a goat. That night I'd read that Etheldreda, on her way back to Ely, after she had fled from her second husband, had placed her stave in the ground. A tree had sprung.

I didn't return to my 'rightful mind' until our return and a good cup of tea!

Who was she? Christian Princess, Queen, Abbess and finally Saint, who'd already felt a Bride of Christ when marrying the Prince of the Fenmen. He'd agreed not to consummate the marriage and given her Ely. Three years later she'd become a widow and then for five years did good works, with the help of her controller, Owen.

Then she was required to marry, in York, the sixteen year old son of the King of Northumbria. Owen went to! Again she'd insisted on no consummation. She'd given her wedding present, of Hexham, to Wilfrid! A few years on her husband had decided he wanted his conjugal rights and had asked Wilfrid to persuade his wife to comply. But no, he'd packed her off to a Nunnery. To cut a long story short, she eventually returned to Ely and founded a monastery for men and women and Wilfrid installed her as Abbess.

In 1988 my friend had thought we should be anointed. I'd come away feeling I was a Bride of Christ, and then eaten almonds, a traditional wedding food.

In 1997, after the Glasgow Congress, I had a strange experience on Iona which you have already read, so I'm omitting it now! Later, I really had to heal myself of the fury I had felt, at Columba and his violation of me. That I felt was the underlying cause of why St. Etheldreda had not wished to consummate her marriages!

She died on 23 June 679, of a throat tumour caused by bubonic plague and buried in a plain wooden coffin. When sixteen years later this was opened, she lay 'as one asleep', all sign of the lanced swelling having departed, no signs of decay, she'd even fitted perfectly her new Marble coffin, found by monks in some Roman remains.

This was accepted as a miracle, final proof that she was a great saint. The wooden coffin and grave clothes were preserved as relics, they held great power. Miracles immediately occurred which went on for centuries.

When a young woman, Etheldreda loved necklaces, Gold and pearls. As she lay dying she'd felt it was a heavenly retribution for her vanity. However that didn't stop women wanting to remember her, by wearing a chain of fine small silk, bearing her name. Cheap lace was given the name Audrey, then came tawdry.

I love jewellery, but unlike Etheldreda, I am aware of the power it holds to transmit energy and you may remember that whilst at the B.S.D. York Congress in 1995, Etheldreda was wanting 1930's glass beads!

Due to surgery, I have a scar on my neck. In 1960 a hard lump appeared but when removed it was benign, not tubercular as my Mother – Christened Ethel – feared. In October 1993, I'd spent three days in bed, very happy, very peaceful, on an antibiotic for a tooth abscess. By the third day, I knew why. I had gone through the death of Etheldreda!

Christian King Anna of East Anglia had four daughters, all became saints. Sexburga, widowed after 24 years of marriage to the King of Kent had plenty of children, and founded the monastery at Sheppey. Then she'd become Abbess of Ely on the death of Etheldreda. I knew about her from the guide book, and soon discovered who she was in this life!

In 1997, Sussex Dowsers went to Glastonbury, Diane was motivated to buy 'Celtic Connections'. It was for me! I'd wondered why. There was a story about the miraculous healing properties of the wells in Sheppey.

Saints and Wells – well, well, well!

Suddenly I'd found myself going to East Anglia for a wedding where I'd met Ian Hughes. My husband had declined so I'd decided to spend four days away, thus was free to visit Sheppey! Driving down the lanes, I'd really felt I was in my sister's territory.

There are three wells in Sheppey. One was found to have a Roman coin at the bottom. A second, an effigy of the Triple Goddess. That had miraculous fertility powers. Written about in the press, infertile women were going to see it from all over the world.

I'd learnt the archaeologist behind it all, Brian Slade, was ill. I'd felt I had to see him and discovered where he lived.

I'd knocked at the door, to be greeted with:

"Don't know whether he will see you".

I'd known he would. He gave me some of his books and then sent more.

From him, I learnt about St. Wendreda of Exning, whose symbol is a horse. That became my next destination. Delia had decided to go on a course at Newmarket, I'd decided I'd go as well, but not to the course, I had other business there!

"Could you dowse where we should stay." she'd said.

"Yes".

Turned out to be an ex blacksmiths! I'd known we had to meet at Exning, have lunch there. She didn't like the look of the pub, but nevertheless, that was where we had to go. Whilst eating she'd said:

"Where do I fit in all this".

Turned out she'd been our brother! We didn't find Wendreda's well, the locals wouldn't let on. Until the plague, Exning was a centre for pilgrims to Wendreda's holy well – the market had to move – hence Newmarket but in the 1960's a trainer took his horses to the well for healing!

Next day, I had another trip to Ely meeting Margaret Schmalz, who'd lived in Lindfield. I'd met her at The Yews, when she'd become Secretary to The Friends. She'd needed help, had come to me and during the healing I'd given her crystals to hold. They had such a traumatic effect, she'd trained as a Crystal healer, and later *knew* she had to move to Ely.

She'd taken me to the market, I'd bought ear-rings, and a wonderful cardigan. This was much admired later in the day when Delia and I met up again and we'd gone to a pub bearing the name 'Jude'! A beer fest was in progress, hardly any seats available, we'd eventually found two and asked the men sitting there if we might join them. They had agreed and mine had kept admiring the woolly.

Home again, retelling my adventure, I'd said :

"Guess what happened last night?"

"I suppose you got picked up by a couple of airmen from Lakenheath (American Air Force Base) husband had replied.

"Yes, mine was a Colonel, a Judge, and Delia's a Major, an Attorney!

After Margaret had left, I went into the Cathedral. In the amazing huge Lady Chapel, there was: 'Potters in the Cathedral' Summer Show'. I bought a wonderful Gecko....Lizard if you prefer, venerated by some religions, others not.

For Egyptians and Greeks it represented divine wisdom, good fortune. Christianity the opposite, evil and the devil, and the Zoroastrians Ahriman and the devil (5) and as for the Old Testament, Leviticus 11. v26 - 30 (2)

' You shall regard as unclean all four-footed wild animals

that go on flat paws.... every type of thorn tailed Lizard

and the Gecko....you shall regard them as unclean..

anyone who touches a dead one will be unclean till evening'

But the Celts venerated him, he is depicted on monuments and I love mine but he doesn't wish to have his photo taken.

I next discovered there was a Church dedicated to Wendreda at March. It was then or never. I had a magical drive through the Fenland to find her Church, which just happened to be open! It has the finest double-hammer beam angel roof in England. Over a hundred angels, which beetle or mankind hadn't succeeded in destroying. Wendreda was buried there, in a coffin encrusted with lapis lazuli and precious stones!

After my visit to Sheppey, I'd sent the Sexburga details to Antoinette in Norfolk, for we knew she had been Sexburga! I'd thought she ought to go to Exning. Learning this, she'd phoned.

"Dereham, where I work, venerates St. Withburga, she's the fourth sister! " There is a healing well by the Church, which sprang up when her coffin was removed and taken to Ely."

In 1994, I'd suddenly decided to go to Norfolk, to stay with William and Mim Topliss-Green. I lunched in Bury St. Edmonds with a school friend, Margaret Harbury, but known then as Tubby Graham! That was an amazing meeting, we both had driven into the station at the same moment, timing perfect! She lived near, I'd come all the way from Sussex, M.25, Dartford Tunnel and all that jazz.

After lunch I went cross country. I'd dowsed the route, which included Dereham. Suddenly I'd found myself going on a very strange journey along very narrow lanes – I'd missed my way. Now I think I know why, nothing to do with the hospital where Antionette worked, but to do with her sister, and mine, Withburga.

In Ely in 1993, I'd bought a cross, I knew I had to lend it to 'Sexburga'. She later reckoned it saved her from a dreadful motorway crash and then it came back to me.

As for Wilfrid, twenty years later, due to the jealous woman Etheldreda's husband then married, he'd fled York, eventually landed on the shores of Sussex.

Three months later fate saw I learnt about him.

I'd gone to Earnley Concourse to learn 'How to Sell What you Write'. I'd been there many times, teaching cake decoration and attending other courses. I'd felt it was my second home. Over the years I'd slept all over the place, usually double rooms, but never in single room No 2!

After an exciting and stimulating Saturday, I'd hardly slept. At 4 a.m. I'd heard the first awakening screech of the peacocks, the symbol of saints. (5) I'd pondered whether to get up, drive cross country to a hamlet, Church Norton, beside Pagham Harbour. A Mecca for bird watchers, it had been like a magnet since finding it at the behest of a very young birder.

Once I'd gone at 6 A.M. and driving along had realized it was foolish not telling anyone where I'd gone. This morning I didn't have to. That was a relief. Lying awake I'd felt 'nunnish' in my single bed and single room.

Five o'clock the peacocks summoned again, I'd opened wide a window, heard half a mile away the distant crunch of sea on shingle, Suddenly, softly, I'd heard:

"Etheldreda, Etheldreda, Etheldreda".

Filled with happiness and awe I went to sleep.

Course over, I had difficulty leaving that room, I'd felt drawn by something intangible. I said a few prayers, then went into the little Church which over the years I'd come to love. I was on a 'high', due to the way the course had ended. I was last to read my story and to my surprise it knocked all the others into a cocked hat!

I brought myself down to earth by singing at the top of my voice:

>'Dear Lord and Father of mankind
>forgive my foolish ways!
>Reclothe us in our rightful mind,
>in purer lives they service find,
>in deeper rev'rence praise,
>in deeper rev'rence praise.
>
>In simple trust like theirs who heard,
>beside the Syrian sea,
>in gracious calling of the Lord,
>let us, like the, without a word,
>rise up and follow thee,
>rise up and follow thee.
>
>O Sabbath rest by Galilee!
>O calm of hills above,
>where Jesus knelt to share with thee

> the silence of eternity,
> interpreted by love
> interpreted by love.
>
> Drop thy stilldews of quietness,
> till all our strivings cease;
> take from our Souls the strain and stress,
> and let our ordered lives confess
> the beauty of thy peace,
> the beauty of thy peace.
>
> Breathe through the heats of our desire
> they coolness and thy balm;
> let sense be dumb, let flesh retire;
> speak through the earthquake, wind and fire,
> O still small voice of calm!
> O still small voice of calm!
>
> *John Greenleaf Whittier (1807-1892)*
> *Hymns Old & New,*
> *New Anglican Edition*
> *Kevin Mayhew Ltd. 1996*

I found a hymn book, sang it again but it would not have been as this version, with the last line of each verse repeated.

Just as I was leaving a man burst through the door, burst into conversation about Wilfrid. He'd written about him, he was John Rusbridge. His wife, the late Yvonne Hudson – had tutored me at Earnley in Small clay Sculptures and I'd been to their home. Yvonne had made wonderful tapestries to adorn local Churches and he'd later sent me some photos.

I mentioned Etheldreda, he didn't know about her! We entered into a deep conversation, exchanged addresses then I returned to the Concourse, I needed a cuppa. Then it was that God dropped his next bombshell.

I learnt St. Wilfrid had landed at Church Norton, where his first Church was built! As I left Earnley, which was so dear to me, I knew I could never return. It was finished.

St. Wilfrid's Chaplain and biographer, Eddius Staphanus, built a chapel on the marshes at Manhood End, near Selsey, immortalized in a poem by Rudyard Kipling.

EDDI'S SERVICE

EDDI, priest of St. Wilfrid,
"How do I know what is greatest,
 In his chapel at Manhood End,
How do I know what is least?
 Ordered a midnight service,
That is My Father's business,"
 For such as cared to attend. Said Eddi, Wilfrid's priest.
But the Saxons were keeping Christmas,
"But – three are gathered together –
And the night was stormy as well
Listen to me and attend.
Nobody came to service,
I bring goodness my brethren!"
Though Eddi rang the bell.
Said Eddi of Manhood End.
"Wicked weather for walking"
'And he told the Ox of a Manger
 Said Eddi of Manhood End.
And a Stall in Bethlehem,
"But I must go on with the service
 And he spoke to the Ass of a Rider,
For such as care to attend

> "That rode to Jerusalem.
> The altar-lamps were lighted,-
> They steamed and dripped in the chancel,
> And old marsh-donkey came,
> They listened and never stirred,
> Bold as a guest invited,
> While, just as though they were Bishops,
> And stared at the guttering flame.
> Eddi preached them The Word.
> The storm beat on at the windows,
> Till the gale blew off on the marshes
> The water splashed on the floor,
> And the windows shoed the day,
> And a wet, yoke-weary bullock
> And the Ox and the Ass together
> Pushed in through the open door.
> Wheeled and clattered away.
> And when the Saxons mocked him,
> Said Eddi of Manhood End,
> "I dare not shut His chapel
> On such as care to attend."
>
>   Rudyard Kipling.

That John Rusbridge had been part of that time, I had no doubt. He'd kept cows, on Christmas Day he would find them kneeling. He felt they knew they were on sacred ground.

Once there had been a great Cathedral at Church Norton, it may have ended up in the sea. Local legend maintains that the bells may still be heard pealing on stormy nights, John had heard them when a child. Was it so surprising I'd heard the name of the woman Wilfrid must have loved. Another Church had been built, then its stones had been used to build the Church at Selsey and Chichester Cathedral. All that remains is the small chapel.

Years before, with great excitement, my birders had spied a white-throat. Remember Etheldreda's throat, perfect 15 years after her death. Then I had put my foot down a rabbit hole, sprained my ankle, driven my carload home in great pain. I had no Rescue Remedy After that revelation I wasn't surprised I'd eaten rabbit when I had been in Ely . I think it was trying to make amends!

So Wilfrid had called to Etheldreda. When I wrote this story I realized he had been watching me ever since we came here. Through our kitchen window, on the horizon we see amongst treetops, the top of a Church tower. In 1967 it appeared to be in the Heart of the country.

One Sunday morning we'd set off and found to our astonishment it was in the local town, Haywards Heath! Not only can he see into my kitchen, he can see through the clear windows, into my bathroom! Over the years much enlightenment has come my way whilst soaking in the bath, as you have maybe read!

I had to meet that man, for the first letter he sent contained the info that he had been to Hurstpierpoint College, a local Public School and that the Chapel was dedicated to St. Etheldreda. I'd nearly fainted with shock. One of my first boyfriend's Dr Stewart Duncan, had written letters to me from that establishment. Alan Hoby, who had known me since before I was born, was a pupil, and above all my accomplice to Ely, had gone there many times!

Why hadn't she told me. Apparently she had, but it hadn't registered, I'd had so many other things on my mind. She'd also been astonished when she'd learnt of Etheldreda's connection. It wasn't until I got to Ely that the name came alive. After I'd been, it did. This goes for so much in life. We maybe told things, see them, but they may make no impact until another piece of the jigsaw slots in.

When Wilfrid had arrived he was given land to build his monastery. The people were starving. He taught them how to catch eels, learnt no doubt at Ely! No wonder Earnley had been my second home. At Church Norton, Wilfrid must have often thought of Etheldreda. In 709 A.D he died in Ripon and was buried in his first monastery.

So to Congress 2000, Ripon again. This time I'd wanted to sing in the Cathedral and I wasn't alone. Two other dowsers were with me for the 9.30 service. I had to put £20 in the 'plate'. Ten from me and ten from my friend – Wilfrid. On being told this, she didn't think much of the idea! An American dowser -Al Heiss - had dowsed it the day before, could find no negative energies. I wonder why! The lesson from Isaiah 35 and the prayer after the Communion were most suitable for us three!

> 'Then the eyes of the blind shall be opened, and the ears of the deaf unstopped, then the lame shall leap like a deer and the tongue of the speechless sing for joy. For waters shall break forth in the wilderness and streams in the desert; the burning sand shall become a pool, and the thirsty ground springs of water.'
>
> 'God of all mercy, in this Eucharist you have set aside our sins and given us your healing; grant that we who are made whole in Christ may bring that healing to this broken world, in the name of Jesus Christ our Lord Amen.

And so ends my tale of Wilfrid and Etheldreda. Whether we have been those people or not, it is how we live our lives now which count. However, from what I have learnt over the years, if you believe in reincarnation, it can make an awful lot of sense of this life and the person you are now.

(1) The Truth Vibrations, David Icke, The Aquarian Press, ISBN 1-85538-136-2

(2) New English Bible, Oxford, Cambridge.

(3) St. Etheldreda Queen and Abbess, C.J. Stranks, Republished 1989 Ely Cathedral Shop

(4) The Fruits of The Tree of Life, Omraam Michael Aïvanhov, Editions Prosveta 32, ISBN 2-85566-467-5

(5) An Illustrated Encyclopaedia of Traditional Symbols, J.C. Cooper, Thames and Hudson, ISBN 0 -500-27125-9

21. Jubilee 2003

Manchester was a new venue for the B.S.D. and as the time drew nearer I thought I should go a couple of days earlier to see some of the new developments. I went to the Imperial War Museum, the Lowrie exhibition and bought a new T shirt emblazoned with Manchester!

Michael Rust had hoped the Congress would repeat the success of the 60th, with a similar number, but unfortunately it was not so, only around 150. It wasn't easy getting from one venue to another. I so admired dear Jenny Edwards, her fortitude to not let her illness stop her from doing the things she loved, as she struggled getting from A to B.

I did however have an enjoyable time. I'd ventured into Manchester on the bendy buses and passed the portals of Manchester's famous music college, Cheethams. Sunday I went to the Cathedral and met a man who knew Cuckfield. He had been a friend of Dr. Nutt, who lived next to what is now Marshalls Manor but in those days had simply been 'Marshalls', the home not only of Dr. 'Cocky' Farr but the then 'Cuckfield Medical Practice'! I rather think it went under the title of 'The Surgery'! I seem to remember one sat on the bench lining the wall, it was all dark wood and rather foreboding!

But I have left, what was for me, the highlight of the Congress, till last. Saturday evening the cake was cut. I gave a little speech, gently pointing out maybe areas where the B.S.D. was going astray.

I was dressed in my very best pink! And that was the last time I went to a Congress and it was the last time the Rusts were in charge, for they also retired from their positions in the B.S.D. that evening.

After the Cake was cut, I met a man who wanted healing. On my return I'd told my husband I'd listened to his list of ailments, it could have been him speaking, but there was a difference! The dowser hoped his problems would not get in the way of a little love affair elsewhere in the world! Oh well one never knows what you may hear! And so my stories close with a story about a very special cake which is roughly where I started!

The B.S.D. 70th Birthday Cake

Placed in the entrance to the Barnes Wallis Restaurant, was a six pointed star made from a very heavy fruit cake, with one tablespoon of brandy for every egg. A white cake, piped top and bottom with pale green icing, as per the Journal. A Silver ribbon frieze of cut out little and large stars ran around the sides. The top bore the logo of the B.S.D. with the name around the outside. On each point of the star and in the centre was a firework candle.

I wished to tell the story of how the cake came about, so before the toasts began I'd stood behind it and six members of the Council slowly walked to either side, bearing a taper. It was a most lovely feeling for me, then I told my story.

"Ladies and Gentlemen, Fellow Dowsers.

I would like to tell you how this cake was created. Ten years ago I made the cake for the 60th Birthday celebrations, a diamond whose board was 36" from point to point.

Our then Vice President, Major General Bill Cooper, had wanted a 'big-un'. At that time I said I had made it because I came from the village, Cuckfield, Sussex, where our founder Colonel Bell had lived and dowsing had changed my life. To my astonishment I'd heard my words quoted by our then President, Sir Charles Jessel in his closing address.

Dowsing has still changed my life. Dowsing can lead to spirituality, as stated in Sig's book, and this is a very spiritual cake. It is a cake for 300 and though we are not that number tonight maybe we are in spirit.

The week before Christmas 2002 I 'saw' the cake which lies before you, a six pointed star. I knew it was for the Dowsers. Knowing the Congress was for 300 I knew it should be another big'un. I worked out it could be made in two hexagonal 14" tins, the flat sides would go together, after cutting into the centre of one to make triangles for the 'star'. I phoned Michael Rust and offered my services once again. He later confirmed the Congress sub-committee would like it but stipulated I had to provide the box.

The Box.

We had a sudden death in the family, the oven died, Within 24 hours another was installed and part of it came in a box.

"The cake will fit in that" I'd thought.

It measured 24". I'd originally measured a 28" box was required. This would just have to do and then I'd had to rescue it from going to the tip!

Next major need was where was I going to get a 24" round board. The cake icing shop couldn't provide it. I had various friends who might do one but I didn't feel like involving them. Suddenly, in the middle of July, a couple came to discuss their Heart shaped wedding cake for 2004. I'd explained my American tins were not quite the same shape as English cake drums.

"Oh that doesn't matter, I can get my factory to make it".

Reeling back in my chair I'd thought:

"May I, Can I, Should I," and I did!

I asked:

"No trouble".

This kind young man brought the board from London the next weekend. The Universe truly did provide that board, all I had to do was cover it with Silver paper.

The day I decided to do that, there was a knock on the door and in entered a fellow dowser. She helped with that and with cutting each flat side, to fit the board.

Then I'd stuck it all together with home-made redcurrant jelly!

Now this is a very spiritual cake, you know the symbolism of a six pointed star, and as you eat it I hope you will send its energy out into the Universe"

To great applause we then lit the seven sparkling fireworks, one for each decade of the B.S.D. . To the great relief of the catering manager and Michael Rust there was no smoke and no fire alarms.

So the cake was cut and eaten, and Monday morning it was time to return from Manchester Piccadilly to London and the strangest thing happened. One of my friends was returning on the same train, she had a special First Class deal, £10 and her seat was in the last carriage. Mine was in the first, I'd tried to upgrade. Being Monday morning it would have cost £70!

So there was a whole train between us but our seat numbers were the same, 07F and to my great regret we never met again.

PS. Michael had the bright idea of selling off the 6 points plus dividing the oblong I had stuck together from those cut offs, £10 each, in aid of the Water For Life Appeal, so that cake made I think £100.00 and some of the cake went to America, for which I was more than truly delighted. It was history repeating again, for you may remember some of the 900 cake of Holy Trinity also crossed the pond.

For those of you who do not know the symbolism of the interlocking triangles of the six pointed star, the hexagon, it symbolises 'as above, so below' the upper triangle is masculine, the lower, feminine, the upper solar, heat, life, fire flame, and the lower the opposite. (1)

And so ends my tale of adventures whilst a member of the British Society of Dowsers, but there is a postscript.

1. An Illustrated Encyclopaedia of Traditional Symbols, J. C. Cooper, Thames and Hudson, ISBN 0-500-27125-9

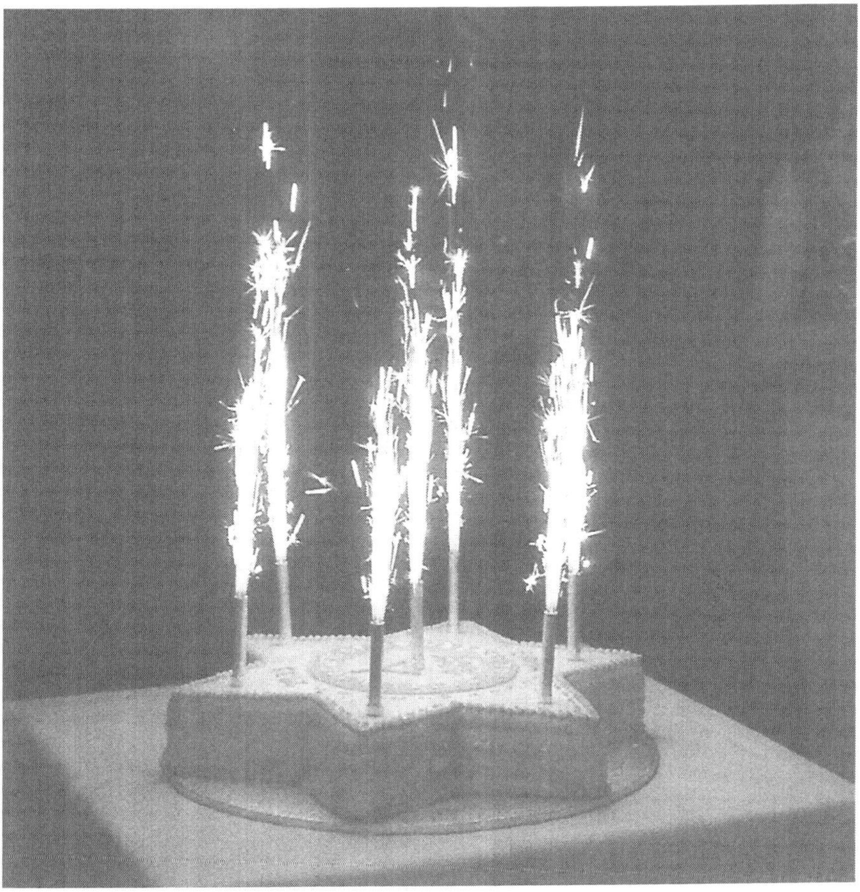

22. Denman College

Now no one knew how I got on the mailing list for 'Ten Years of Dowsing at Denman' at Denman College WI Residential Adult Education College in October 2007.

I'd returned from Egypt to find a flyer about the course celebrating Rosemary Hudson's ten years of teaching Dowsing. I'd immediately **known** I had to go.

I'd first heard of Denman probably over thirty-five years ago. Walking up Broad Street I'd seen someone either loading or unloading her car and though I hardly knew her, I'd asked where she was going or where she had been! Her answer was Denman, and that she tutored floristry.

It was through that meeting that I made the decision that if I could ever get involved with a residential college to teach cake decorating, I would. You could say I put the thought out to the Universe and in the fullness of time the Universe saw that it came about. I became a tutor at Earnley Concourse, near Chichester.

So I got to Denman and learnt of a new Pendulum. A Polo mint! It's brilliant and I also learnt how to deal with dusty blankets!

At the beginning of this Memoir you may remember I met Bob Harris and so I will end with his advice about blankets! Hang them on the line in lovely sunshine and that will kill off all the microbes or whatever it is that makes the dust in them. It solved a problem, for when my husband was alive we used to vigorously shake the blankets together, and oh boy, what a lot of dust sometimes flew out. It had worried me, how I would do it, if he was not around, now I knew.

I had a wonderful time at Denman that weekend and it was all agreed that it was a good thing I went. So I now have a polo mint Pendulum on a white cotton thread, which I think is better for me, than all the polos I ate in my younger days for they probably contributed to my mouthful of fillings but I ate them to stop me from fainting.

I was known as the Polo girl when in the Choir of St. Judes-on-the-Hill, Hampstead Garden Suburb and one Christmas one of the choirmen gave me a box containing four packets! Just think how many Pendulums that would make!

23. Postscript

This journey couldn't have been achieved without dowsing. It led to my learning about myself, looking through the looking glass, just as Alice did.

In May one of my granddaughters, Hayley, had an Alice in Wonderland birthday party and Granny was invited. At the beginning of this book I said I was a Dowser not a Dancer. Well I now have to correct that latter statement!

I'm on YouTube performing The Mad Hatters Granny Dance! I was reminded to add this when on the bus to Lewis and three girls from Plumpton Agricultural College studying Small Insect Science got on and started talking about YouTube, and me, being me, told them I was on it, which resulted in a lovely conversation! So my message is be a dowser, a dancer and don't be shy of talking to strangers when appropriate! But I have to add I wasn't asked by my Grandson Matt if I wanted to be, he just put me on!

So this adventure of mine has truly been a wonderland, the means by which God made the Unseen – Seen and showered me with many blessings. I hope that through reading this epic you will also be showered with the Blessings of God, or if you don't believe in him, you have found it of interest and help.

Now you have read the story, do you want to give it a go, for:

Dowsing is fun!

Dowsing is measurement!

Dowsing makes the unseen seen!

Now try it!

This epic saga was born because *I knew* I had to go to the Lake District on a course with The Friends of Iona and it was at Rydal Hall, opposite Rydal Mount, the last home of Wordsworth. I'd thought I was going to learn about him, because of my love of Keats, but THE LORD I think had another reason. On the first night I'd met Hugo who'd published a book on Stonehenge. I'd said I wanted to do the same but had no money and he said it could be done almost without it and that he would edit it. Little did he know what he had let himself in for.

Added to this the day before I'd met Andy Harrison, me with my apron and heavy hammer in my hand, for my garden was being opened for the NSPCC. I was banging in a notice. I saw this man with his head in the hedge opposite, and seen this happening before and in my inquisitive nature wanted to know *What On Earth He Was Doing.*

"Picking dandelion leaves for my tortoise " and then he'd said: "Aren't you are a friend of Rosie Baxter?"

"Yes" said I, "and Now what do you?"

The result is the book cover. I tell this tale because it shows that when something should be born it will be. Hugo Jenks MSc, is a member of Sussex Dowsers and of the B.S.D. .

P.S .If you want a book to help you on your way, why not try a recently republished timeless book by Dennis Wheatley, a Master Dowser, for it 'is the only introduction you will ever need' :

The Essential Dowsing Guide

Dennis Wheatley

ISBN 978-0-9560733-1-0

www.theaveburyexperience.co.uk

Email: mariawheatley@aol.com

Telephone: 01672 511427

24. The Stepping Stones

I send my love to all the Stepping Stones whether on Planet Earth and elsewhere. If I have left anyone out, please forgive me.

Anderson, Richard feather
Arnold, Anthea
Arnold, Duncan
Ball, Sue
Baxter, Rosemary
Beadon, Wing Commander
Beale, David & Elizabeth
Beattie, John
Bell, Colonel A.H
Bentine, Michael
Bernadette
Betz, Dr. Hans-Dieter
Bezant, Anthea
Bird, Christopher
Breene, Tina/Christina
Brewer, Bob
Brown, Marion
Brown, Sue
Bruce, Jill
Bull, Margaret
Burgess, Hazel
Butler, Jill
Butler, Tom
Campion, Margaret
Carlebach, Sir Philip
Carver, John
Chapman, Ann
Clark, Pam
Clifton, Jean

Collett, Julia
Collins, Seanaid
Collins, Stephanie
Cook, Michael
Cooper, Major General Bill
Cottington, May
Cowan, David
Crampton, Jane
Crossland, Jim
Cuninghame, John and Pru
d'Auria, Paul
Darke, Dorothy & Michael
Davies, Pat
Dawkins, Peter & Sarah
Diamond, Jo
Dubrov, Prof. Alexander
Dulverton, Lady
Duncan, Dr Stewart
Ede, Eric
Edmonds, Philip
Edwards, Jenny
Elaine
Elcome, Delia
Elliott, Marilynne
Ezen, Sylvia (Sylvia Franke)
Farr, Dr. 'Cocky'
Fawcett, Edward
Fellows, Linda E.
Felsenreich, Dr. Maria

Flexman, Celia
Flint, Dr
Fortlage, Kate
Francke, Sylvia
Garcin, Beulah & Philip
Gibson, Mr. and Mrs.
Gola, Albino
Grafe, Dr. Gernot
Granny Hazel
Grushevaya, Dr. Irina
Gubbin, Evonne and Ruby
Guest, Gavina
Guest, Michael
Hancock, Sheila
Harbury, Margaret
Harold, Edmund
Harris, Bob
Harris, Frederick Vivian
Harrison, Andy
Hawkins, Brenda (Tills)
Hazel
Hazell, Will
Heiss, Allen
Higgins, Ann
Hill, Rosemary
Hoby, Alan
Holderness, Charles
Holmes, David
Hubbard, Ethel May
Hubbard, Rose
Hudson, Rosemary
Hudson, Yvonne
Hughes, Ian

Humeston, Eric
Ison, Mary
Jenks, Hugo
Jessel, Sir Charles
Joachim, Bogdam
Judy
Kenton, Leslie
Kenyon, Dr. Julian
King, Joyce
Le Carpentier, Ronald
Lonegren, Sig
Lyons, Jim
MacManaway, Bruce
MacManaway, Patrick
Mainey, Dr
Malins, Ernie
Marjorie
Mayne, Alison
Mayne, Very Revd Michael
Mayo, Veronica and Madeleine
McKenzie, Sandy
McKie, Peter
McLauchan, Madeline
Mehta, Jehanne
Miss Mansell
Mouat, Kit
Peacock, Jenny
Pike, Cyril
Pilkington, John & Elizabeth
Pinna, Jane de
Pope, Pat
Porter/Steele, Jude/Judy
Prisbie, Barbara

Rene, Joan
Roberts, D.W.
Roberts, Julia
Roberts, Mimi
Roll, Michael
Rubie, Judith
Rusbridge, John
Rust, Deirdre
Rust, Michael
Sarah
Sayers, Liz
Schmalz, Margaret
Scofield, Anthony M.
Scott-Elliot, Major General
Scott, Valerie
Sephton, Bob
Shaw, Mike
Shillingford, Diane
Sinclair, Claire
Slade, Brian
Smith, Dr. Cyril
Smith, Raymond
Stenning, Diane
Stevenson, Annie
Stewart, Daphne
Stewart, Gordon
Stewart, Katie
Stone, Barbara
Stringer, Heather
Strong, Christopher and Veronica
Stuart, Professor Peter
Sullivan, Elizabeth

Swann, Rev. Ellionna (Jane)
Tait, Janice
Temple, Jack
Thompson-Walker, Philip & Betty
Thornton, Carole Anne
Tidy, Miss
Tintern, Janet
Tonks, Ruby
Topliss-Green, William & Mim
Tout, Mr
Wallace, Kathryn
Ward, Evelyn
Watson, Michael
Watts, Antoinette
White, Pam
Wilkins, Donovan
Williams, Audrey
Williams, Emma
Williams, Hayley
Williams, Keith
Williams, Madeleine
Williams, Matt
Williams, Maureen
Williams, Rebecca
Williams, Tom
Willings, Heather
Willis, Janet
Wilson, Dan
Woods, Valerie & Claire
Wootton, Jilly
And not least my three sons,
and my husband!

25. Index

Abbess....199, 200, 291, 325, 326, 335

Abbey....122, 127, 141, 173, 195, 198, 202, 205-207, 210, 211, 220, 222, 223, 232, 238, 239, 266, 273, 276, 284, 288-291, 294, 295, 300, 301, 305

Abigail..85

Aborigines...94

absent healing............................81, 255

Adrenals...45

Advanced Dowsers Day Course.........11

Adverse Earth Radiation....................19

Aesculapius.....................................315

Age of Reason.................................278

Ahriman...328

Ainu..136

Aïvanhov, Omraam Mikhaël....90, 115, 120, 138

Alabaster..................................316, 319

Alconbury...71

Alice in Wonderland........................344

All Souls Day 1990......................8, 82

Allen, Benedict.....................87, 94, 120

Alsatian..12

Althorpe...276

Aluminium.........11, 96, 108, 244, 273, 279, 280, 314

Alzheimer's..............................273, 280

Amalgam..271

Amazon..316

Amen.........42, 252, 253, 256, 310, 335

America...............................201, 278, 339

American.....71, 72, 93, 129, 206, 211, 278, 320, 328, 335, 338

Amethyst........205, 206, 209, 211, 219, 267, 296

Ammon.....................................252-256

Amphitrite..203

Amun..252

anaconda...316

Ancient Man......................................61

Angel of Air.....................................126

angle Iron....................................11, 91

Anglican............................276, 291, 331

Ankh..48, 49

Antakarana......................................255

Anthropologist..................................316

Anthurium Scherzerianus.....................53

Aquarius..265

Archangel..........................116, 117, 126

Argyll..174

Armistice Day....................................185

Army.......................100, 228, 281, 290

Arnica..108, 110

Aromatherapy..........110, 144, 152, 248

Arran...198, 202

Arrow of Love.....................................59

Art Deco...78

Art Nouveau..79

Ascension Day............................283, 284

Astarte..272

Astrology..........114, 148, 150, 229, 240

Atlantean.............................56, 110, 198

Atlantis..............................48, 56, 97, 200

atomic...............................18, 57, 60, 169

Aubrey, John..............................130, 137

Aukland......................................303, 304

Aura.....37, 75, 84, 104, 107, 110, 160, 170, 186

Aura Soma....................................75, 104

Auric Field..................................250, 255

Australia........37, 87, 94, 156, 170, 189, 232, 266, 303

Austria......................22, 49, 79, 103, 104

Autumn Equinox...............................131

Avebury..........126, 129-131, 137, 139, 272, 286, 306

B.S.D. 7, 11, 12, 47, 51, 68, 69, 91, 96, 119, 124, 140, 143, 153, 171, 177, 181, 183, 286, 294, 304, 306, 315, 320, 326, 336, 337, 339

Babar..211

Bach......................22, 76, 128, 176

Balcombe..283

Baltic..131

Banbury...167

Banks, Joseph....................................156

Barrowfield..51

Basalt...........79, 96, 103, 104, 195, 215

Beaconsfield......................................50

Beadon, Clive....................................295

Bedhampton......................................172

Belarus..217

Belladona..280

bells.....46, 61, 66, 150, 164, 165, 242, 243, 289, 302, 333

Bells Publishing.................................12

350

Belsize Park..................................184
Beltane...110
Bennu Heron..................................241
Benton Castle................................166
Bergamot.......................................209
Betelgeuse.....................................224
Betjeman, Sir John..................121, 130
Beverly...147
Bible...67, 77, 119, 181, 253, 280, 335
Big Ben..97
Binah......................................114, 117
Biochemistry.............................135, 139
Biro..39, 52
Bishop Colman.............................236
Black Death..................................291
Black Mountains..........................283
Black Watch..179-181, 192, 208, 281
Blake, William...............................318
Bloodline................................237, 240
Bloody Mary...................................80
Boerickes Materia Medica..............96
Boron..29
Bosnia...131
Brass......41, 61, 75, 84, 125, 256, 294, 314

Brecon Beacons............................283
Brennan, Barbara Ann............248, 270
Briar Rose...........................254, 258, 259
Brighton.............71, 183, 267, 268, 271
Bristol Cancer Centre..................10, 18
Bristol Diet.................................11, 13
Bristol University's Geophysics Department.................................272
Britain........54, 61, 138, 139, 169, 170, 278, 282, 290, 304
British Museum.........................260, 270
British Society of Dowsers..6, 7, 63, 82, 340
Bronze.........................61, 78, 165, 272
Buddha..........................23, 77, 165
Buddhism..................................78, 110
Buddhist.......................................77, 78
Burial Ground...............................294
Bury St. Edmonds.................278, 329
Cabbalah................................114, 116
Caduceus......................................315
Calcium...................................28, 262
Calendar Club...............................287
Calvary..258
Camberley.......................................12
Canada....................................74, 219

Canadian................97, 104, 112

Cancer................9, 11, 13, 118

Cancer Contact................75

Cancer Contact Fund................18

Cancer, Zodiac................293

Cancers................9, 150

Cancerwise................279

Candida................246-249, 270

Canterbury................47, 112, 131, 212

Carrot, Jasper................96

Cathedral.....17, 22, 88, 105, 112, 130, 149, 153, 155-157, 163, 186, 194-197, 212, 215, 277, 280, 297-300, 305, 322, 328, 333, 335, 336

Catherine Wheel Inn................137

Celeste................211

Celtic.....135, 191, 194, 212, 236, 243, 275, 326

Celtic Benediction................243

Celts................328

Centre for Implosion Research........168, 170

cervix................9, 13, 72

Chakra 23, 37, 42, 44, 45, 54, 94, 118, 148, 150, 156, 160, 161, 174, 176, 202, 210, 211, 251, 254, 258, 260, 269, 294, 310

Channel Tunnel................126

Charles Clarke................12

Chartres................109

Cheethams................336

Chernobyl................217

Chevy Chase................64

Chi Kung................162, 170

Chi Rho................242

Chichester...22, 50, 88, 112, 140, 156, 280-282, 333, 342

Chichester Cathedral................280, 333

Children of the New Forest................277

china................78, 258, 264

China................251

Chinese.229, 230, 251, 257, 258, 265, 303

Chiron................126, 142

Chokmah................114

Christ........46, 52, 62, 79, 88, 113, 125, 160, 175, 209, 237, 258, 310, 311, 325, 335

Christian................10, 46, 258, 259, 272

Christianity................328

Christmas.......51, 73, 92, 96, 123, 236, 247-250, 255, 256, 263, 265, 278, 298, 300, 314, 332, 333, 338, 343

352

Chrome..271

Chromium...28

Church. .17, 46, 53, 63, 71, 77, 87, 88, 90-92, 123, 130, 145, 146, 150, 162, 165, 191, 194, 207-211, 214, 215, 236-238, 274, 281, 284, 291, 297-301, 306, 307, 320, 323, 328-334

Church in 1991...................................278

Church Norton..........................329, 332

Cinderella..68, 84

Cirencester....121, 124, 127, 142, 174, 271, 274, 286, 287, 305

Cistercian.................................... 290, 291

Clair Hall..263

Clairvaux..290

Cleopatra's Needle.................................97

Clumber Park..149

Cocks..46

Colchester..271

Collins, Joan..233

Colm..194, 215

Columba.........174, 176, 194, 209, 210, 212-215, 236, 239, 293, 301, 325

Communion......87, 149, 155, 158, 205, 291, 297, 322, 335

Complimentary Centre...................10, 47

Concourse..331

Congress.......28, 47, 48, 50, 51, 57, 62, 68, 72, 74, 88, 90, 95, 105, 111, 118, 121, 124, 126, 134, 143, 144, 147, 149, 168, 171, 173, 174, 176, 181, 185, 195, 199, 209, 214, 218, 239, 243, 271, 272, 274, 286, 288, 289, 293, 294, 296, 303, 304, 315, 320, 325, 326, 335, 336, 338

Conquistadors......................................316

Constantine..242

Constantinople..............................77, 320

Copen, Bruce...............................257, 270

Copper...16, 23, 24, 28, 29, 56, 58, 59, 61, 62, 75, 190, 252

Corinthians..62

Cornish Sinfonia..................................277

Cornwall..121

Cosmic.................45, 241, 315-317, 319

Cosmic Egg of Creation......................241

Cosmic Serpent..................315-317, 319

Cosmic Tree..107

Cove..132, 137

Cowfold...147

Crawley..21, 162, 263

Crickhowell..................................283, 285

Cronus..60

Crop Circle...307

353

Cross Pattée..................................95
Crown of Thorns........................254
Croydon......................................287
Crucifixion.................................237
Crystal....43, 51, 52, 56, 58-60, 62, 72, 73, 90, 99, 105, 137, 164, 179, 185-187, 196, 200, 219, 245, 260, 269, 270, 288, 289, 327
Cuckfield....8, 9, 24, 37, 41, 49-51, 63, 75, 87, 88, 141, 143, 160, 182, 184, 191, 277, 281, 283-285, 290, 297, 302, 312, 336, 338
Cuckfield Medical Practice...............336
Cumbria......................................135
Curie, Marie................................251
Curry......................16, 22, 23, 25, 26, 44
Curry, Dr. Manfred........................26
Cygnus Magazine..........................175
Cyprus..228
Dalai Lama...................................110
Danish..217
Darke, Harold..............................236
Dartford Tunnel.......................70, 329
Daventry.....................................275
Dead Orgone Energy...................248
Dead Sea Scrolls...............66, 98, 120

Dear Lord and Father 330
Denman College...........................342
Dereham.....................................329
Desdana......................................316
Devils Dyke.................................183
Diana...................................175, 272
Dilgo Khyentse Rinpoche 93, 109, 110, 112
Divine Inspiration..........................68
DNA.............................316, 317, 319
dodecahedron..............................323
Dolphin.......................................203
Dominic................................194, 215
Doors of the Mind....................55, 74
Dove Clinic..................................318
Dulwich Health Society...........21, 29
Dunlin..205
Duodenum............................247, 248
Earl of Crawford..........................181
Earnley........................331, 332, 334
Earnley Concourse............50, 329, 342
Earth Energies Group.....181, 183, 286, 306
Earth Goddess.............................248
Earth Radiations................16, 21, 25

354

Earthdome Ltd	98
East Anglia	326
East Barsham	275
Easter	236, 237
Ebony	221, 224, 232
Ecology	71
Ecumenical Church Council	77, 320
Edinburgh	210, 216, 233
Edward King House	153
Edwardian	151
Egypt	113, 141, 142, 251, 252, 256, 342
Egyptian	48, 118, 223, 244, 249, 252-254, 257, 270, 315, 328
Electricity	28, 45, 46
Electrolux	39, 40
Elephant	72, 156, 211
ELF	28
Elijah	77, 321
Ely	79, 156, 200, 222, 234, 300, 320, 321, 325-327, 329, 334, 335
Emerald Innovations	244, 269
Emsworth	279
Encyclopedia	61, 62, 66, 97, 239, 240, 270
Endocrine Glands	23, 37
England	87, 113, 122, 129, 147, 149, 180, 219, 274-276, 300, 328
Enoch	66, 98, 120
Epiphany	160, 251
Epping Common	285
Escape Society	155
Esplanade	151
Essene	56, 65, 66, 98, 99, 120
Estonia	131
Etheldreda	79, 87, 144, 301
Ether	57, 90
Euston	175, 231
Evensong	78, 146, 322
Evesham	275, 282
Exning	327, 328
Fakenham	275
Far Memory	55
Faro	48, 56
Fasciolopsis buskii	244
Federation of Master Builders	98
Ferguson, Sarah	289
Fingal's Cave	195, 197, 198, 206, 209, 210, 216
Fionnphort	193
Fleche d'Amour	59

Flint....................40, 41, 133, 136, 185

Folkestone................................126

Fondant Icing..........................313

Fort William.............................188

Fountain International...........218

Fountains Abbey......................291

France..............................150, 200

Francis Holland School......184, 234

Francium..................................258

Franklin, Benjamin................211

Free Will..................................143

Freemasonry...........................237

French..49, 62, 75, 215, 222, 278, 294

Fulham....................260, 262, 263

Gabriel....................................116

Gaelic...............................194, 215

Gaia..248

Gall Bladder...............52, 53, 110

Gallery of Modern Art......223, 232

Garcin, Beulah & Philip..........294

Garden of Eden......145, 148, 151, 152, 239

Gatekeeper Magazine........174, 239

Gatekeeper Trust....................198

Gaviscon..................................280

Gecko..328

gelatine paste..........................313

Geomancy..................................52

Geopathic Stress 11-13, 15, 16, 22, 25, 28, 91, 248

Geophysicists..........................272

Georgian....................123, 145, 164

Germany..............................15, 21

Gerson, Max..............................38

Gianni Schicchi.......................268

Girl Guides..............................273

Glasgow..........171, 173, 177, 179, 180, 186, 187, 205, 210, 218, 220, 221, 223, 226, 230-233, 242, 287, 302-304, 322, 325

Glastonbury............281, 302, 306, 326

Glenny, Evelyn..........................61

Gloucester........................244, 269

Gloucestershire...............121, 167

God.....7, 12, 19, 35, 54, 60, 62, 65, 67, 77, 78, 83, 84, 94, 95, 97, 107, 114, 116, 117, 123-127, 138, 139, 144, 156, 159, 160, 181, 199-201, 209, 218, 228, 231, 232, 249, 253, 272, 285, 307, 311, 315, 321, 324, 332, 335, 344

Goddess...61, 141, 165, 203, 229, 248, 326

Goddess of Love...............................61

Gold...41, 46, 74, 75, 90, 110, 123, 143, 157, 200, 207, 222, 241, 260-262, 315, 326

Golden...59, 63, 81, 104, 113, 114, 124, 292

Gonads..45

Goodwood House.........................279

Gordon, Rolf....................................23

Gors Fawr......................................166

Gothic...............127, 134, 138, 196, 242

Granite..............................186, 217, 239

Graves, Robert........................223, 240

Great Brington..............................275

Greek..........................59, 242, 301, 315

Greeks..................................60, 258, 328

Green Jack.......................................61

Green Man....................................277

Gregory, Bottley and Lloyd......262, 263

Guardian of the Threshold................116

Guinness....................133, 157, 219, 292

Guinness Book of Records.............50

Hafnium..28

Hall, Jerry.....................................289

Hampstead................173, 228, 236, 343

Harper Collins.......................113, 120

Hartman..16

Hartmann, Dr. Ernst......................27

Harvey, Andrew............................77

Haskins, Susan.............................113

Hatchards..73

Hatton Garden.......................260, 268

Havant.....................................47, 172

Hawkwood..........................168, 241, 243

Haywards Heath..........9, 12, 19, 51, 63, 113, 158, 182, 190, 191, 237, 263, 291, 334

healing...12, 52-54, 60, 61, 73-75, 81, 84, 85, 95, 96, 99, 103, 107, 112, 118, 120, 123, 130-133, 136, 141, 143, 147, 156, 157, 160-163, 165, 167, 178, 179, 185, 186, 190-192, 208-210, 213, 244-246, 249, 251, 254, 255, 260, 262, 264, 267, 270, 272-274, 276, 281, 284, 291, 296, 297, 302, 304, 309, 312, 315, 317, 321, 322, 326, 327, 329, 335

Healing Force..................................61

Health Centre................................294

Heart.........3, 16, 37, 38, 42, 44, 45, 80, 116, 119, 148, 182, 187, 190, 198, 202, 226, 228, 253, 257, 267, 310, 315, 334, 338

Heathfield..55

Hebrides	197
Heliocobacter pylori	249
Helmsley	287, 288
Henrietta Barnet Junior School	183
hexagon	340
Hexham	144, 286, 289, 300, 301, 325
Hieroglyphics	252
High Altar	295, 298, 299
Highland Chieftains	215
Highland Regiment	180
Highley Manor	9, 18
Hindu	231
Hoffman	44
Hoggarth, James	7
Holland	45, 235
Holst, Gustav	60
Holy Grail	237, 240
Holy Trinity	182
Holy Trinity Church Magazine	285
Holy Trinity Young Mothers	50
Homoeopathic	9, 55, 96, 135, 176, 177, 218, 219, 249, 257, 280
Homoeopathy	10, 137, 239
Horsham	200, 256, 293
Horus	253
Houghton St. Giles	275
House of Commons	97
House of Eliott	61
House of Fraser	223, 233
Houses of Parliament	306
Howards Way	277
Huguenot	9
human sacrifice	53
Hunmanby	145, 286
Hurstpierpoint College	334
Hydrogen	133, 158, 230, 254
hysterectomy	9
Icke, David	77, 119, 335
Icomkill	215
Imperial War Museum	336
Incorporated Dental Hospital	225
International Association for Humanitarian Cooperation	218
Io	272
Iona	79, 141, 171, 173–176, 187, 190, 191, 193–196, 198, 199, 201–203, 205–208, 212, 213, 215, 219, 220, 225, 232, 237, 272, 293, 301, 325
Ipecacuanha	257
Ireland	131, 176, 194, 201, 215, 217, 239

Irish.............................194, 201, 215, 236

Iron. 11, 16, 19, 20, 24, 26, 28, 29, 91, 126, 289, 294

Isis...244-246, 256

Islington District Colposcopy Clinic 177

Islip window...222

Jade...80, 86, 229, 261, 262, 264, 265, 267, 269

Japanese...136

Jehovah..114

Jejunum..247

Jerusalem....................209, 210, 219, 333

Jesus......62, 66, 77, 113, 125, 147, 195, 236, 254, 298, 300, 308, 310, 311, 330, 335

Jones, Dr. Wynn......................................283

Journal..........12, 49, 70, 210, 256, 304, 320, 321, 337

Jupiter...................................61, 252, 272

Justinian..320

Karnak.............244, 249-252, 254-258

Keats.......171-173, 193, 195-197, 213, 215, 239, 270

Keiller, Alexander...................................132

Kelvin....171, 174, 177, 178, 189, 190, 192, 208, 219, 225

Kelvin Conference Centre.........171, 178

Kether....................................114, 116, 126

King Aldfrith..301

King Edward House..............................157

Kingley Vale..167

Kings Cross..............174, 175, 233, 234

Kings Lynn..275

Kipling, Rudyard....235, 324, 332, 333

Kosmed..312

Kremlin.....................................92, 113, 209

Krishna...77, 78

Labour Party...206

Labradorite.................................185, 289

Labyrinth......72, 73, 85, 86, 90, 94, 97, 99-101, 104, 107, 109, 117, 118, 125, 135, 144, 166, 241-243

Lady Richeldis de Faverches.............276

Lakenheath...328

lapis lazuli...268

Larkin, Jill..302

Laser............28, 72, 123, 151, 177, 260

Latin...59, 147

Lawrie, John...218

Leicestershire...181

Lemurian...110

359

Leptons 169

Lethbridge, T.C ... 11, 13, 20, 35, 36, 43, 60, 66

Leviticus 328

Lewes 185, 278, 281

Ley Line. 11, 15-19, 21, 22, 25-28, 36, 38, 41, 45, 97, 198, 256, 270

Light Emerging 248, 270

Limestone 186, 217, 239

Lincoln..153, 155-159, 171, 179, 189, 294

Lindfield 270, 327

Lizard 328

Loch Katrine 231

Loch Staonaig 202

Lockerbie 80, 81, 83, 84

Lockyer, Sir Norman 256

London 29, 47, 99, 120, 123, 124, 137, 140, 166, 220, 232, 234, 243, 246, 248, 260, 262, 265, 268, 288, 315, 323, 339

Long Meg 135

Lord's Cricket Ground 266

Lorraine 49

Loughborough University 149

Lowrie 336

Lycidas 196, 197

Lyttelton 303

M.25 .... 70, 329

M.Y. Club 9, 190

Mabey, J.C 55

Macdonel 215

Mackintosh, Rennie 176, 188, 220, 224

Macleans 215

Mad Hatters Granny Dance 344

Magdalene, Mary..222, 230, 237, 299, 317

Mager 38, 294, 295

Mager Rosette 38, 294, 295

Mager, Henri 294

Magicians 60

Magnesium 28, 262

magnetic field 168, 247

magnetism 36, 41, 46

Malketh 117

Malmesbury...121-123, 127, 128, 138

Malta 91

Maltese Cross 91, 95

Manchester 105, 336, 339

Manhood End 332, 333

Marble.....78, 186, 203, 206, 217, 218, 239, 325

Marlborough..................................130

Mars................................148, 254

Marshalls Manor..............................336

Marx, Carl..97

Mary Magdalene...113, 120, 223, 236, 237, 316

Mary of Egypt...................................113

Master Number................................175

Matthew, Gospel of 77, 320

Maze..72, 76

MCC.....................105, 137, 266, 267

McLellan Galleries............................226

McLeod Centre................................211

Mecca..329

Medicine..............................13, 315, 318

Medieval glass....................................78

Melissa..248

Mendelevium.....................................28

Mendelssohn..................................198

Mercury..................................271, 272

Meridian Associates..........................126

Merlin...............121, 123, 126, 130, 133

Mermet...75

Metatron..126

Methodist..274

Middle Ages......................................60

Middlesex Hospital............................22

Milton...197

Minsk..216

mobile phone masts........................306

moon..58

Moorfields Eye Hospital....................166

Mother Earth...............23, 132, 174, 247

Mother of Pearl....................118, 119

Mother Teresa..................................198

Mothering Sunday.............................53

Mousehole Cat................................277

Mozart..273

Mt. Olympus.....................................60

Mull........171, 193, 195, 205, 208, 216

Naishpur...204

Napalm..151

Narby, Jeremy..................................316

National Federation of Spiritual Healers.................................99, 132

National Gallery......................210, 237

National Railway Museum................151

Nazareth...276

Nazi..15
Negative Green........233, 244, 245, 247, 251, 257, 270
Neolithic..17
Neptune..203
New Testament...........................237, 320
New York.....................................230, 248
New Zealand 156, 192, 210, 287, 303, 304, 309
Newbury..122
Newcastle..144
Newmarket................................286, 327
Nitrogen...29
Norfolk..107, 126, 171, 277, 328, 329
Norman...276
north 62, 71, 121, 168, 194, 205, 211, 215, 272, 287, 289
North....23, 26, 71, 121, 145, 245, 303
Northumbria.................144, 194, 325
Norton......................................333, 334
Norwegian.......................................215
Norwegians............................194, 215
Norwich..277
NSPCC...263
Numerology..............120, 163, 170, 175
Nunnery...............................194, 324, 325

Nutt, Dr...336
Nystatin..248
oak..................................41, 125, 136
Oban......174, 187, 188, 192, 193, 214, 219
obelisk....56, 58, 59, 86, 87, 90, 92, 94, 107, 132, 206, 301
Oberammergau...........................49, 108
Occident..258
Old Cuckfieldians.........................183
Old Testament...............................328
Olive Oil..................................62, 296
Omar Khayyám......202, 203, 238, 239
Opal.................123, 249, 250, 309, 310
Ophiuchus......................................315
Orient..258
Osiris...............................244, 245, 248
Osmium...28
Oxygen..262
Padmasambhava..................94, 109, 110
Pagham Harbour............................329
Paine, Thomas......................278, 282
Pakistan..107
Palace of Westminster....................124
Palmer, Magda................................260

Pancreas..45
Papua New Guinea........................87, 88
Passion Play......................................49, 108
Passover...236
Pastilage..313
Patron Saint of Sinners......................113
Paul d'Auria Centre............................274
Pauli..169
Peace Chapel......................................293
Pendulum. 7, 9-11, 18-27, 35, 36, 38-42, 51, 52, 58-60, 72, 73, 75, 79, 84, 91, 96, 98, 103, 105, 119, 125, 127, 137, 141, 153, 164, 174, 179, 183, 184, 186, 188, 193, 198, 222, 224, 233, 244-247, 249-252, 254, 255, 257, 258, 270, 271, 288, 291, 294, 296, 312, 317, 342
Pendulum Kit................73, 119, 129, 139
Penny Brohn Centre..............................10
Pentagram....................................58, 60, 81
Pentatonic..........................211, 243, 269
Periodic Table..........................29, 251, 255
Persia...204, 269
Peru...74
Peterborough......................................275
pheromones...96
Philistine..202

Phoenix..239, 241
Phosphorus.........................176, 177, 247
Physics.................................170, 183, 301
Piccadilly..............................73, 140, 339
Picts...194, 215
Pilgrims Way..61
Pineal...44
Pisces..229
Pitcheblend..251
Pituitary..44, 46
Planet Suite..60
Planetary Spirits................................125
Plato...56
Pleurisy..291
Plumpton Agricultural College........344
Pluto...232
Poet Laureate....................................121
Poland..251
Poldark..277
Polonium...................251, 252, 255-258
Polovtsian Dances............................265
Pont Hywel Mill...............................166
Portugal...48
Poseidon..203
Pot Basil..172

prayer..310

Presbyterains.....................................215

President........48, 49, 70, 72, 74, 80, 81, 90, 93, 104, 125, 181, 218, 288, 293, 304, 338

Prince of the Fenmen............................325

Princess Diana............................176, 276

Princess Elizabeth...............................267

Psoriasis...317

Ptah...249, 250, 253

Public School.....................................334

Puccini...268

Pugin.................124, 127, 134, 138, 139

Pyramid..............73, 118, 190, 245, 301

Pyrites...74, 75

Pyrites, Fools Gold................................74

Pythagoras....................................57, 60

Qabalism..114

QE2.....................................69, 74, 112

Quantum..169

Quarks...169

Quartz. 26, 59, 62, 105, 179, 233, 260

Queen.........22, 79, 146, 161, 187, 221, 223, 224, 231, 233, 268, 325, 335

Queen Elizabeth..................................268

Queen Etheldreda................................79

Quicksilver...272

R. Holt & Co......................................260

R.I.C.S..164

Ra...253, 256

Radi Corder...16

Radionics..........126, 127, 133, 245, 297

RadiTech......................16, 21, 23, 35, 44

Radium..22, 251, 257

Rameses....................................252, 253

Ransome, Arthur.................................184

Rectory............................63, 145, 147, 288

Reichel-Dolmatoff, Gerardo.............316

Reiki..125

Rein, Dr. Glen....................................160

reincarnation...77, 213, 238, 320, 335

religion................37, 253, 270, 278, 328

Requiem..302

Rescue Remedy........128, 176, 221, 231, 291, 334

rhododendron......................................54

Rievaulx...........289, 290, 292, 300, 305

Ring our Wild Bells..............................61

Ripon...38, 68, 85, 286, 292, 293, 295, 298, 300, 301, 303-305, 315, 320, 321, 334, 335

River Kennet............................122, 131

364

River Thames................................124

Robin Hood...................................149

rock crystal..............................52, 60

Roman......53, 56, 60, 61, 76, 147, 237, 258, 301, 315, 323, 325, 326

Roman Catholic.....147, 236, 237, 301, 323

rose Quartz...................................233

Rosicrucian...................................116

Rossetti, Dante Gabriel.......................226

Rota, L.G.V......................................55

Roughton.......................................277

Round Table...................................192

Royal Agricultural College.....121, 124, 138, 142

Royal Commonwealth Society for the Blind......................................19

Royal Exchange...............................223

Royal Fusilier........................180, 258

Royal Regiment..............................180

Russia...79, 83, 92, 111, 269, 312, 318

Rutile...59

Rydal..344

Sadalfon...117

Salisbury..................................10, 59

Salvation.......................................281

Samarian..28

Sanctuary.........................9, 131, 141

Sapphire....................................96, 97

Sarum Hall.....................................184

Sauchiehall Street.............226, 228-230

Saxa Rubra.....................................242

Saxon...........17, 76, 122, 300, 332, 333

Scalar Field................................49, 57

Scarborough.............144, 145, 147, 151

Schumann.............................16, 27, 45

Scotland..........171, 175, 180, 210, 219, 223, 233, 239

Scott, Sir Walter..............................187

Scottish Dowsers..............................72

Scrumpy Jack.............................92, 97

Sea of Tranquillity..60, 91, 93, 94, 103

Seaweed................................108, 110

Secretary......12, 47, 80, 120, 218, 233, 304, 327

Selenium....................................27, 28

Selsey.....................................332, 333

Seneco Greyii..................................113

Sephirah...116

Sephiroth...............................114, 117

Sephirotic..............................114, 126

Serpentine	203
Setterington	184
Seventh Heaven	230, 302
Severn Vale	241
Sexburga	326, 328, 329
Shakespeare	7, 272
Shamanic Wisdom	311
Shamanic Wisdom cards	308
Shamans	107, 308, 316
Shanti	77
Sheppey	326, 328
Sherwood Forest	149
Shoreham	158
Shropshire Blue Cheese	250
Signal Hills	202
Silbury	130, 281
Silica	29, 133
Silicon	262
Silver	20, 95, 97, 123, 129, 165, 212, 216, 233, 251, 260, 261, 271, 272, 298, 314, 337, 339
Silver Birch	107, 112, 113
Singer, A.	177
Siva	231
Sleeping Beauty	259
Smith, John	206
snake	37, 315
Sodium	28
Solar Energy	66
Solar Plexus	37, 42, 45, 54, 118, 150
Solomon's Temple	295
Souls	77, 78, 82, 94, 227, 294, 331
South African	233
Southampton	10, 47
Southlands Hospital	158
Southwell Minster	149, 150
soya milk	10
Spanish	74
Sparsholt	47, 68, 72, 92, 97, 98
Sparsholt Agricultural College	47
Spider Web Coil	304
Spiritual Dowsing	129, 135, 138
spirituality	12, 129
St. Bartholomew	238
St. Bartholomew's Hospital	22, 160, 206
St. Bernard	150, 290
St. Bride	210
St. Catherine	137
St. Catherines Hospice	263

St. Columba...174, 176, 192, 199, 201, 202, 204, 205, 212, 213, 236, 301

St. David.................................162, 163

St. Dunstan...................................322

St. Etheldreda..........200, 236, 320-326, 329-331, 334, 335

St. George.............................173, 266

St. Hughes Monastery............................147

St. John...........65, 68, 85, 236, 286, 320

St. John the Baptist.................53, 77, 321

St. Joseph of Arimathea.......................237

St. Jude..312

St. Judes-on-the-Hill..........................343

St. Luke.............................160, 318

St. Mary........................66, 163, 195

St. Matthew....................................62

St. Michael...................................131

St. Mungo........................186, 221

St. Peter..................236, 237, 298

St. Simon.....................................312

St. Wendreda..................................327

St. Wilfrid......236-238, 291, 293, 298, 299, 301, 303, 320, 332

St. Withburga.................................329

Staffa................................196, 215

Stamford............................171, 191

Stannum.......................................135

Stansted...........................172, 248

Staphanus, Eddius................................332

Steiner, Rudolf.....................66, 116, 243

Stepping Stones...........................

   Anderson, Richard feather..72, 100, 104, 118

   Arnold, Anthea................................19

   Arnold, Duncan................................68

   Ball, Sue................................186

   Baxter, Rosemary.....................24, 345

   Beadon, Wing Commander....94, 95

   Beale, David............54, 73, 125, 296

   Beale, Elizabeth................................128

   Beattie, John...22

   Bell, Colonel A.H. 6, 8, 9, 12, 48, 49, 55, 59, 61, 63, 73, 75, 119, 127, 128, 133, 136, 140, 144, 151, 153, 181, 183, 234, 303, 323, 338

   Bentine, Michael........55, 66, 72, 74, 113, 119, 120

   Bernadette..129

   Betz, Dr. Hans-Dieter......................90

   Bezant, Anthea................................272

   Bird, Christopher...............72, 93, 94

   Breene, Tina/Christina..................143

Brewer, Bob..........................271
Brown, Marion.......................18
Brown, Sue.....................272, 273
Bruce, Jill............145, 151, 152, 239
Bull, Margaret.....................200
Burgess, Hazel..............37, 278, 282
Butler, Jill..........................160
Butler, Tom............52, 104, 111, 133
Campion, Margaret..................306
Carlebach, Sir Philip...............180
Carver, John.......................183
Chapman, Ann.....................190
Clark, Pam.........................156
Clifton, Jean......................263
Collett, Julia......................273
Collins, Seanaid................117, 172
Collins, Stephanie.................185
Cook, Michael.....................144
Cooper, Major General Bill 49, 166, 181, 338
Cottington, May....................21
Cowan, David......................183
Crampton, Jane.....................9
Crossland, Jim....................127

Cuninghame, John and Pru........168, 271
d'Auria, Paul.................273, 274
Darke, Dorothy & Michael..........235
Davies, Pat........................180
Dawkins, Peter....................173
Dawkins, Sarah...................174
Diamond, Jo......................167
Dubrov, Prof. Alexander..........83, 92
Dulverton, Lady...................128
Duncan, Dr Stewart................334
Ede, Eric.....................184, 246
Edmonds, Philip..................186
Edwards, Jenny...91, 105, 124, 149, 336
Elaine.......11, 36-39, 43, 44, 47, 48, 75, 81, 83, 91, 121, 129, 131, 135, 137, 165, 174, 180, 220, 226, 312, 315, 317
Elcome, Delia....................167
Elliott, Marilynne........10, 51, 63, 69
Ezen, Sylvia................61, 79, 117
Farr, Dr. 'Cocky'..................336
Fawcett, Edward...................57
Fellows, Linda E..................126
Felsenreich, Dr. Maria..............103

Flexman, Celia..................................263
Flint, Dr..54
Fortlage, Kate..........................135, 286
Francke, Sylvia..................................79
Garcin, Beulah & Philip...................158
Gibson, Mr. and Mrs..........................63
Gola, Albino....................................304
Grafe, Dr. Gernot.............................103
Granny Hazel...................................321
Grushevaya, Dr. Irina.......................218
Gubbin, Evonne...............................107
Guest, Gavina......................63, 65, 303
Guest, Michael.................................184
Hancock, Sheila.................................21
Harbury, Margaret............................329
Harold, Edmund................................43
Harris, Bob....48, 52, 55, 57, 58, 97, 342
Harris, Frederick Vivian......................6
Harrison, Andy.................................345
Hawkins, Brenda................................10
Hazell, Will..........................49, 72, 126
Heiss, Allen...........153, 178, 184, 296
Higgins, Ann......................................42
Hill, Rosemary.................................138

Hoby, Alan...............................277, 334
Holderness, Charles...181, 187, 202
Holmes, David.........................28, 279
Hubbard, Ethel May..............................6
Hubbard, Rose..................................285
Hudson, Rosemary............................342
Hudson, Yvonne...............................331
Hughes, Ian......................................326
Humeston, Eric............................11, 18
Ison, Mary.......................................102
Jenks, Hugo.....................................345
Jessel, Sir Charles....48, 70, 81, 178, 338
Joachim, Bogdam.....................244, 251
Judy..171
Kenton, Leslie..................................279
Kenyon, Dr. Julian.....10, 25, 27, 49, 57, 83, 90, 279, 318
King, Joyce...............................50, 160
Le Carpentier, Ronald.............284, 285
Lonegren, Sig........73, 129, 138, 139, 306
Lyons, Jim..183
MacManaway, Bruce.........20, 38-40
MacManaway, Patrick..........73, 166, 168, 183, 241

Mainey, Dr 90, 92

Malins, Ernie 8

Marjorie 69, 71, 104, 125, 129

Mayne, Alison 237

Mayne, Very Revd Michael 220

Mayo, Veronica and Madeleine 278

McKenzie, Sandy 141, 242

McKie, Peter 74

McLauchan, Madeline 236

Mehta, Jehanne 61, 67

Miss Mansell 177

Mouat, Kit 21, 75, 198

Peacock, Jenny 290

Pike, Cyril 41

Pilkington, John & Elizabeth 47

Pinna, Jane de 264

Pope, Pat 40

Porter/Steele, Jude/Judy 143-147, 150, 151, 153, 156, 158, 162, 166, 167, 170, 171, 173, 209, 273-276, 281, 286, 287, 306, 312, 317, 318, 327

Prisbie, Barbara 320

Rene, Joan 9-11, 17, 18, 41, 246

Roberts, D.W. 103

Roberts, Julia 87

Roberts, Mimi 162

Roll, Michael 169, 170

Rubie, Judith 304

Rusbridge, John 331, 333

Rust, Deirdre 12, 47, 49

Rust, Michael 68, 140, 153, 158, 336, 338, 339

Sarah 85

Sayers, Liz 147

Schmalz, Margaret 327

Scofield, Anthony M. 126

Scott-Elliot, Major General 141

Scott, Valerie 65

Sephton, Bob 47, 85

Shaw, Mike 11, 18, 19, 21, 37, 74

Shillingford, Diane 281

Sinclair, Claire 73, 136

Slade, Brian 327

Smith, Dr. Cyril 96, 98

Smith, Raymond 284, 285

Stenning, Diane 50, 160

Stevenson, Annie 132, 133

Stewart, Daphne 51

Stewart, Gordon 50, 138

Stewart, Katie 9, 63, 263

Stone, Barbara..................................200
Stringer, Heather.............................50
Strong, Christopher and Veronica 274
Stuart, Professor Peter....................315
Sullivan, Elizabeth................144, 166
Swann, Rev. Ellionna (Jane)........219
Tait, Janice..304
Temple, Jack 11, 12, 27, 42, 71, 73, 95, 96, 124, 135, 176, 185, 247, 260, 280, 289, 305
Thompson-Walker, Betty.............137
Thompson-Walker, Philip...........137
Thornton, Carole Anne.......118, 177
Tidy, Miss...182
Tintern, Janet.........................117, 218
Tonks, Ruby...................................55, 59
Topliss-Green, Mim..126, 171, 237
Topliss-Green, William......222, 321
Tout, Mr..123
Wallace, Kathryn............................279
Ward, Evelyn.......................................38
Watson, Michael.................28, 55-57
Watts, Antoinette............................277
White, Pam..63
Wilkins, Donovan................135, 136

Williams, Audrey.............................171
Williams, Emma..............................303
Williams, Hayley.64, 138, 321, 344
Williams, Keith.......................156, 167
Williams, Madeleine............172, 256
Williams, Matt.................................344
Williams, Maureen...........................81
Williams, Rebecca.................138, 321
Williams, Tom..................................303
Willings, Heather............................140
Willis, Janet...21
Wilson, Dan......................................168
Woods, Valerie & Claire................191
Wootton, Jilly.........................170, 316
Stepping Stones into the Unknown 274
Stilton..250
Stockholm...............................241, 269
Stone Circles..........................135, 139
Stonehenge..............................17, 256
Stroud.........................67, 168, 241
Structured Water............................318
Subterranean Streams....16, 23, 25, 38, 45
Subtle Energy..........................49, 246
Sue Rider..171

371

Summer Solstice..................184, 256

Sunday Express......................277

Sunday Telegraph 68, 71, 83, 105, 119

Supreme Spirit..........................107

Surrey..............................37, 270, 286

Surrey Dowsers........................286

Sussex. 12, 17, 37, 140-142, 147, 167, 171, 172, 176, 191, 270, 275, 282, 316, 323, 326, 329, 338

Sussex Downs...........................17, 183

Sussex Dowsers.........12, 140-142, 167, 183, 243, 281, 326

Sweet Violet..................................9

Swindon.....................................133

Swiss Cottage............................184

symbol...16, 35-37, 44, 46, 49, 60, 62, 66, 90, 101, 110, 111, 114, 115, 120, 132, 136, 138, 141, 161, 165, 204, 230, 232, 237, 239, 240, 253, 254, 259, 260, 298, 301, 309, 323, 327, 329, 335, 339, 340

Synod..236

T.B. 173, 176, 177, 190, 193, 244, 268

Tail Bone......................................46

Talisman....................................265

Tangent...................158, 192, 238, 247

Tartan......86, 179, 180, 192, 198, 212, 219, 225, 239, 281

Taylor, Allegro.........................267

Tekels Park...........................12, 95

Teleradethsia............................25

Television Aerials....................46

Telos...318

Temple Hall.......71, 72, 75, 79, 90, 102, 104

Tennis..................................86, 266

Tetbury......................................123

Tetragrammation...................114

Tewkesbury.............................271

The Breath of God...................65

The Guardian..........................141

The Healing Power of Crystals. 96, 120

The Observer..........................141

The Old Vicarage...............8, 9, 63, 64

The Proving Grounds............87

The Reluctant Jester........113, 120

The Rights of Man................278

The Royal Northern Hospital....72, 123

The Symbolic Language of Geometrical Figures.................90

The Triangle Healing Centre. 143, 287, 312

The Wandsworth Cancer Centre....274

The Yews 190, 327
Theodora 77, 320
Thetford 278
Third Eye 37, 73, 80, 161, 254, 269, 318
This Sunrise of Wonder 272
Thomas The Tank Engine 264
Thrush 248, 249
Thymoma 273
Thymus 44, 273
Thyroid 44
Tibet ... 78, 93, 109, 110, 120, 165, 302
Tiddlywink 260-262, 265, 269
Tiger's Eye 287
Tin 135, 255
tingshaws 302
Tintagel 123
Tiphareth 150
Titan 59
Titanium 59-61
Titans 60
Tithe Barn 133
Tomb of the Holy Sepulchre 209
Tonbert, Prince of the Fenmen 79
Transformative Pathways 72, 86

Treasurer 51, 233
Tree of Life 73, 99, 101, 114-117, 120, 126, 138, 148, 150, 335
Tribune Poet 21
Trinder, W.H. 9, 137
Tsaphkeil 117
Tunnel of Light 221, 223, 224, 233, 250
Tupperware 314
Ty Croeso Hotel 283
Underworld 232
United Kingdom 131
Universe 125, 175, 296, 315, 339, 342
University of Sydney 278
Uranium 59-61, 186
Uranus 60
Uriel 117
urine 54, 113
Valley of the Kings 251
Vanadium 28
Vegan 10
Venus 58-61
Vicarage 145
Vilsbiburg 20
Viola Odorata 9

Virgin Mary..276
Vitamin E..17, 27
von Poh, Gustav Freiherr.............20, 22
Waden Hill...272
Wakaito...210
Wales..................73, 162, 180, 281, 286
Wallis, Barnes.....................................337
Walsall..152
Walsingham..171, 274, 276, 277, 287
Wammee...113
Wanderlust Magazine........................141
Warrior..............................87, 275, 308
Warwick...275
Washington...64
Water Divining............................138, 139
Water Violet Remedy...........................75
Watkins, Alfred.....................................17
Wells-next-the-Sea............................276
Welsh.................................54, 163, 180
Wen Di..265
Wentworth House..............................279
Wessex Cancer Centre........................28
Wessex Cancer Help Centre............279
West Brompton..................................263
West Pallant House...........................156

Westminster Abbey..........220, 222, 223, 238, 273
Whangaparaoa....................................304
Wheatley, Dennis...............................345
Whichford Pottery..............................167
Whitby..236
White Horses...............................306, 307
White Rays..246
Wiggle, Wiggle, Wiggle.312, 314-318
Wilfrid, St..298
Willow..122, 135-138, 191, 220, 221, 226-229
Wiltshire...306
Winchester......................................47, 79
Wisbech..275
Woolger, Dr. Roger.............................273
Workhouse....................................283-285
World Healer...................128, 131, 142
Worthing..42
Wrangham House Hotel............145, 146
Xenon..28
Yang..28, 230
Yellow Pages.......................................312
Yesod..116
Yin..28, 230

Yod He Vau He 125

York 68–71, 73, 75, 76, 79, 81, 86–88, 92, 99, 105, 108, 109, 111–113, 117, 119, 121, 125, 133, 135, 143–147, 151, 153, 159, 176, 199, 200, 208, 209, 230, 233, 236, 239, 248, 272, 289, 296, 305, 325, 326, 329

York Minster 75, 86, 88, 92, 208

YouTube 344

Zeus 252, 315

Zinc 61

Zirconium 29

Zodiac 264, 293

Zoence 173

Zoroastrians 328

Copyright Notice

Copyright © 2010 by Sally Hubbard Harris The right of Sally Hubbard Harris to be identified as author of this work has been asserted by her in accordance with the Copyright, Designs and Patents Act 1988.

First published 2010.

Brontovox Publications   www.brontovox.co.uk

All Rights Reserved. No part of this publication may be reproduced, stored in a retrieval system, or transmitted, in any form or by any means, electronic, mechanical, photocopying, recording or otherwise without the prior permission of the Copyright owner.

To obtain further copies of this book

Visit the website of Brontovox Publications   www.brontovox.co.uk

The book can be ordered online.

If you would like a signed copy, contact the author directly:

email: sally@williams24.plus.com

tel: 01444413944

Printed and bound in Great Britain by
CPI Antony Rowe, Chippenham and Eastbourne

My Next Book

will be

'SAILING IN THE WIND'

Tales of Adventure

on

LAND, SEA, & SKY!